Dream
Beyond Borders

Dream
Beyond Borders

Priceless Lessons
for Every Entrepreneur

Reza Sarshoghi
with Calvin Bowry

Canadian Cataloguing in Publication Data

Sarshoghi, Reza, 1966-

Dream beyond borders : priceless lessons for every entrepreneur / Reza Sarshoghi with Calvin Bowry.

ISBN 978-0-9877397-0-4

1. Sarshoghi, Reza, 1966-. 2. Businesspeople--Québec (Province)-- Biography. 3. Iranian Canadians--Québec (Province)--Biography.

4. Success in business. I. Bowry, Cal, 1968- II. Title.

HC112.5.S27A3 2012   338.092   C2012-906514-5

Cover design by Dan Graham, Allan Graphics, Kingston, Ontario

www.dreambeyondborders.com

For Azita,
who has always believed in me.

Contents

Preface

Pedaling my red bicycle through dusty narrow laneways in Iran in the early 1970s, I often imagined that I was riding a rocket ship through outer space. I loved the feeling of the wind rushing through my hair as I raced down hills and stuck my feet out in front of me. I bought that bicycle with money I had earned working for my father and uncles in their shops.

While I held onto that childhood dream of one day flying through outer space, it was coming into contact with foreign tourists in my uncles' carpet shop that inspired me to set goals that were somewhat more earth-bound. From that very young age, I was fascinated by the West. To me, it represented a world where almost anything was possible, so long as one had the determination and the will to work hard.

Ultimately, my dream brought me to Canada. The business path I carved out after arriving in Canada has led to both immensely satisfying experiences, and personal challenges that have shaken me to my very core. When I first dreamed of running my own small business, I never imagined that I would encounter such hardships. I was new to Canada, and spoke only broken English and no French whatsoever. I was alone in a foreign land. I didn't know anyone who could provide business advice or explain Canadian business practices. I had common sense and a will to succeed, but I didn't have the business sense that comes from experience. I have paid a heavy price over the years for not recognizing what I didn't know.

For the uninitiated, running your own business can be brutal. I have spent my fair share of time in court pursuing delinquent loans, fighting with insurance companies, and arguing with government officials. I learned about doing business the hard way, as many people do, through tough but invaluable lessons. Having completed an MBA program recently, I can also say that many of these lessons are not taught in the classroom. They are learned through real-life experience.

I have written this book for people who are pursuing their dreams of running their own small businesses, but who may not have the educational or the practical experiences to help guide them along the way. While the characters' names in this book are fictional, the stories are not. They are based on my real-life experiences of starting and running small businesses in Canada.

This book is not a silver bullet. When it comes to business, there is no such thing. But I hope that you, the reader, can learn some important lessons from my twenty-plus years of experience as a successful entrepreneur. Unseasoned business people don't often see the depth of risk they are facing until they are already fully immersed in a difficult situation. In sharing my experiences, I hope to help aspiring entrepreneurs improve their chances at success by identifying risks, on the one hand, and good practices on the other. I wish there were a similar resource for me when I was starting out.

May this book serve as a coaching tool to help entrepreneurs avoid the landmines of business that I didn't see along the road to achieving my dreams. May it also help you make good decisions that will allow you to one day fly your own rocket ship through outer space.

Reza Sarshoghi

2

Chapter 1: Set Goals and Believe

Once upon a time, there lived a king named Bahram. He enjoyed hunting very much, and had an extremely accurate shot with a bow and arrow. When King Bahram travelled, he was usually accompanied by a number of officers and servants. On one of his excursions, his entourage included a beautiful woman named Azedah.

King Bahram wanted to show off his skills to this beautiful woman, so he asked her if she would like to see him pin a deer's leg to its ear with his bow and arrow. She shook her head, doubting that he could achieve such a feat.

"I know you think it is impossible," he said to her with a grin. "Just watch me."

First, he loaded his sling shot with a stone, fired it off and just grazed a deer's ear. When the deer stopped and rubbed its ear with its hind leg, the King shot another arrow, and pinned its leg to its ear.

King Bahram looked at Azedah and smiled proudly.

"I think anyone can do that with hard work and practice," she said, unimpressed.

The King became very angry. He summoned an officer and told him to seize the woman at once and have her banished. She was no longer welcome in his kingdom

The officer had a very soft heart. Even though he feared for his life, he took Azedah to a secret place. She pleaded with him to spare her, and go back and tell the King that she had been taken care of. The officer decided that if the King had tears in his eyes, he would allow her to go back and live inconspicuously among the others in the servants' quarters of the castle; if the King welcomed the news, then the officer would fulfill the King's orders.

The next day he returned to the King and informed him that the woman would no longer be a problem. After relaying the information, he noticed a sad look in the King's eyes. The King paused and stared silently down at the ground for a moment, reflecting on what he had done. Sensing the King's heavy heart, the officer lived up to his agreement and found shelter for Azedah in the servants' quarters of the palace, located sixty steps above a beautiful garden.

Upon arrival, Azedah asked the officer to find her a fawn. Every day for two years she would put the fawn on her shoulders and climb the sixty steps until it matured to a full-size buck. She then asked the officer to invite King Bahram to watch her hoist the deer up the steps.

At the officer's request, the King peered out from his balcony high up on the hill and looked down onto the garden. He saw a beautiful woman carrying a large deer up the stairs on her shoulders.

"What do you think about this, Your Highness?" asked the officer.

It is a sight to behold, but with much hard work and practice, one can do anything." The King's eyes welled up with tears. "Someone once said that to me, which prompted me to make a terrible decision. I would give anything to reverse what I did."

As Azedah got closer to the King's balcony, the officer revealed her identity to the king. He married Azedah and she became Queen. King Bahram had acknowledged that, with a goal, hard work, and perhaps a bit of patience, one can achieve anything that seems impossible.

I grew up in a middle-class family in the central part of Iran. The second of four children and the eldest son, my parents made me responsible for many of the regular household chores. Of all my little responsibilities, the one I was least fond of was going to the local bakery every morning to fetch bread for my family. I had to wake up at five o'clock to get to the bakery in time to buy the bread fresh from the oven. I remember often having to wait in a long queue, sometimes for more than an hour. There were times when I would actually doze off while standing in line. My head would sometimes jerk out of a blissful few seconds of extra sleep. It was not easy, but I did what I had to do.

My parents always taught me that anything is possible, and that you can achieve anything you wish as long as you are focused, disciplined and are willing to work hard. As I grew up, those values became increasingly clear to me, and I used them as principles to guide my life.

For practically as long as I can remember, I have worked to earn money. My father ran his own business distributing household cleaning products. He worked out of a tiny shop in the commercial district of Isfahan, one of the largest cities in Iran and a place of significant Persian cultural heritage. From a very young age I worked in his shop after school most days of the week. During my summer holidays, I spent ten hours a day at his shop doing little jobs like piling boxes, sweeping, counting inventory, and other tasks that were appropriate for a young boy. The hours were long, but the rewards for me were huge. When I was ten years old, I bought my first bicycle with money I had earned working for him. Purchasing that bike with my own money was one of my proudest childhood memories.

My father's business typically quieted down at around three or four o'clock in the afternoon. To amuse myself, I would often visit some of the neighbouring merchants. It was exciting for me to hear the local politics and gossip. In fact, even though some of them were my father's direct competitors, they did not mind sharing information because we were also each other's customers.

The merchant next door to my father's shop called me "the little fox" because he thought I was quick, smart and always wanting to know what was going on around me. He gave me a piece of advice once that I have always remembered: "Little Fox, every man's jacket has two pockets: one for gains, the other for losses. You have to watch both of them."

When not hanging around other merchants' shops during slow summer afternoons, I would set up a stand on the sidewalk in front of my father's shop and display small items for sale, like chewing gum, biscuits, and candy, just like a lemonade stand in North America. I was quite successful at talking passers-by into buying my goods. Even then I had a strategy, which was to target grown-ups by telling them how good their teeth would look after chewing my gum, and that purchasing my biscuits would make their kids very happy. If a grown-up challenged me on the latter point, I would tell them that they should listen to me because I was a kid, too.

I remember one situation when I was seven years old, involving a middle-aged man with a moustache. Every day he would walk by and I would call out to him to buy something from me. Day after day he would ignore my solicitations and pass by with an indifferent shake of his head. I hounded him for weeks. Finally, one day he stopped and said, "Look, kid, you always ask me if I want to buy something, and I always say 'no.' Will you stop asking me?"

"Sir, if you buy something from me I will not ask you again," I responded. He smiled, shook his head, reached into his pocket and bought two pieces of candy from me.

"You certainly have persistence and ambition. Keep going," he said.

I had five uncles on my mother's side. Together they owned a carpet shop, selling mainly to foreign tourists. From time to time during my summer holidays, my parents would let me work with my uncles in their shop. It was there that I learned how to "flip" carpets as a young boy. Carpet dealers always stack their carpets in piles up to a couple of feet high, which makes searching through the piles quite awkward. When a customer sees an appealing design, the flipper obediently pulls the carpet out and rolls it out onto an open floor. Dignified salespeople never handle heavy carpets. They employ carpet flippers to do the physical work.

At ten years old, I absolutely loved working with my uncles in their shop. While my father dealt almost entirely with the same local clientele, my uncles' customers were wealthy tourists. I helped carry carpets out of the shop and load them into customers' vehicles. And for good reason, too: I earned a lot of extra money in tips. Most customers got a kick out of seeing an enterprising young boy on his summer holidays so engaged in the business.

One of the most valuable lessons I learned at my uncles' shop came from watching a skilled carpet master meticulously fix damaged carpets. He would often spend hours repairing damaged silk, strand by strand. After finishing a repair job, he sometimes challenged us to find the area that he had just repaired. We always lost. The look on his face when we could not find the damaged area was a reflection of the tremendous pride he took in his work. Everyone held a great deal of respect for his expertise and the commitment he gave to his craft.

Every Friday, my parents religiously took me and my siblings to visit my maternal grandparents. My grandfather was the best story teller I have ever known. I remember often being entranced as he would recount his many amazing adventures growing up in Iran. He was completely captivating when he told traditional Persian folk tales.

On one of those Fridays, after greeting us at his front door, he asked my father if I was being helpful in the shop. My father said, "Well, it is the summer holiday, and while Reza does come to the shop, there is not much for him to do there. But , still, he is tired."

My grandfather then called me over, kneeled down to my level, put his hands on my shoulders, and said, "Reza, from now on I will call you Mirzuly."

Everyone gave him a puzzled look. He then explained:

"Once upon a time, there was a woman who had a teenage son, whose name was Mirzuly. She took him to a nearby coffee shop and asked if they had a job for him. The owner of the shop said that, unfortunately, there was not much to do, but he was welcome to stay and learn the business. The mother and the boy agreed. For awhile, Mirzuly came home every night very tired."

"Why are you so tired?" his mother asked. "I thought the master said there was not much for you to do."

Every time Mirzuly answered, "The master was right. He does not have much for me to do."

As soon as Mirzuly arrived each morning, he would go to his boss and ask if there was anything to do. 'No,' his boss would say. 'But you could run over and get some sugar from the store on the corner.' On his way over, another merchant would often ask Mirzuly to pick up something for him as well. This pattern would continue till late in the afternoon."

"And that is why, young Reza," said my grandfather, "I am going to call you Mirzuly. No doubt, you are kept busy while spending time around your father's shop, aren't you?"

My grandfather understood that I was quite a busy boy.

My father would often join in when my grandfather started telling tales. He always had stories about his suppliers, his interactions with customers, his inventory, and advice on when to buy and when to sell. He loved talking business. Even after spending a long day in his shop, he would return home and talk about work with our family.

I can remember my father telling me the things I would have to do when I became a man. It was typical fatherly advice. He was very focused on the importance of work, to the point where he told me to avoid playing too much with other children because there was always work to be done. He said that I should know by heart the cost and selling price of each item in our shop, as well as those of the competition! Not to worry; I always found time for play as a child. But my father's focus on business, which for him was a labour of love, shaped the way I see the world.

I respected my father's values. Despite the fact that I did well earning money as a young boy, I wanted to continue my education after finishing high school and try new things the world had to offer. I was not anxious to rush into the world of work. Both of my parents, especially my mother, wanted me to continue with school.

I was thirteen and in my first year of high school when the Revolution erupted in Iran. I still clearly remember focusing on a math problem our teacher had given us when there was a sudden commotion outside. It scared many of us out of our seats. We ran to the window and saw the school's main gate being violently shaken by a mob of students trying to break in.

The gate burst open and about a hundred high school students swarmed our school. They broke windows and vandalized everything in sight. They ripped down the pictures of Iran's king, threw them to the ground and stomped on them. It was terrifying.

It was the beginning of the Islamic Revolution. A military curfew was imposed and a long lasting national strike took root. Goods of all sorts fell into a critically low level of supply across the country. Food was rationed through government- issued coupons. The new regime closed down all universities for five years in order to reinvent them according to Islamic law. Basic survival for the average person became quite challenging.

I was in my early teens during those years, and I worked at a number of jobs to earn extra money. I was quite handy with electrical work, having learned the basics of electricity from my father. Family and friends hired me to fix appliances, simple electronics, and even electrical systems in their cars. I had my own little workshop in my parents' home. I loved doing business. The problem was that my work would often be curtailed by a scarcity of materials due to government rationing.

Dream Beyond Borders

Just one year before I finished high school, universities across the country reopened with a curriculum to reflect the new religious ideology. I had to write the national university entrance examination. To prepare for it, I participated in a year-long extra-curricular program that one of my high school teachers offered for free in an effort to help promising students succeed on the exam.

The chances of being accepted to a university in Iran at that time were one in a thousand. So, I was absolutely stunned to learn that, perhaps with divine intervention, I was accepted to the electrical engineering program at a university in a northern Iranian city called Tabriz, about a thousand kilometres north of Isfahan. The odds of being accepted to such a specialized professional program were even higher.

During my undergraduate studies, I received a small monthly stipend from the government, in the form of a loan, but it was hardly enough to live a decent existence. In the beginning, I tried to find work, but it was impossible since I could not speak the local language – Turkish – and the local people were not overly hospitable to university students. My options were either to work for someone, doing absolutely menial tasks and earn paltry wages, or to take my destiny into my own hands and work for myself.

After some brainstorming and a bit of market research, I came up with an interesting idea. My hometown, Isfahan, was known for a special confection, which I could sell to pastry shops in Tabriz. Meanwhile, I could also buy the high- quality Turkish hand tools that were only available locally in Tabriz and ship them to retailers in Isfahan.

After living in Tabriz for two years, I could speak Turkish almost fluently, and this helped me enormously to operate a small trading company. I sold confections in one direction and hand tools in the other for all four of my undergraduate university years thereby increasing my income by over four hundred percent compared to the government's monthly stipend. It was my first real foray into the exciting world of business.

Trading goods substantially improved my quality of life. I learned that taking initiative, believing in myself, and setting goals would be the key to a better life.

While at university, I observed what was happening in my country. A national strike had crippled Iran's economy. As proud as I was to be born and raised in Iran, and of its culture and my family's heritage, I knew that Iran could not offer me the life I sought. I wanted desperately to see the world beyond Iran's borders, to learn a new language and to experience a new culture. I wanted to fly as high as I could. I wanted nothing more than to live my life in America or Europe. Traveling outside of Iran was extremely restricted for Iranian citizens, but I remained focused on achieving what was possible, and I refused to be dissuaded by the chances of failure. I established a goal to obtain a passport, but like all Iranian men, I first had to complete two years of national military service to become eligible for one.

When I finished my engineering degree, I moved back home to Isfahan and rushed to the military recruitment centre to register for service. Two years of military service was mandatory for all men in Iran. Back then, the military draft was held only twice a year for university graduates. As luck would have it, I had just missed a draft by a couple weeks. It would be another five months' wait for the next draft, which was simply too long for me to wait. I was motivated to move on to the next stage of my life.

I talked to dozens of people in search of a solution that would allow me to start serving in the army right away. One of them was a neighbour of mine in Tabriz who owned a men's clothing store. I got to know him while attending university. He was an older man with a gentle disposition. He often told me about the importance of having clear goals, strong determination, but most of all, good values. His son, whom I did not know very well, was very well connected. I introduced myself to him over the telephone one day and told him about my desire to join the military quickly.

"Hmm…" he said. "You know, I have a friend who works in the human resources department of a newly established division of the military. This department is completely independent and will accept people with specialized skills, so long as they have strong references. Let me talk to him. I will be in touch with you in a couple of days. I think you might even be able to get posted in Isfahan, your hometown."

In two days he called me back. "Reza, the door is open. You can go and apply for service on the base in Isfahan. You don't have to wait for the next draft."

I was overjoyed.

I drove to the base the next day. The installation specialized in remanufacturing Russian and Chinese tanks captured from Iraq. The Iranian army would refurbish them and send them back to the field.

I made my way to the human resources department after passing all the security requirements at the various checkpoints. A young, charismatic fellow met me there. He joked with me, which really surprised me. He asked if I would be willing to start the next day because they were trying to recruit as many university graduates as possible.

"Uh… absolutely!" I responded. I just had to provide some documents by the next day.

I left his office that day excited, but extremely nervous. My life had just turned a corner. I could not wait to start my service, as it would expedite my passport to the West.

Most of my friends were either in the army or had illegally fled the country to avoid military service. If I had to fight in the field, there was a real possibility of being injured or even killed. But I resigned myself to simply doing what I had to do, knowing that I could not control my destiny for the next two years. Deserting the military would jeopardize all of my rights as an Iranian citizen. I also felt a sense of obligation after years of consuming my country's resources as a university student. I wanted to be able to say to my children that I had defended my country. It was a matter of personal honour.

The next day, I returned to the base and met the same fellow. He had finished my paperwork and informed me that my military service officially began that day, but that I had to go to Tehran to register my acceptance. I was to report back for duty by six o'clock in the evening ten days later. With those orders, the first step had begun towards obtaining a passport to my eventual new life in the West.

I was eventually posted to the war zone on the Iraqi border. It was a humbling and terrifying experience. I clearly remember the trip to the front line of the war. As my group first set out from the base, the atmosphere in our vehicle was as though we were on a camping trip. We were fifteen young guys, full of energy. But along the route, we passed waves of Iraqi war refugees who had fled the chemical bombs unleashed by Saddam Hussein. Men and women, young and old, were carrying whatever belongings they could. Their children walked beside them, often in bare feet. It was a desperate scene. The roads were muddy since it was the beginning of spring and the rainy season. It made me proud to welcome these people to my country.

As we approached Iraqi territory, our convoy suddenly found itself under a mortar attack. Shrapnel were flying everywhere. Our vehicle pulled over and two of us ran for cover inside a nearby stone shelter that had a heavy metal door. Machine gun shrapnel were pinging off the door as we ran inside and slammed it closed behind us.

We remained in that location for a few days until our commander ordered us to move back. We spent most of the time securing the shelter to protect ourselves from ground and aerial attacks. We reinforced the roof with layers of corrugated metal, and bolstered the main entry with tires to absorb any potential explosions. All fifteen of us slept in an area that was about twenty by fifteen feet.

After two weeks in the war zone, I received a special order to return to Isfahan. I had initially agreed to serve in the war zone because of a law stating that if half of one's military service was not in a war zone, an extra three months' time would have to be served. I simply did everything to avoid serving extra time. Thankfully, one of the commanding officers in the field recognized my electrical engineering background and realized that those skills could be better utilized back on the base. I felt lucky to be posted back to Isfahan, but like most major cities in Iran at the time, Isfahan was facing daily aerial strikes from Iraqi air forces.

My work in Isfahan was in an electronics shop, where my main responsibility was to refurbish electrical circuits of the incoming tanks in preparation for their return to the battlefield. It was very challenging because they were Chinese and Russian tanks, whose parts were not easily sourced. But we did our best. I was on the base from seven o'clock in the morning until two o'clock in the afternoon, after which time I would go to my father's shop and help him with his work. Shops in Iran generally closed at around nine o'clock in the evening.

After just two months, I became the assistant manager of the base electronics shop. Normally, it was next to impossible for a soldier to rise to an officer's position, but somehow I did it. Two months after that, I became the base Technical Lieutenant Colonel, a very high-ranking position.

After completing my military service, I had to wait one year for the military to process my certificate. During that time, I started to work in private industry for a steel mill called the Mobarakeh Steel Company. New recruits underwent one month of broad training, which included lessons in English and Italian. Just shy of my first anniversary at the company, I became the head of quality control and was chosen to go to Italy for special long-term training. It meant that I could be issued a diplomatic passport and the company would pay for all of my travel expenses. However, by that point, my military certificate was ready and I was eligible to apply for a regular civilian passport.

The dilemma I faced at that point was ironic. I had risen very quickly through the ranks of this company while waiting for my military certificate. Such a high- ranking position at such an early point in my career guaranteed me a comfortable lifestyle if I chose to stay with that company in Iran. People ten years senior to me envied my position, and all its executive perks. Only four of the four thousand candidates who applied for these positions were chosen.

I had to make a major life decision. I could accept the exciting opportunity to go to Italy with the company, but in return, I would have to commit many years of my life to them. Alternatively, I could just leave the company and take the extremely slim chance of getting a visa to Europe or America through normal procedures.

It was a difficult decision, but my goal had always been to pursue my dreams in the West. I decided to resign from the company and apply for a regular passport. Everyone said I was absolutely out of my mind to give up such an opportunity.

It was January 1991. Iraqi forces had invaded Kuwait the previous summer. More than one travel agent I talked to said that the global tensions created by the invasion were making international travel from the Middle East quite challenging. Apparently, it was next to impossible to get a North American or European visa for unofficial travel. I was forced to change my plans. Instead of applying for a U.S. visa, I applied for a visa to Dubai. Back then, Iranians could get a Dubai visa without too much difficulty through a travel agency for around two hundred dollars. My chances of getting a U.S. visa from inside Dubai were much higher.

I submitted my application, purchased a plane ticket and was ready to leave. Ten days before my flight, I had to send my passport to the airline for approval. The day after I submitted it, I returned to pick it up and was told that it had been lost. You can't imagine how devastating that news was for me. It took me two very long, tense days to track it down. Meanwhile, the war drums were beating harder. Tensions between the United States and Iraq were escalating. I listened to media reports every moment of those two days.

The day before my scheduled departure to Dubai, I visited most of my friends to say farewell. I was packed and ready to leave. Then, at midnight, President George H. W. Bush announced that the United States was leading a coalition to bomb Iraqi forces in Kuwait. The next morning, all flights to and from Dubai were cancelled, and along with them, my visa. My world was beginning to crumble. My only options were to get to Italy by going back to the company – which would be difficult, let alone awkward since I had already resigned – or to secure a new visa for another country. But how?

I talked to friends and relatives in search of a solution. One of my cousins had a connection who could get me an appointment at the Swiss embassy in Tehran. Apparently, I stood a reasonable chance of being allowed to apply for a tourist visa to Switzerland. The earliest appointment I could get was in two weeks' time.

The days passed slowly. I made my way to the Swiss embassy and, after a two-hour wait, sat down with a consular official. Among thirty-two applicants, only two visas were approved. After waiting for forty-eight hours, I learned that mine was one of them.

I returned to Isfahan from Tehran right away. Even before going home, I went to the travel agency and purchased an airline ticket for Switzerland. I was anxiously looking forward to the departure date. I tried to be positive, yet remained cautious, given what had happened with my previous travel arrangements. I did not say goodbye to anyone except my family, and packed a very small suitcase.

My flight from Tehran to Zurich was scheduled to depart at five o'clock in the morning. I had to leave Isfahan for Tehran by bus a day earlier, which got me to Tehran International Airport at around ten o'clock the night before. Finally, I was there, at the airport, waiting for my flight to take me to my new life. Was it really happening? Was I dreaming? If so, I did not want to wake up. For the next few hours I counted almost every move of the minute hand on the clock in the boarding area. Finally, boarding began. After more than three years, my dream was beginning to take shape.

Lessons Learned

In this opening chapter I recount stories of my early personal life because I believe therein lies important lessons for entrepreneurial success. Early experiences will shape you, and you must have a clear vision of where you want to go and what you want to do. I knew, for example, that my destiny was not in Iran, but somewhere in the West. I envisioned it every day. Anyone is capable of having a dream, but dreams can only take shape if you believe in yourself and convince yourself that you have the ability to achieve them. I was not afraid of failing on the path to reach my goal. I knew with all my heart that I could achieve it.

The barriers to getting out of Iran were formidable: getting accepted to university and being granted a foreign visa in the face of almost impossible odds, fighting in a war, having my passport misplaced, and the Gulf War breaking out. when I was ready to leave the country. I experienced a roller coaster of emotions throughout those years. But like anything else that's worth achieving, it took focus, cast-iron will, and unwavering belief in myself to get to where I wanted to go.

I want to emphasize that point. I cannot overstate the truth in the words of Thomas Edison: "Genius is one percent inspiration and ninety-nine percent perspiration." Any successful business person will tell you that the key to success is determination and hard work. I have heard the stories of many successful business people. Some started as floor clerks and rose to executive level positions. Others started their businesses driving from town to town to sell their merchandise and ended up owning a national chain of stores. All of them started with an idea, a dream and a goal. They didn't let obstacles like failed deals or even bankruptcy get in their way. They got right back on the horse when they fell off.

Very few successful people reach their goal quickly or easily. Whether you are a free- market entrepreneur or a corporate employee, success comes from passing the primary steps to get to the top.

Dare to dream. Set goals. Believe in yourself. And don't let anything stop you.

Chapter 2: Master Your Domain

A legendary potter used to sit at the front door of his shop in Isfahan. He would size up every customer who entered the store and then, while customers browsed his merchandise, quietly coach his apprentice on how to sell to that customer for best results.

The potter's accuracy in reading people as they came through his door, and his ability to use that information to his benefit, continued to amaze his young apprentice. "Just how do you read people so well?" he asked the old potter one day.

"First, I look at their shoes to know what kind of budget they have. You can learn a tremendous amount about a person from their shoes, my son. Then, I look to see which direction they are coming from. If customers approach my shop from the left, it means they have already visited my competitors, which tells me what kind of merchandise I can offer them and in what price range. If they come from the right, I know that I am likely the first shop they have visited. Of course there are many other

considerations, but you really must have a profound knowledge of your business and your customers."

The apprentice had always admired his master for the fine pottery he made. "I have been working for you for years, but still cannot achieve the quality of your fine work, nor your art of dealing with customers. What do I have to do to be like you?"

"Ah," the potter replied, nodding his head at his young apprentice. "You need to learn the secret technique of blowing on the pot before you display it on the shelf."

The apprentice gave him a puzzled look. "The what?" he exclaimed. "Why didn't you tell me about it before, master?" he asked. "You must teach me this technique right away."

The old potter started to laugh and placed his hand on the young man's shoulder. "Son, there is no mysterious technique to selling merchandise, and no pot to blow on. You simply need a passion for your business and a hunger to learn about every possible thing there is to know about it. When you know everything there is to know about this business, especially about the customers who walk through that door, you will have mastered the secret blowing technique.

After touching down in Switzerland, my plan was to stay just long enough to secure a visa to the United States. The five-hour flight from Tehran to Zurich arrived late in the afternoon. With the help of a patient airport information assistant, I located a hotel on the outskirts of the city. He also told me how to get to the central train station in downtown Zurich, where I would be able to take a train to Berne, home to the embassies.

Dream Beyond Borders

I fell in love with Switzerland right away. The snow-capped mountains, meticulous social order, and wealthy economy were a captivating contrast to what I had just left in Iran. The barrier, however, was language. There are three main spoken languages in Switzerland; German, French, and Italian. I didn't speak a word of any of them. Furthermore, Switzerland has extremely strict immigration rules that make it difficult, even for neighbouring Europeans who speak the official languages, to immigrate to Switzerland. As enticing as it was, staying in Switzerland was not an option for me. I had to stick to my goal of going to America.

In Berne I found a modest hotel that offered long-term room rentals. I knew that the visa application process would take me many weeks.

My initial target, which I had been planning for years, was to secure a visa to the United States. It took a week just to arrange an appointment with a consular official to review my situation. While I was prepared to face a certain degree of bureaucracy, I was naïve to just how challenging the process would be. I was aware that my situation was rather suspect. I was a young, single Iranian man with no employment ties back to Iran, barely able to utter a sentence in English. And here I was applying for a U.S. visa from a third country. I might as well have written "refugee" across my forehead.

It took me a full day to carefully fill out the application form and append the supporting documents in the required format. And then I had to simply wait, helplessly, for a decision. While killing time around Berne, I happened to meet another Iranian man, similar in age to me, who had been working for a local engineering company for about two years. It was comforting beyond words to meet somebody who spoke my language. He taught me a great deal about the lay of the land in Berne: where to find low cost food and accommodations, emergency services, and how to make cheap phone calls back to Iran. Through him I was able to build a tiny social network of people who were in a similar situation.

Eight days after my initial application, I picked up a letter waiting for me in the American embassy.

"Denied."

I refused to simply roll over and walk away. After overcoming so many challenges to get to this point, giving up was not an option. I made another appointment to appeal the decision. More waiting, this time for four days. I was able to speak with a different consular official who, despite what seemed to me to be a balanced approach to my file, advised me that I would simply not be granted a visa if I chose to apply again. "Sir," he said, "I know this was not the outcome you wished, but there is clearly no chance for you to be granted a visa to the United States."

Years of planning and dreaming came crashing down like the chunk of the official's red ink stamp on my application form.

What was I to do? My father suggested that I consider Canada, now that that door had been closed to the United States.

Even though Canada had never really been part of my dreams, it seemed to be a natural option. Besides, I had a distant family connection in Montréal who might be able to help me out.

Off to the Canadian embassy I went, to submit a visa application.

"Denied," read the bold red letters across my application three weeks later.

It felt like I was in a World War II Spitfire that had just been shot out of the sky. The issue, apparently, was not whether I would apply for permanent residency in Canada, but rather the perceived risk of me claiming refugee status.

No. I was not the person the embassy staff perceived me to be. I was not a refugee claimant; I wanted to create a new life for myself in Canada, just as thousands upon thousands of people are granted to do each year. I had to convince the officials that I had good intentions.

I waited for three weeks to let the dust settle, and then visited the embassy again. All the while, I focused on doing a better job of communicating my situation. Lucky for me, my second appearance at the embassy involved an interview with a different consular official. By now, after going through the visa application process a number of times, I was beginning to see the pattern in the interview questions. This time, even though my circumstances and intentions had not changed, I understood the key information that the interview questions were designed to uncover. I was able to answer them with confidence.

The Canadian official opened a file for me and asked me to return the next day. The good news, he said, was that I was eligible to apply again for a visa. The bad news, however, was that if my application was again refused, I would not be permitted to apply for another six months.

The anxiety I felt over the next twenty-four hours was physically draining. I slept less than three hours that night and was too nervous to eat. The next day, I arrived at the embassy by taxi at the specified time and went inside to the pick-up window. After showing identification, the person behind the window handed me a brown manila envelope with the Canadian coat of arms on the top left corner. Inside, I found my passport with a six-month Canadian visa stamped onto one of the pages. My eyes welled up as I slowly looked up at the person behind the window. After three months of living in limbo, the next leg of my journey, to Montréal, Canada, was about to begin.

My arrival in Montréal was followed by all the little steps necessary to start building an existence. My family connection there, a distant cousin on my father's side, was kind enough to invite me into his home for a few days while I found my own place to live. I started looking for a job two days after arriving, and within a week I found work in a carpet store called Collage Tapis. It was a small store located in an upscale neighbourhood known as Westmount. Knowledge about the carpet trade that I had gained from working in my uncles' shop helped me to impress the owners. The store was owned by two women who were actually in the early stages of dissolving their partnership. One of them, Marta, was buying out the shares of other, Arlene. I arranged with them to work in the afternoons so that I could spend my mornings in English school. My responsibilities were very general. When there were clients in the store, my job was to flip carpets for the owners. When the store was quiet, I had to tidy up.

Marta and Arlene sold a mixed product line of wall-to-wall carpet and custom designed area rugs. When a client placed an order for a custom piece, they would simply order a second one from the designer to keep in stock. It was surprising to me that they did not offer Persian carpets.

In the beginning, I could sense tension in Marta. For weeks I noticed that she was visibly agitated, so I approached her one day and asked her if there was anything I was doing that did not live up to her expectations.

"No, not really," she answered, brushing me off with uncertainty.

"Are you sure?"

"I don't think you can help me, Reza," she replied.

"I will try, Madame," I said.

"Well, I am going to see an accountant soon to seek advice on bankruptcy protection. Collage Tapis has huge debts and there is not enough money coming in to cover them. In three days, I have to pay my rent."

It was 1991. The world was in the middle of a recession. Storefront signs advertising going-out-of-business sales were popping up daily throughout Montréal. With few options in front of them, most retailers facing hard times were choosing bankruptcy. It was a tough economy.

When Marta talked to me about her financial problems, the solution seemed straightforward. I asked her if she wanted to consider other options besides bankruptcy protection.

"Yes, of course!" she replied. "But what?"

Together we looked at her problems in a different light.

The first thing I did for Marta was to buy her some time with her landlord. That month, he got a carpet instead of his rent payment. Both sides were happy. It bought Marta thirty days

What seemed obvious to me, but surprisingly not to Marta, was the mismatch between the products she was selling in Collage Tapis and her clientele's tastes. The people walking past her Westmount store were very well heeled. Yet, even her custom-designed rugs lacked a degree of refinement. In fact, she sold duplicates. When a client designed a rug to their own tastes, she simply had two of them made at the same time to save costs; one for the client and another one to display in the store. In effect, she was not meeting her customers' expectations for uniqueness.

Her presence in the store was another reflection of her lacklustre commitment to her business. She spent barely two hours a day in the store. The salesman and I were her front line to her customers. But she wasn't involving us in her operation in a way that inspired our commitment. We were simply working for money. Trusting us to hold the fort while she was out, doing who knows what, isolated Marta from her customers. She didn't have an intimate sense of their needs, and the performance of her business was showing it.

I sensed an opportunity, so I pitched an idea to her. First, I addressed her line of custom-made carpets. She wasn't approaching this stream of her business properly, and it would take a very long time to turn it around. Yes, these rugs were beautiful in their own right. But I made the case to Marta that if somebody was willing to spend thousands of dollars on a custom-made rug, they wanted a unique piece of art, not something off the rack. I convinced her to liquidate her large unsold inventory of custom rugs at a seventy-five percent discount.

She also had to move her slow-selling mainstream inventory. To do that, I convinced Marta to auction it off. I felt that she still needed to expand her product line-up to get people excited about purchasing a carpet when they walked into the auction room. To help do this, I visited carpet dealers around Montréal and made deals to get some very good quality carpets on short-term consignment. I combined Marta's existing stock with these new carpets and sold them in a few auctions at rented hotel ballrooms in suburban Montréal.

After each auction finished, if there were any visitors in the crowd who could not find just the right carpet, I would invite them to Marta's store. From there I had another chance to get to know them better and help increase the chances of them purchasing something from Collage Tapis.

My strategy worked. Sales increased in the first month by over two hundred percent. More importantly, these special auctions allowed me to gather incredibly useful insights about the specialty carpet market in Montréal. I talked to the buyers and kept their contact information.

I believe that the key to my success in this case was two-fold: a combination of determination and an understanding of the market. Keep in mind that, at this point, my job was still to flip carpets for Marta's salesman. Even though I was only a hired hand, I spent my first three months looking at Marta's customers' shoes, just as the fabled potter taught his apprentice to do.

Marta became convinced of the need to better align her products with the market. She shifted her focus away from large and custom-designed area rugs to selling high- quality handmade Persian rugs.

Two months after I started organizing auctions to help move Marta's inventory and increase sales, she called me into her office. She told me how much she appreciated my help and hard work, and that she wanted me to replace her existing salesman. She would increase my base salary and pay me a commission.

It was fantastic news for me. I accepted her offer. I was now in the position of having to find a person to flip carpets for me. I actually found two men in their early twenties, who had immigrated to Canada from Egypt. I have always believed that, if you want to succeed, you must surround yourself with the very best people. I hired these two men because I saw in each of them a sense of integrity that would help me, in spite of their menial responsibilities to flip carpets and keep the store tidy. My aim, or more truthfully my preoccupation, was to make sure that these two new assistants knew absolutely everything about the products we were selling, and could quickly size up our customers' needs.

In a few weeks, the three of us had developed an extraordinary sense of coordination. Marta had around six hundred carpets in stock, all in different dimensions, colours, prices and styles. I knew every detail about every carpet, and I made sure that my teammates did as well. They could quickly locate each carpet in stock based on its size, colour and region in which it was made. Our customers were continually impressed by our professionalism.

I worked to build a trusting relationship with my assistants. Flipping carpets was neither easy nor highly rewarding work. On top of it all, dealing with retail customers was not always pleasant. I remember once, after spending hours with a customer, flipping through dozens of carpets, and enduring a great deal of flip-flopping in her decisions, one of my assistants said to her, "I don't think we have what you are looking for, lady!" I just about died on the spot when I heard those words come out of his mouth.

Later that day I had a chat with my assistant. I recounted a story my father had told me years ago:

Once upon a time a landowner hired a well digger. He marked a point for him and asked him to dig until he hit water. The man dug and dug and dug, but there was no water. Not even moisture. After days of digging he looked up from the bottom of the deep hole and said to the landowner in exasperation, "Sir, why are you asking me to dig here? You will not find water."

"Don't stop," the landowner shouted from the top of the hole.

"But there is no water here! I have a lot of experience! I am absolutely certain there is no water here."

To which the landowner replied, "If digging this well will not bring me any water, I know it will bring you bread! It's your choice. If I were you, I would dig.'"

My assistant understood the moral of the story.

I was determined to learn every dimension of the carpet business in Montréal. I made a point of visiting every one of my competitors to learn about their products, their suppliers, their prices, and how they sold their carpets. Armed with that knowledge, I gradually gained a reputation as a highly knowledgeable source of information on top quality carpets, which is what Marta's customers wanted. People who pay thousands of dollars for a carpet are not concerned about price, so much as quality and value. They don't just want to purchase a carpet; they want to buy art. My obsession was to educate myself about my product so that I could speak with authority about anything related to carpets. I was careful not to come across to my customers as a salesman per se, but rather, as a consultant. I never pushed anyone into buying anything from me; an approach that I believe helped me gain many long-term relationships. If a customer wanted something that I did not have in stock, I always knew where I could get it quickly. A customer would never leave my store empty handed.

For the first few months in my new sales position, everything went smoothly. I stabilized Marta's business and I was making a good living. But with the new-found confidence that accompanied the rejuvenation of sales, Marta began to look for ways to squeeze more profit out of her business. Her new mission was to reduce overhead expenses. Without consulting me, she decided to move to a less expensive location. Marta believed that since I continued to enjoy success at auctioning her carpets in rented hotel ballrooms, the actual store location would not be so important. I didn't agree with her strategy, but then again, it was not my business. Little did she know that this decision marked the beginning of the end of her enterprise.

Marta found a cheaper location between two well-known furniture stores far from Westmount. Immediately across the street was a cemetery, which was not exactly a drawing feature for retail customers or walk-in traffic. I was sure we would lose a lot of our regular clients. The landlord would not make any leasehold improvements, so Marta had to completely remodel the space to fit her needs. Her husband, an architect, designed the layout—a showroom, two small offices and a bathroom.

A combination of events sounded the death knell for the business. Other dealers began to notice the success we were enjoying through our auctions, and started copying us. Competition grew, which forced our prices down. Customer traffic to the new store did not reach the level that Marta had anticipated, despite the referral fees we had arranged with neighbouring furniture stores.

The turning point for Marta came about four months after moving to the new location. The lower operating cost of the new location could not compensate for the unexpected reduction in sales. She was ultimately forced to sell the business. And with most of her inventory being held on consignment, the business wasn't worth a lot of money.

It was an opportunity that landed in my lap. I understood the business better than Marta. I had established very good relationships with wholesalers in Toronto and New York, through whom I could source almost any type of carpet. My client list was strong and growing, and I was clearly building a solid reputation for myself among high-end carpet buyers throughout Montréal. I decided to go for it.

I bought Collage Tapis from Marta for a song, with money that I had been diligently saving since arriving in Canada and working for Marta. Effectively I was buying the business name and a little bit of equipment in the store. Marta seemed quite happy to sign it all over to me. I was thrilled to be buying a business in my new adopted country. To me, it was the deal of the century.

It didn't take long for reality to hit. I had about as many employees as weekly customers, so I had to lay off my two trusted assistants, which was not easy. Furthermore, I was locked into a five-year lease on a poorly performing location, of which more than four years remained. Two months later, one of the adjacent furniture stores went out of business, followed soon by the other one announcing its relocation, which spelled impending doom for me. An important portion of my business was referrals from those stores.

I knew I needed a strong base of high income customers, so I decided to start looking for a new location. The question of the lease would have to be faced later, for changing locations was a matter of survival. I quickly came to realize that, while I had become an expert on the local carpet market, I knew nothing about commercial real estate.

After weeks of searching for the just the right location, I discovered a beautiful historic four-storey stone building back in lower Westmount. It was built in the mid-1800s and had stately Victorian windows at street level, which would be a perfect for displaying carpets. It was on the corner of a high traffic street and in close proximity to two museums, two luxury hotels, a Cartier jewellery store, several high-end antique stores, and a number of expensive condominiums. It was perfect.

With a bit of sweet-talking and a Persian carpet, I was able to break my five-year lease by paying the landlord a three-month penalty. I signed a two-year lease for two floors in the beautiful building in Westmount. I also decided to focus the business exclusively on selling high-end Persian carpets to distinguish myself in the market.

Admittedly, I got ahead of myself. I did not have enough cash— after paying the three-month penalty and the deposit on the new location— to pay the first month's rent. It was impossible to get a line of credit from a bank since I was still relatively new to Canada and had no credit history. So, I did what I knew best: I held an auction. Of course, I had to pay for the hall, advertising and the auctioneer's fee, but payment for some of these expenses could be delayed for thirty to ninety days. I used the cash from that auction to pay for moving expenses and the first month's rent at my new location.

The strategy behind this new location for Collage Tapis paid off. Customer traffic improved significantly and, most importantly, so did sales. But with the average customer paying thousands of dollars for one of my Persian carpets, their expectations for service were high.

Soon I had a salesperson working for me, but I still made a point of being around the store at all times to talk to every customer myself. I was like a chef coming out of the kitchen to chat with guests. It was important for symbolic reasons, but it also enabled me to communicate my passion and knowledge for my product, and to glean an intimate understanding of my customers' needs. These people wanted the experience of acquiring a piece of art: learning the story behind their carpet, what made it valuable and knowing why it represented a better investment than a carpet from another retailer. Perceived value was my customers' highest concern,; not price.

It was on this point that Marta had failed. She allowed discerning customers to deal entirely with commissioned salespeople, who had only a surface-level commitment to Marta's business and her customers' interests. My approach was to gain a customer's trust by demonstrating knowledge and commitment. If I could achieve that goal, I was convinced that sales would come naturally. Sometimes, it took a great deal of time and patience— days, weeks, or even a year or more to make a sale. I would spend hours with some customers, discussing carpets and negotiating terms. But it was truly a labour of love. Afterwards, I always personally delivered the carpet to make sure my customers were truly satisfied, and admittedly, to also identify opportunities to sell them something else in the future. I learned that the key was to satisfy customers' complete needs, not simply to sell them a carpet. And if they were happy, they would always refer people to my store. This personal commitment to customers' needs, and to knowing every possible dimension to the local market, allowed me to grow the business far beyond what Marta had achieved. I tried to build a customer-centric culture among my employees, too.

One of the most basic principles of marketing is to identify other products that compliment yours. I developed partnerships with furniture stores in Montréal, Ottawa, and Quebec City, and a couple of carpet retailers that sold non-Persian and wall-to-wall carpets. I provided the furniture stores with complimentary carpets to enhance their displays. If they directed a customer to me, I paid them a referral fee.

Aligning with a competing dealer in the same city might be a puzzling strategy on the surface, however, it was a great way to build relationships with future buyers. Many people came into my store who were not quite ready to purchase the quality of carpet that I was selling. I treated them just as royally as my top clients, except I referred them to one of these other stores whom I trusted would provide the level of service I expected. Ultimately, the strategy brought me a lot of reciprocal business.

One year at my new location, Collage Tapis was doing very well. My cash flow was positive, I had the right merchandise, the right location, and the right customers. Until, that is, something happened that was completely unexpected and personally devastating. One night at around midnight I received a phone call at home from my alarm company. The representative told me that the motion detectors in my store had been activated. I ran out to my truck and drove to the store.

Dream Beyond Borders

It was not the first time this sort of thing had happened. But the difference this time was that all of the motion detectors had been activated, not just the typical one or two. I was puzzled as to what could have triggered all of them at once. It was either the alarm system malfunctioning or, at worst, someone had broken in and stolen a couple of carpets, in which case I would not even submit a claim to my insurance company.

After parking my truck, I raced up to the front of the store. There was no sign of police. The windows were fine. The door was still secured with bars. I could not imagine how anybody could have broken in. I walked around to the back of the store and met a police officer. He stopped me, and I told him that I was the owner.

We walked in together through the back entrance. The security bars had been ripped from the door frame, likely with a rope tied to a truck. All of the motion detectors had been smashed. I walked inside and immediately saw a bare display stand that had once showcased a stack of fifty of my finest Persian silk carpets. They had all been stolen.

The police could not conclude anything. They simply filled out a report and left. So, there I was at my store, at two o'clock in the morning, windows broken, no alarm, and missing tens of thousands of dollars of precious inventory. There was no way I could come up with the capital to replace it. I felt absolutely sick. Who could have stolen so many carpets? There were formidable obstacles to overcome, suggesting that it could have been an inside job.

Curiously, two days after the robbery, my salesman had a big argument with me, which was uncharacteristic of him. He resigned on the spot and disappeared. His outburst was just too abnormal for me to consider it a coincidence. I just could not help but feel suspicious.

The insurance company concluded that they had grounds to refuse my claim. I called the adjuster and asked him why, even after I had provided all of the requested documentation to prove that I had purchased the carpets.

"You should be thankful, Mr. Sarshoghi. There is a clause in your policy stating that we can refuse your claim if we can prove that this was an inside job. I chose to ignore that clause. If I had gone down that route, you wouldn't have a legal leg to stand on. I am at least giving you the option to pursue this matter in court."

"But you know I had nothing to do with it. I have even passed the lie detector test."

"I trust *you*, but not the people who work with you. Look, from now on I can't talk to you. You can get any information you need through your lawyer."

I thought about what he had said. I tried to recount the events in my mind, step by step, the day the robbery had occurred. Our closing time was six o'clock in the evening. I remember stepping out of my office and saying to the two employees, "It's six o'clock, everyone. Let's go home." I armed the security system, locked the doors and wished everybody a good night. Ken, the employee who later had an argument with me, came out from the back storeroom and said that the loading entrance was secure. I did not bother to check it myself. In fact, I had not been back in the storage room all day, as I had been busy at a customer's home and running errands around Montréal.

Had Ken been busy loading the carpets into his truck? Did he come back later that night to rip open the door and disappear? I raised these possible scenarios with the police but they told me that I couldn't rightfully accuse anyone without evidence or witnesses. I had no proof. I knew my business well, but did I know enough about my employees? I fought the insurance company in court for the next eighteen months. I had to make great personal sacrifices to build up my inventory once again.

Collage Tapis thrived. In 1996, I decided to search for yet another location, one that I could purchase instead of continuing to waste money on a lease. Since the economy was still in a downturn, it was not difficult to find commercial real estate for a good price. Nevertheless, I realized that purchasing real estate would be a challenge.

Within a couple months, I found a repossessed commercial building for sale, close to my existing store, on the south side of Sherbrooke Street. The building had four floors, with two beautiful large bay windows at street level. It couldn't be more perfect. Of course, at the time I could only fill two floors with merchandise. But to find something like that in downtown Montréal at a relatively low price was a once-in-a-lifetime opportunity. I wanted that building.

Through one of my acquaintances, who was a real estate broker at the time, I made an offer to purchase the building for a price that we estimated to be about twenty-five percent of its true value. After a few days of negotiation, the vendor miraculously accepted my offer. I could hardly believe it because my offer was ridiculously low. Timing, as they say, is everything. The bank just wanted to unload the building as quickly as possible.

My next challenge was to finance the deal. I needed to secure about a half million dollars in financing to complete the transaction. During the due diligence period, I tried securing a loan from a number of banks. The answer I got every time was a resounding "no.".

It was a very stressful time. With only one day left before the deal was to close, and potentially fall through, I decided to talk to the vendor's broker and ask for more time. The vendor agreed to give me forty-five days to secure the financing, but he demanded a fifty-thousand dollar security deposit. If I could not close the deal in that period, I would forfeit the money.

I accepted his terms despite the high stakes attached to them. I was determined to find a solution. For this final kick at the can, I worked with a mortgage broker, who introduced me to the Business Development Bank of Canada, a government- owned agency that specializes in business financing.

The loan application process was not easy. I had to demonstrate to the bank in my projections that I would generate enough revenue in this new location to cover all of the overhead expenses and the mortgage payments, and still be profitable. However, it wasn't an extremely tough sell. In the bank's view, the value of the loan I was seeking was easily secured by the building.

The bank accepted my numbers and granted me the loan to purchase the building. Within just a few years of arriving in Canada from Iran as a carpet flipper, I now owned my first piece of real estate in Canada. I moved Collage Tapis for the third time, closing off the existing location with a moving sale and opening in my own building with a grand opening sale.

My new challenge was to maintain revenues and costs according to my projection. I now had to generate more sales to cover my taxes, utilities, insurance, and many other cash outflows, which I had not foreseen. When I was renting, I would simply call the landlord for anything in the building that needed to be repaired. If there was any delay in rectifying the issue, I would simply put pressure on the owner. But when you are your own landlord, there is nobody to hear such complaints. The other big difference was that my monthly mortgage payment was firm. Back when I was a tenant, if I was short on cash I had greater flexibility to delay rental payments. The bank that held my mortgage, however, would be much less flexible. There was little chance of them accepting a carpet in lieu of a monthly payment.

My knowledge of the market got me through the launch period. I knew my products, my customers, my suppliers and my competition inside out. Bigger challenges, however, had just begun. For the first few months, business was not bad because of the timing of the move. Sales were strong from November to March, but dropped off significantly from March to June, which reduced my cash flow. Financially, I was heading down a river with a large waterfall in clear sight. Pouring every possible penny I could find into the business, I was just scraping by. I was left with just a few hundred dollars a month to feed and clothe myself.

Financially, things were becoming quite tense when I encountered a sudden windfall. I received a call from my lawyer to inform me that my insurance company had made a settlement offer for the stolen silk carpets . The timing couldn't have been better. But as tempting as the settlement appeared, I did not accept the insurance company's first offer. I had been advised as a matter of principle never to accept any first offer from an insurance company. After a week of negotiations, I settled with them for fifty percent more than they had initially offered. That money provided me the necessary cash flow to maintain Collage Tapis through the period of slow sales.

By no stretch were my sales always slow. I established myself as the leading retailer of high-end Persian carpets in Montréal. My customers included a former Canadian prime minister and many politicians and business people from the Montréal establishment. I can say with confidence that my intimate knowledge of my product, customers' needs, the new location, and my well-trained staff were the formula for my success. I had succeeded in building Collage Tapis into a profitable business out of one that was near the end of its life.

After finishing up at the store in the evenings, I used to frequent a Persian restaurant. I was a good customer, so the staff would always give me special attention. One evening, while I and one of my employees, Fred, were enjoying a delicious dinner at this restaurant, a woman sitting at a nearby table caught my attention. She had long, black, curly hair. She was absolutely stunning. But what also captured my attention was her accent. She was speaking English, but I could tell from the way she spoke that she was from my region back in Iran.

"Reza...Reza, are you listening to me?" Fred said. My attention had drifted completely away from him to this woman.

"Fred, do you hear her?" I replied. "She is from Isfahan!"

"Do you know her?"

"No," I said. "But I can tell from her accent that she is from Isfahan. I'm absolutely sure of it. Fred, look at her! She is gorgeous! Mark my words, Fred. One day I am going to marry that woman."

But I was too shy to approach her in the restaurant. After she left, I asked the restaurant owner if she knew anything about her. Unfortunately, she didn't. It was the first time she had ever seen her. Whenever I returned to the restaurant, I would ask the owners if she had come back, but she hadn't. Months went by and I just could not get her out of my mind.

Later that year my mother came from Iran to spend a couple of months with me. It didn't take long before she started to ask about my plans to get married. Ironically, I ignored her. Every time she brought up the subject, I pushed back, telling her that I was too busy and not ready to get married. But without my knowing it, my mother was secretly searching within the Iranian community of Montréal for an Iranian bride.

One day, when I was busy with a customer, two women walked into Collage Tapis. I just assumed they were customers. Since I was busy, I asked Fred to help them. He went over to greet them, but quickly returned.

"They wish to talk to you. They asked for Reza," he said.

At about the same time, my mother walked into the store. She went straight to those two women and started to talk with them in Persian. It took me by surprise. I didn't understand what was happening.

After finishing with my customer, I walked over to them and introduced myself. I shook hands with the two women who had asked for me. They were both Iranian, so we all spoke in Farsi.

"Reza, this woman has a daughter in university who is similar in age to you," my mother said. "Maybe you should get to know each other." The two women were the mother and grandmother of the university student, whose name was Azita.

Quite honestly, I was very reluctant to pursue what was being laid out in front of me. My focus in life at that point was my business, not a romance. I know my mother was just trying to be helpful, but I felt that she was being a bit too helpful. However, after a half-hour of chatting, it was decided that I would meet the daughter. Besides, there was more to life than just business. I was young and I had always wanted a family, but the intensity of moving to Canada and establishing myself had distracted me from pursuing a relationship. The women left me Azita's phone number.

Azita and I spoke on the phone and then decided to meet over a cup of coffee. I arranged to pick her up at her home on a Wednesday evening. Walking up the stairs to her front door, I remember thinking that I had no plans to get married at that point, and that I would probably not be attracted to her, anyway.

I rang the doorbell, and through the frosted glass I could see the outline of a woman walking toward the door. The door opened. It was the mother who had come to my store a week earlier.

"Why don't you come in, Reza?"

I'm not sure why, but I politely declined. "No, thank you. But could you please ask Azita if she is ready?"

"I will get her."

Moments later, Azita appeared at the far end of the hallway. Suddenly, I realized that I had seen this woman before. I froze. Yes! Yes! She was the woman I had seen in the Persian restaurant months earlier! I was so overwhelmed that I didn't know what to say. We had planned to go for coffee, but suddenly those plans seemed out of place.

Overcome with anxiety, I extended my hand to greet her. At first, she seemed serious and reserved. I wondered if she had been pressured into going on this date the same way that I had been.

We walked to my car and I opened the door for her. All I could think about was finding a very good restaurant that didn't require a reservation.

"I have seen you before" I said.

"I don't think so."

"I saw you about nine months ago in a Persian restaurant on Sherbrooke Street! You were with a group of people. The moment I saw you, I wanted to marry you."

"Excuse me?"

"I am serious. When I saw you, I was absolutely stunned by your beauty. I promise you I will make you happy."

We had not even known each other for five minutes and I was talking about marriage. True, I was being forward. But I was so excited that I could not contain myself.

"How about an Italian restaurant?" I proposed.

"That would be fine." I sensed hesitation in her voice.

It was one of the most memorable evenings of my life. I was on a cloud. Meeting Azita, purely by chance, months after I first happened to notice her in a Persian restaurant—on a blind date of all things—was nothing short of a miracle. But it became obvious that the evening was not such a thrill for Azita. I could sense that she did not feel the same spark that I was experiencing. But I was determined to earn her affection.

I called her a few days later.

"Reza, I respect you very much, but I don't think we have anything in common."

It was as though someone had held a balloon to my face and pricked it with a pin. But I was not willing to let my chance die there on the spot. I am the type of person who gets what he wants. I came up with all sorts of points over the phone about how similar we were. But I couldn't convince her to go out again, even though our families hoped that a relationship would develop between us.

A week later, I learned through my mother that Azita was sick with a cold. So, I sent her a bouquet of flowers. She called to thank me, but I could tell she was still not convinced that we had anything in common. She was cordial but very distant with me.

I felt totally deflated, but I was still not willing to give up. I believed with all my heart that we were right for each other. I knew that I had found my soul mate. I was determined to win her over.

After Azita got over her cold, I persisted and asked her out on another date. I could almost hear her sigh in response. But something made her think twice and she accepted the invitation. I was not going to let my pride get in the way. She made me feel like I had never felt before, and I was willing to risk my pride in order to get what I wanted.

Over the next year, I asked Azita out on dates as often as I could manage without overwhelming her. It didn't take long before she stopped distancing herself from me and started expressing an interest in seeing me again. Even though it was hard to contain myself, I felt that slow -and -steady would win the race.

We spent a fair amount of time together, gradually becoming closer despite some ups and downs that are typical in relationships. We got to know each other better by spending time with each other's family. In doing so, we saw each other from different perspectives. I knew that, to win Azita's heart, I would also have to prove myself to her family.

One fall weekend about a year after we first met, I joined her family on a short getaway to a nice resort north of Montréal. I drove an SUV at the time, and invited Azita to go for a ride with me through the mountains while the rest of her family was relaxing at the cottage.

We drove on a road that carved its way through a forest. The fall colours were spectacular. Soon, it began to rain so hard that I had to pull over to the side of the road. The moment was as good as any. I turned to Azita, pulled a small ring box out of my pocket, and opened it to reveal a beautiful diamond ring. She was taken completely by surprise. After getting over her initial shock, she nodded, eyes welling up slightly.

"Yes," she said, reaching for me. "Yes."

Within two years of that first blind date, Azita and I got married in Montréal. Our wedding day was the most joyful day of my life and it was everything that Azita had wished for since she was a child. She truly looked like a princess in her wedding dress. I have always loved her and I am continuously thankful to have her in my life.

We slept past noon the following day. It was the first day of my entire life that I had gotten out of bed so late. I have to admit that I just could not stop working. The day after my wedding, I had to go to my store to check up on things because weekends were the most active sales period of the week. What's more, I actually delayed taking a honeymoon for six months after our wedding. When I did set aside time for our honeymoon, I chose a destination where there was a carpet expo. Perhaps this offers a sense of what it was like for the first few years of our marriage. Yet Azita never complained.

Lessons Learned

My first few years in Canada were highly eventful and dynamic. I went from flipping carpets as a newly -landed immigrant, to reinventing the store owner's sales strategy, to buying her business and growing it into one of the most respected high-end carpet stores in Montréal. I even got married. Those first few years in Canada were like surfing a giant wave.

I believe that the key to my early business success was an unrelenting desire to learn everything possible about my business domain. I landed in Canada with a basic knowledge of carpets that I had learned from hanging around my uncles' shop in Iran. As a retailer, I could speak with authority about my product, which gave customers confidence in purchasing from me. Perhaps working with my father from a very young age helped me to develop my business acumen. But overall, I believe that it was the in-depth knowledge I acquired about Persian carpets, prices, my suppliers, the competition, their suppliers and customers' needs that was at the root of my success with Collage Tapis. I considered myself to have a PhD in the Montréal high-end carpet business. That knowledge gave me the confidence to work with my competitors, not against them. In fact, referring people to other carpet retailers actually generated sales because they began to do the same in return.

The knowledge I developed reflected my passion for my business, which, in turn, gave me integrity in my customers' and competitors' eyes. If people trust you, they will keep coming back and they will tell their friends about you. In business, building trusted relationships is the name of the game.

Chapter 3: Find Your Niche

King Abbas, who ruled Persia in the early 1600s, called for a gathering of scientists, mathematicians and philosophers at the royal palace in Isfahan. At that time, a sheikh named Bahai was one of the most knowledgeable people in the land. He traveled a great distance to participate in this gathering of leading thinkers in Isfahan. With no facial hair and a petite frame, Sheikh Bahai had a boyish appearance. Furthermore, his old worn clothes gave him the air of a peasant.

When he arrived at the palace entrance, the guards stopped him and asked who he was. "I am Sheikh Bahai," he replied. They laughed and pushed him away, refusing to grant him entry to the royal conference. He tried again and again to convince the guards of his identity, but to no avail. So Bahai turned and left, disappointed and frustrated.

He soon found himself at a bazaar at the dusty centre of the city. A man weaving traditional blankets in a small shop caught the sheikh's eye. The man was chubby with dark, leathery skin and a thick white beard. Bahai had an idea. He approached the man and asked him how much money he was earning in that shop. "I will pay you twice your salary to come and help me," he offered. The man accepted Bahai's offer and locked up the store.

"The first thing," Bahai said, "is to go to the public bath. I want you to wash well." Just before rounding the corner to the bath, Bahai told the man to wait for a moment. He ran ahead and announced to the bath keeper that the most famous sheikh in the land was coming to this bath.

The bath keeper asked for the sheikh's name. "This is none of your business!" Bahai replied. "Your status is too low to know his name!" Bahai soon returned with the blanket weaver, and the bath keeper received him with reverence and awe. While he took his bath, Bahai rushed back to the bazaar to purchase a well-decorated donkey and a special costume worn only by the nobility.

The nameless sheikh finished his bath and donned the costume. Bahai told him to get on the donkey, and then led them back to the bazaar. Along the way, he whispered in people's ears that the person riding the donkey was one of the most important sheiks in all the land, and was visiting the city at the personal invitation of the King. Bahai had instructed the blanket weaver not to talk to anybody, and to simply direct people's questions to him.

After a day of parading the "sheikh" around in the city and allowing word of his presence to spread, Bahai took him to the palace. News of this revered figure had already reached the guards, and without asking any questions, they opened the gate, bowed and escorted him to the special room where the scholars had gathered. Bahai announced the presence of the great "Sheikh Bahai" and everyone stood as he entered the room. Bahai and his cohort sat quietly at the centre of the room, the great Bahai himself posing as the sheik's young apprentice. Questions that this conclave of forty people could not answer were directed to the "sheikh," and each time he quietly motioned to his assistant to provide a response. Bahai, a man of great wisdom, would silence the crowd with his answers.

The following day, a palace staff member informed the King of the mysterious genius that had joined the conference. He explained to the King how the most complex problems were so far beneath this man that he directed his junior apprentice to provide the answers. The King ordered for them to be brought, one by one, to his chamber. He wanted to meet this mysterious pair.

"I have a huge room in the palace, for which I have no immediate use," the King said to the great "Bahai." "What would you suggest?"

The disguised carpet weaver thought of his dark, tiny shop, and what a comfortable workplace it was. "A room for the tailor for weaving beautiful warm blankets for your staff would be the best use," he answered. The King excused him and asked for the man's apprentice to appear in front of him.
Bahai entered and bowed to the king. "How can I be of assistance, Your Highness?" Bahai asked. The King presented him with the same question.

Bahai had always wanted a big library, since he didn't have much space for his books. He knew that a library would benefit many people. "The best use would be to make it into a library, Your Highness, a place where great knowledge could be created and shared," Bahai answered.

The King was a very wise man and sensed what was happening. "Young man, just who is the wise teacher and who is the student?"

The moral of this tale: the way you present yourself has a very powerful effect on your ability to reach your market niche.

Dream Beyond Borders

Previously, I described how I purchased Collage Tapis from Marta, moved it to a higher profile location, and then purchased a commercial property in downtown Montréal and used it for the new, permanent home of Collage Tapis. All of this took place within my first few years of arriving in Canada. However, even before purchasing the commercial building and moving the store, I had my first experience of seeking start-up financing from a bank to launch a new small business alongside the carpet store.

Collage Tapis attracted just a handful of clients per week. It was enough to sustain me financially, but I needed something to occupy my time between customers. I was restless to do more than just sit, hour after hour, and wait for the next person to walk in from the street. I was young and had too much ambition to sit and wait for the next sale. I wanted to achieve more.

I knew, at that early point in my career, exactly what I wanted to achieve in life. I had experienced enough, growing up in Iran, to realize the opportunities in front of me in North America. Many people around the world would walk on broken glass to have the opportunities that Canada granted me. I wasn't about to squander them. I have heard it said that you only get out of something what you put into it.

The coffee craze was just beginning to sweep North America. The likes of Tim Horton's and Starbucks were making a big mark on the business landscape. More and more, I noticed people carrying a cup of coffee in their hands while on the go. Drinking coffee was becoming a pastime. Gourmet coffees seemed to be proliferating as well. I figured that it was a business concept I was easily capable of mastering. Furthermore, I reasoned that growing a chain of coffee shops in Montréal was a greater likelihood than growing Collage Tapis into a chain of high-end Persian carpet stores.

I ventured forth and put my free time at Collage Tapis to work. My goal was to find a high traffic location for a coffee shop of my own. Without yet having gained any experience in the food services industry, I knew I was jumping in blind. But I convinced myself that smart thinking and determination would lead to success, much the same way as when I was planning my way out of Iran. Besides, how hard could it be?

I have experienced a lot of challenging obstacles in my career, but the coffee shop, which I named Café Saison, was where I really cut my teeth on the harsh reality of starting and operating a business. I learned enough about business from Collage Tapis to know that having a business plan would be essential, so I wrote one in about two days. More than half of the plan focused on the visual identity and atmosphere I was aiming to create with Café Saison. There was a section on the equipment I needed to get financed, and an outline of my projected cost and revenue structure for the first two years of operations. But I especially wanted to be sure that any loan officer who read the plan knew that I had the proper vision to attract a loyal clientele.

And so my adventure began. In stark contrast to my experience with the banks in purchasing the building for Collage Tapis, every single bank I approached for a start-up business loan turned me down. First, my business plan had a number of large holes in it, especially regarding my cash flow projections. A business plan should illustrate to any prospective investor why your business idea will succeed and, among many, other considerations, accurately outline the start-up and operating costs for the first two years. While my plan did a good job of portraying how I was going to attract customers, it fell short on explaining how much I was going to have to spend to do it. Combined with the fact that fifty percent of all new restaurants go out of business in the first two years, the banks saw a huge risk in me. I was turned down by all of them. So, to move ahead with the idea, I had no choice but to finance my equipment through the manufacturers at punishing interest rates.

After being turned away a dozen times by property owners and managers, who looked at my credit history and either shooed me away or simply ignored me, I happened to come across an old storefront in suburban Montréal. With a beautiful stone facade, the building had loads of character. For the last twenty-five years, it had been used by a husband and wife for their business office. The woman was a notary and used the main floor, while her husband used the upper floor for his insurance business. But they were now both retired and wanted to rent the building to generate income.

The location was outstanding. It was in the heart of a suburban Montréal business district. There were two banks nearby, the municipal office was just across the street, and there were a variety of retail stores in the immediate vicinity, providing heavy foot traffic at all times of the day. The downside was that the building had been sitting unused for fourteen months and had never been well maintained in the first place. It would need significant renovations to be converted from an office to a restaurant space. But I didn't see any of those factors as problems. I could only see the possibilities.

The landlord was very rigid and flatly refused to negotiate his terms, but at least he was willing to work with me. Full of exuberance and a dash of naiveté, and wanting to be sure not to let a good thing slip between my fingers, I signed a lease agreement with the landlord that very day. Lacking in experience, I didn't even make the agreement conditional on a professional building inspection. My real-estate broker was coaching me through the process, but looking back, I now realize that he, too, was just as inexperienced as I was, having only closed a couple of transactions before this one. And of course, he had one eye on his commission the whole time. Like me, he just wanted to sign the agreement and was not so concerned about what was lurking beneath the surface.

And so the escapade began. The next day, I walked in with a contractor named Mohsen Kazemi, who had been referred to me by my real-estate broker. He simply went by the name Moe. Moe was Middle Eastern, like me, which made me trust him far too easily. I had been in Canada for a relatively short time at that point. You naturally gravitate to people who speak your own language.

Moe hadn't seen the building before I signed the lease agreement. I led him inside and we surveyed all the renovations that would be necessary to accommodate my vision for Café Saison. He walked around and made everything sound so easy.

"Oh, Reza, this will be fantastic! I can build a partition wall here, lay tile flooring in the entrance, and you can have a new cash counter over here. This is going to be beautiful!" Moe could talk a fantastic line.

The plan was to redesign the space with mostly cosmetic changes and a few minor alterations that required construction. I needed to build a vestibule, a new serving counter, and a cash counter, but that was the extent of the construction. Moe sketched out the plans by hand. I agreed to his concept. He anticipated that the job would take approximately six weeks.

I should have recognized the telltale signs. Anytime I asked Moe a question about what needed to be done, he would never give me a direct answer. But he exuded the confidence of an expert. "Oh, that's no problem, Reza. I'll take care of it," was a line I heard repeatedly. My father used to say that one who knows everything knows nothing. But I was too excited to have found somebody who would lease me their property to remember my father's words.

I paid Moe a deposit of one-third of the estimated costs, which was uncommonly high for a commercial renovation. He and his team started work the following week, just two weeks after I had signed the lease agreement. I dropped by the site a couple times a week to watch the work unfold and to address any questions or problems that came up.

Moe made reasonably good progress during the first two weeks, but then things began to slide. I began to notice that precious little was being accomplished between my Monday and Thursday visits. I let it go for a couple weeks. Eventually, it reached the point where I had to express my concern. Moe was nowhere near reaching the milestones he had originally proposed, and as time slipped away, so did the rent money that I was paying on an expensive and unproductive piece of commercial real estate.

Right away, the situation improved, at least for a while. Moe put his full crew on the job and the pace picked up noticeably for about a week. And then I found myself playing the same game again. A week would pass with no progress. By the tenth week, I estimated that Moe had completed only about a third of the work.

About that time, I received a phone call from a friend to say that officials from La Commission de la Santé et de la Sécurité du Travail du Québec, or CSST—the agency that upholds Quebec's occupational health and safety laws—had been seen at a nearby job site the day before, and that they would probably conduct a surprise inspection. I didn't think much of it, but I mentioned it to Moe when I was talking with him on the phone that afternoon. "Oh, really?" was his response.

I dropped by the café first thing the next morning and was surprised to see two CSST officials waiting at the front entrance. Moe and his crew were nowhere to be found. The officials introduced themselves and explained that the CSST was the government agency charged with upholding Quebec's workplace safety laws.

"Mr. Sarshoghi," one of them asked, "could you please give us the name of the general contractor who is performing the work?"

I did.

They were there to verify that all members of the construction team were CSST members and to survey the job site for safety hazards.

Coincidentally, Moe happened to call me on my cell phone to say that he and his crew had been called to attend to a pressing situation on another job site, and that they couldn't make it.

"Hmm." I thought to myself.

The CSST officials spent about twenty minutes looking around, making notes as they went.

"We need to ensure that all the people working on this job site are properly insured to carry out work on a commercial building. We need to report this information to our office," the official said.

"What does that mean for me?" I asked.

"We will call you later this afternoon," the CSST official replied. "It's outside of our jurisdiction, but did you secure all the proper permits for converting this from an office to a restaurant space?"

"Yes, I did."

"Thank you very much for your time," he said in a friendly tone. He shook my hand and left.

Indeed, I received a call from a different CSST official that afternoon informing me that Moe was not properly insured to be employing construction workers in a commercial construction zone. If anything happened to cause an injury to one of his workers, I would be liable. They could sue me for medical costs and future wages. I was putting myself at huge risk, the official said.

I had been looking for an excuse to liberate myself from Moe, anyway. He had been working at such a glacial pace that the renovation was going to be at least three months overdue. I phoned Moe and asked him not to return. I didn't realize when I hired him that he and his workers were required by provincial law to hold appropriate licenses and insurance for conducting a commercial renovation.

I took over the work myself. Friends advised me to get city building code inspectors in to approve the changes I was making, since I was going to be operating a public eating space. My renovations would have to meet local standards in order to be granted a license.

It was good advice. What started out as a simple renovation in Moe's eyes quickly turned into an extensive construction project. I had to upgrade the washrooms and plumbing to commercial standards, and adjust my plans in order to make the space wheelchair accessible. The city required minimum distances surrounding walls, counters, the entrance and doorways. I had no idea that the building code was so specific. Luckily, Moe had not started the major construction portion of the project, otherwise I would have been forced to tear out most of what he and I had envisioned in the original plan.

A city inspector came in and pointed out that the floor, which sagged slightly, did not have nearly enough support underneath. Perhaps it was fine when the building was built in the previous century, but by modern standards it was a disaster waiting to happen. I would be forced to raise the floor and reinforce the joists underneath. The inspector also recognized that the electrical system was woefully inadequate to support power-hungry kitchen equipment, and that the heating system was also inadequate by modern commercial standards. The inspector estimated that the aluminum wiring was installed in the 1940s. The existing 60-amp service needed to be upgraded to a three-phase 200-amp service. All the wiring needed to be torn out and replaced with copper.

Oh, my God.

But I was too far into the project to turn around. I approached the landlord to see if he would fund the upgrades. He refused, stating that our agreement still stood. If I wanted the building, I would have to fund the upgrades myself; if I walked away, he would seriously consider suing me for the remaining portion of the lease. We had a legal agreement.

While I was waiting for a new construction crew to begin, I began removing the old ceiling tiles myself one night after closing Collage Tapis. Behind them I found a hidden treasure. The original ceiling was four feet higher than the ugly drop ceiling that I was tearing out. It was covered in decorative tin tiles, which called back to the time when the space housed a hardware store. I could hardly believe my eyes. The landlord said that the building was at least a hundred years old. The tin was likely original. Unfortunately, the tin tiles were covered with dull grey paint that did nothing to bring out their rich historical character. All of a sudden, I had a new vision for the interior theme of Café Saison.

With great excitement, I tore down the entire drop ceiling that evening. Over the next two weeks, I and a friend cleaned the dull, grey paint off the tiles and refinished them in a classic copper toned paint. My plan was to apply a brass finish to the antique radiators to compliment the ceiling. I could hardly wait for it all to be finished.

During the renovations, the city inspector dropped by periodically to monitor every tiny detail: the emergency exit door, the type of glass on the front windows, the fire resistance of the walls, the need to install a sprinkler system, among many other things, all of which pushed the renovation costs much higher than my budget. I complied with all of the requirements, except the sprinkler system. It was just too expensive.

I couldn't open the coffee shop without the inspector's approval. I used every creative bone in my body to propose workable alternatives, but the inspector flatly refused to accept any of my ideas. It was a commercial space and the law was clear. I needed to install a sprinkler system before I would be granted an occupancy permit. I gave in and started looking for a company to install a sprinkler system.

The sprinkler problem continued to worsen. I contacted three companies and went with the one that would install the system at a competitive price and seemed to offer responsive customer service. Fine. But after I agreed to hire them, four days passed without hearing anything about when they would start the job. I called the sales rep and asked if he had any news for me. He said, "Well, we are waiting for the city to provide us with some information regarding the water main."

"Is there a problem with it?" I asked.

"Possibly," he said. "The existing water main from the street is only two inches in diameter. According to code, we need four inches for a sprinkler system," he said.

"What is the city going to do?" I asked.

"They might force you to replace the pipe coming in from the street," he said.

I sunk down in my chair and gazed up at the ceiling above me. "What next?" I thought to myself, in desperation. I thanked him and hung up. Right away, I called the city to find out more background information. I then found out that the inspector who had given me so much grief over a sprinkler system had gone on maternity leave. After reviewing my file, the new inspector said that he would accept one of my earlier proposals to install a fire alarm system.

Five months after I had parted ways with Moe, Café Saison was ready for business. It was absolutely exquisite. I installed beautiful tall windows facing the street, which took advantage of the added height I had discovered above the false ceiling. The walls inside were lined with rich wood paneling. The focal point of the café was a huge brass chandelier that I had imported from Iran. People's eyes were immediately drawn to it as they entered the cafe. The brass radiators and the dark covered chairs complimented the warm, luxurious atmosphere inside Café Saison. I was proud of my accomplishment, although I had invested practically every spare dollar I had to complete the renovation.

After opening the doors, my next goal was to ensure Café Saison attracted people's attention. I gained a lot of experience promoting Collage Tapis, but I didn't have experience running a coffee shop, nor a working knowledge of the local restaurant industry. I knew it would be essential to hire someone to oversee the day-to-day management of the café.

I interviewed a few different people and finally hired a young man named Denis Giroux. He came across as being motivated and experienced, and he demonstrated leadership qualities. I hired him and made him responsible for overseeing the café's operations.

Denis soon made a case to me that he needed an assistant. His arguments sounded reasonable, so I approved his request. He interviewed and hired a wonderful young woman named Judith

Heffernan, who was to help him in the mornings and on weekends, when the shop was busiest.

Six weeks later, when I popped into the café one morning, Judith asked if she could have a word with me. We went to a corner table and sat down.

"Reza, I would like you to raise my salary," she said.

"Oh?" It was the last thing I expected from a new employee. "Judith, you have not been here two months. I can't pay you more than what I pay Denis." I paused and shrugged my shoulders. "I'll certainly consider it when the café becomes more established, but for now I just can't do it."

"But why can't you pay me more than Denis?" she asked, quite forcefully. "He is never here and I am the one who does almost everything! I also have a lot of ideas that could increase your sales and create more traffic. But Denis is never here to discuss them." I read between the lines. I sensed that Denis was not being totally forthright with me. I knew things were going fairly well with the café in my absence, but perhaps that was because of Judith, not Denis.

"Interesting," I said to her. "Judith, I hear what you're saying. I promise you that I will look at this issue very seriously. But first I need to hear your ideas."

"Reza, you know how important marketing is, don't you?" she asked.

"Yes, I do. I also know how expensive it is."

"That's not necessarily true,," she said. We talked for over an hour about her ideas to raise Café Saison's profile. We also set a date for the same time the following week to meet and discuss her ideas further.

That week, I observed Denis closely and became convinced that his heart was not in his job. There were instances where he simply didn't show up, and left the serving staff to run the café. When I asked him for an explanation, he said that he had been meeting with suppliers. But when I called my suppliers, they were not aware of such meetings.

I eventually learned that Denis was a guitarist in a band, which was occupying his time late into the evenings. When it came to the day-to-day running of the coffee shop, I could certainly say he wasn't fully engaged. He was delegating most of the work and responsibilities to Judith. She was actually the one taking care of the details. It became clear that Denis was using me. Just before my next meeting with Judith, I met Denis at the shop and asked him not to return.

Judith had a lot of experience in the hospitality business. I have to hand it to Denis: he made a good decision in hiring her. The next time I sat down with Judith, I told her that she was right. I was convinced that Denis had clearly not been pulling his weight, and that he was no longer an employee. I promoted Judith to manager. I made it clear that the promotion was on the basis of trust, and that there would be a probation period for the next two months, during which time I would evaluate her performance. She was thrilled.

Judith and I continued the conversation that we had started a week earlier. We concentrated mostly on how to attract more customers and how to encourage them to keep coming back. In the hospitality industry, location is extremely important. Since we couldn't spend a lot of money on advertising, we had to make sure the business was visible.

"Fortunately, Reza," she said, "you've got an amazing location on a main street. The location alone gives you high potential for visibility. You just have to capitalize on that potential."

"What do you mean? I already replaced the front door, which I think is very classy." I realized that a main entrance makes an important impression on people. The new door was elaborate; solid wood with thick mouldings and a polished brass handle. It hinted at the atmosphere inside.

"Absolutely," said Judith. "But the money that you would normally throw away on traditional advertising could be spent much more effectively to increase your visibility."

"Oh?"

"Yes..The way you have extended those windows at the front, to take advantage of the high ceiling, is great. But I would have chosen windows that can completely open like a door onto the street during the warmer months. It would give your café a special flair."

"That's an interesting idea."

"And while we're talking about the front of the café, I think that sidewalk would be a perfect spot for a patio. Look at the width of that sidewalk, Reza! There is plenty of space. Having a patio out there would create a real buzz in this area."

"I never thought of that," I said, nodding my head in agreement. "A sidewalk patio would definitely compliment the café."

"Exactly. Look at the area. We're located on the main street of town. Almost every major bank has a branch within three blocks. City Hall is literally across the street from the café, which means that anyone living in this city has to eventually pass by the café for some reason, be it municipal court, a construction permit or paying a parking ticket. There is free parking located behind us. A patio would increase the number of customers we can serve at a time. I could go to the city and apply for the permit to use part of the sidewalk for a patio. I think we could fit another twenty-four seats out there!"

Her enthusiasm was a breath of fresh air.

"Reza, do you realize that this café is located on the warm side of the street?" she asked.

"What?"

I'll guarantee you that this side of the street gets more pedestrian traffic than the other side. It's warmer over here because of the angle of the sun."

Judith was right. I remember from my childhood how the business owners around my father's shop would talk about the advantages of being on the warm side of the street. It was said that the morning sun was warm, but not hot, and it lasted longer than the afternoon sun.

There was no stopping Judith. "Reza," she continued, I think this business is competition-proof. There are no other cafés around and it is in a neighbourhood with above-average incomes. I want to put plants by the four tables at the windows, to draw people to them. I think that will have a positive effect. Pedestrians will see the people at the windows and the shop will appear full. In any business, the appearance of a crowd is the best way to attract a bigger crowd. I would also like to put some plants at the back of the café to give that end a warmer, more inviting atmosphere. It's rather dark back there because there are no windows," she said.

"But plants need sun, Judith."

"I'll look after them. Don't worry about that.."

I was pleasantly surprised. Judith was completely right. Being so busy with planning the renovations and the start-up, I didn't consider the obvious, but Judith did. Since I didn't have the start-up capital to fund an elaborate advertising campaign, the café was entirely dependent on walk-in traffic. Obviously, I would have to use a promotional strategy that was oriented to a particular customer.

"I have to say, Judith, that I am extremely impressed. Good work. I like your ideas. Let's try them and see how they fare. And why don't you go ahead and inquire with the city about creating a patio out on the sidewalk. I like that possibility."

Judith was thrilled that I trusted her with such responsibility.

"Can I ask you something?"

"Sure," I replied.

"How did you finance this coffee shop?"

I snickered slightly, recalling the ordeal I had in trying to get a bank loan. "It's quite a story. I approached many banks but they all turned down my loan application. The failure rate for new restaurants is about fifty percent," I said.

"I'm not surprised," Judith replied, nodding slightly.

"The first question every loan officer asked me was if I had any previous experience in the restaurant business. I didn't, which was the first fatal strike against my loan application. But I had written a business plan, about fifteen pages long, and presented it to each bank."

"Well, that's a good start," Judith said.

"Not really. Everything was clear in my mind about how I was going to make the café successful. I included some demographic information about the area, which I had researched in the public library, and a substantial section on the aesthetic aspect of the café, such as the business logo, and the design of napkins, place mats, and coffee mugs. I even included a sample of the material I wanted to use to cover the chairs. In my mind, these were the things that would encourage business and drive my revenue."

"So, what was the problem?" Judith asked.

"The problem, I think, was that my cash flow projection was not realistic."

"Ah, I see. They want to know that you have made realistic projections of how much revenue you're going to generate, and that you have accurately predicted all of your costs."

"Exactly. It was clear in my mind, but it was not clear in the plan. In addition, though, I did not provide a marketing plan, even though the interior design that I described in the plan, in effect, was my marketing plan. Anyway, I seemed to strike a chord with one of the loan officers. He told me that he believed in me, but not necessarily in my business plan. He said that he could use his own limit to approve a loan, but the amount was less than forty percent of what I was seeking. I felt insulted. I let pride get in the way, and made a huge mistake by turning down his offer. I told him I truly didn't need bank financing and I could finance the start-up myself, which was not true."

"So how did you get started?" Judith asked.

"I actually financed all the equipment through the manufacturers."

"That sounds good."

"As a last resort, yes. But the interest rate charged by the manufacturers is outrageously high. I'm paying double the interest that the banks would have charged me. It's hurting my cash flow."

"May I have a look at the business plan you are talking about?"

"Sure. I don't have it with me, but next time, I will bring it along."

We finished the conversation at about eight -thirty that evening. Judith immediately started to reposition all the chairs and tables with the plants behind the windows. She also relocated some of the paintings to make the café more inviting.

Call it feng shui or a woman's touch, but it worked. It didn't take much time before we saw an increase in walk-in traffic. Positioning the tables beside the windows so that their occupants looked out onto the street drew new customers, like kids to a candy store. Judith was absolutely right. Her design strategy was well executed.

One Monday morning, a few weeks later, I walked into the café and immediately noticed that Judith had changed the location of the gift section. I

"Wow, that's different," I said to her.

Judith walked toward me and asked, "How do you like it now?"

"Well, it's—"

She cut me off before I could say anything. "I've sold over two hundred dollars in gifts since yesterday when I repositioned the gift display. I called the sales rep and asked him to bring me a wider variety of items to display," she said proudly.

We hadn't sold two hundred dollars' worth of gifts in a month, let alone a day.

"Judith, that's great! Well done!"

"Did you have a chance to get me that market study?"

"Yes, I actually have it in my car. I will get it for you."

Dream Beyond Borders

On my way out the door a customer stopped me and asked, "Do you work here?

"Yes, how can I help you?" I responded.

She handed me a piece of paper. "I got this coupon, and that is my friend over there."

I had no idea what she was talking about. The paper had a drawing of a mug of coffee and "Café Saison—Bring a Friend and Get a Free Cup of Coffee" written on it. I had never seen it before. There were some other details, but I didn't bother to read them. I walked over to Judith and handed her the coupon with a puzzled look on my face.

"Do you know anything about this?" I asked.

"Of course. This customer has brought a friend. I will go and meet them and ask them some questions," she said to me quietly. She walked toward the woman and her friend, and, after bit of chit-chat, she offered one of them a free cup of coffee.

I was very intrigued. I didn't ask any questions, and just went to my car and brought back the Café Saison business plan. We sat at an empty table at the back of the café. A server was taking care of customers while Judith and I spoke.

She took a quick look at my business plan package. While flipping through the pages, she asked me how I came up with the name.

"That is a very interesting story. I spent at least three months trying to come up with a name that would be easy to pronounce, easy to remember, and would portray as much information about the business as possible. I actually faced a bit of a dilemma when choosing the name."

"How so?"

"To my mind, it was like a golf-pro scenario. Does one have to be rich to start golfing or should one start golfing to get rich? If we look at famous brand names, they seldom portray their business lines. In fact, some of them are simply the family names of their founders, such as Ford, Heinz, Johnson & Johnson, and Toyota. They are among the most highly recognized brands in the world, yet their names don't have to incorporate what they sell. Unfortunately, I didn't have the luxury of time that these companies had in building recognition for their brands. I had to come up with a successful name.

"The only widely known coffee shop in Quebec at the time was Coffee Van Hoot. There were a small number of Second Cup franchises, and Starbucks had yet to hit the scene. I wanted the name to have impact."

Judith was listening closely, nodding her head.

"What I did was combine the French words for coffee and season. Together they produced a nice feeling for me. Coffee beans are green before they are roasted, so I chose green for the colour of the logo. For me, the logo and name just felt right."

"I love the name." Judith said. "And you have done a great job with the graphics and the interior concept. What was the inspiration behind your choice of colours?"

Actually, I think you know the designer. He is a middle-aged guy with long grey hair, always smiling. François….."

"François Ducharme?" she asked.

"That's right."

"I know him! That's why he acts like he owns this place! He comes here often," she said.

"François helped me with the plans. Right after signing the lease, he and I took a trip to Boston to get some ideas from Starbucks. Starbucks was starting to establish outlets in western Canada at that point, but it was still not a popular name in the east. I had heard about the sensation it was creating in the United States. Fortunately, François is not a very good follower. He is an innovator. He believed that he could create a much more effective visual presentation than what we saw in Starbucks. I realized on that trip that my customers would be completely different than those of Starbucks. Based on my research, I knew that they would mainly be over thirty years old and would likely prefer a higher level of service and be willing to pay extra for it. They wouldn't want to stand in line and pick up their coffee from a counter. I knew these people would prefer to be served at their tables. They would be more willing to pay healthy tips, too. So François and I designed a long counter and placed all the tables along the counter and this wall. On one side, customers would enjoy seeing the paintings on the wall, and on the other side they would see all the products we were serving. The idea was to stimulate the customers by displaying our desserts, coffee and beverages. We also added this nice little section of gifts and promotional items."

"Reza, what do you think about printing t-shirts, and perhaps creating other products, with the Café Saison logo?" Judith asked. "We can use the t-shirt for our employees and also display it for sale in the gift section. It would be very good publicity."

Judith was full of great ideas to promote Café Saison in thrifty, unconventional ways. She also suggested that we start gathering information about Café Saison's customers and use it to gain insights into our market. She wanted to personalize the coffee shop and tailor it to their interests and needs. She wanted everything—the coffee, seating, menu items, opening hours—to be perfectly compatible with their tastes, which would be the first step in creating customer loyalty.

So far we had done a good job of positioning the coffee shop in the market. The branding was coming along, too.

I was very busy with my other business affairs, but fortunately I could rely on Judith. I made time to walk around and meet the business owners and managers in the area surrounding the café.

Three weeks later, Judith telephoned me to say that she had finished gathering customer information and that it revealed a great deal about their tastes. She asked if we could meet the next day.

"How about six o'clock?" I asked.

"We can't meet at that time, Reza. I gave permission to a local dance group to hold their practice here, so long as they order from our menu."

"What? Dance practice?" I asked. It caught me completely by surprise.

"Yes," she said. "They are a professional Latin dance group. It will be amazing to watch them dance. They'll come here, bring their own music, and likely bring friends. The other customers will love to watch them dance. It will be a free performance for them."

"Judith, you're a genius," I said. "Okay, how about meeting me at three o'clock tomorrow instead?" I asked.

"Sure, that's fine."

The next day I arrived at the café at three o'clock. I intended to stay and watch the dance group. "Okay, Judith, I am here to listen to your ideas."

She grinned.

"I have to say again how impressed I am about you welcoming the Latin dance group. Well done."

"One of the dance group members came in for a cup of coffee last week and I happened to strike up a conversation with him. It taught me that simply talking to people is very important for uncovering opportunities."

"It's true," I replied.

"Well, back to the marketing plan," Judith said. "I started with our opening hours. To begin with, we were open from nine in the morning until ten in the evening, every day. In talking with our customers, I found out the hours that best suit their needs. Most of the morning customers are business people who start their work day fairly early in the surrounding offices. For that crowd, the food has to be ready by no later than seven o'clock in the morning. The next wave of customers tends to start at about ten o'clock, with retirees and office workers taking morning breaks."

"Okay," I said.

"I think we need slightly different menu offerings for the early and mid-morning crowds," Judith pointed out.

Just then, a tall man with a long ponytail walked into the café and came toward us exclaiming, "I did it, I got it!"

He came up to our table, extended his hand to me and said, "You must be Reza."

"Yes, that's right."

"I'm Daniel. Everyone calls me Danny the Artist," he said.

I must have had a very puzzled look on my face. Judith quickly jumped in to help me understand what he was talking about.

"I promised Danny that if he could get some artists together, I would talk to you, and if you agreed, we would display their artwork here in the coffee shop. I proposed that they organize an exhibition and keep their paintings here for one month. For every sale they make, they will pay the Café a small fee to help cover our overhead costs."

I couldn't believe how creative Judith was.

"What do you think, Reza? I am sure this will go a long way to filling the café every moment of our opening hours," Judith said.

Even though I thought her idea was great, I didn't want to express too much enthusiasm without seeing the results. I paused for a moment and then replied, "Okay. I will try it for one month and see how it works."

It worked perfectly. Café Saison became *the* cafe known for its unique interior design, service, and, thanks to the rotating art displays, its sophisticated atmosphere. Everything came together so nicely—the antique brass chandelier, the tin plate ceiling and tall windows, the plants and the artwork. In fact, Café Saison was more like a community cultural centre disguised as a café. In providing local artists a space to display and sell their work, we helped them gain exposure. In turn, they helped Café Saison gain exposure by introducing their social networks to the café. These were people who would never be found in a franchised coffee shop. Café Saison was the perfect match for their tastes and budgets.

Café Saison soon developed a cult following. It became *the* gathering place for a certain segment of the local community. Some people were attracted by the art; others were captivated by the ambience. Café Saison had firmly established itself as a destination. Its reputation even attracted film crews. Two production companies approached Judith in eighteen months to rent the café for Hollywood movie shoots.

Judith also came up with a great idea for packaging. She was aiming to supply our customers not only with food and drink in the shop, but with something for them to take home that would get our name out onto the streets. Specially-packaged gourmet food, pastries, and coffee beans grew as take-out items. We even changed the colour of our packaging to match each season.

Judith's ideas prompted my own, too. I devised a simple card system to help customers explore the many varieties of coffee we sold. It also helped them to discover the flavours that appealed to them. The cards kept track of the customers by name and phone number. To encourage people to start using the system, I offered one hundred grams of dark roasted Colombian coffee beans for free. People would try it and record their comments on the card. The next time they came in, I would again offer one hundred grams of a slightly different roasted bean for free, and I would do it until the customer found the coffee bean they preferred. From that point, they could walk in anytime, give either their name or phone number to any staff member, and purchase coffee beans that were tailored exactly to their tastes.

These days, there are many new inexpensive ways of marketing through social networking. We didn't have the luxury of using the Internet the way we can today. But rotating art displays, dance classes, a simple loyalty card system and even the location of the flowers allowed us to entice a unique market niche without spending a great deal of money.

Lessons Learned

I've watched small business managers throw money at traditional advertising media, thinking that the return would be instant. The lesson that I learned from Café Saison was that effective promotional strategies need not be expensive nor follow the status quo. They just have to be properly targeted and well thought out in order to speak to the particular niche that you are targeting.

One of your primary goals as a small business manager is to differentiate yourself. The easiest first step is to look at the physical design and presentation of your business. Don't underestimate the power of appealing to people's senses. At Café Saison, my business was coffee and light snacks. Did the taste and price of my coffee define me in the local marketplace? Hardly. People came to Café Saison because of the atmosphere. It takes years to develop a brand through advertising alone; Café Saison impacted people's senses through atmosphere and design. Be imaginative and don't be afraid to hire someone to help you get it right. Remember, I hired a designer and we traveled to Boston to do research so we could get the design for Café Saison just right. Everything about Café Saison—from its logo to its interior colours and design features—was the advertising strategy. It all worked together to appeal perfectly to a certain niche of the local market.

Defining and understanding your audience is also essential. Think in terms of networks. Judith brilliantly tapped into networks of artists and dancers. Café Saison was compatible with their tastes, and filled a niche in a way that nothing else in the area had done. We provided those networks with something they needed, at no cost to them, and in turn they loyally supported the café. Remember, if your business has an impact on people, they will promote it for you through their network. Word of mouth is very powerful.

Chapter 4: Think Like a Banker

When he was a young man living in the city of Isfahan, my grandfather bought and sold antiques for a living. He was well known as somebody who travelled the region on a constant search for rare, valuable pieces. He would buy large quantities of merchandise for a good price and then sell the items individually. But to make a large purchase he had to borrow cash through a local financier. My grandfather would pay him interest on the borrowed money every month until he sold his inventory, and then would pay him back the principal.

The financier became quite a bully when people didn't make their payments on time. If my grandfather didn't happen to have enough money on collection day, he would refer the financier to his brother-in-law, who was a giant of a man with an intimidating presence. His brother-in-law took pride in supporting family members in need. He was always able to deter the financier until my grandfather sold enough merchandise to make his payments.

This arrangement ended after my grandfather had a falling out with his brother-in-law, which meant that he could no longer rely on him for protection. And in that small district in the heart of Isfahan, the smallest bit of gossip became local news very quickly.

Word of their falling out reached the financier. Two weeks later, on the day my grandfather failed to make a payment, the financier paid him a visit. After hearing the banging on his door and knowing that it couldn't be anyone but the financier, my grandfather leapt from his chair and grabbed some money that he kept hidden in a tin can for emergencies. He actually had more than enough money in the can to pay his entire debt to the financier, but only took out enough for one month's payment.

My grandfather opened the old wooden door and greeted the angry looking man. Without saying "hello" in return, the financier said in a very threatening tone, "I am not here for a social visit. I want my money."

"Oh, sir, I was actually just on my way to give it to you." "Here you go," my grandfather said, and he handed him the money. It was business as usual from that point on.

My grandfather told me this story many times. "Reza," he would say, "why use your own money if you can use somebody else's? But never borrow so much that you can't manage the payments. And remember one of the most important things in business: always have money set aside for a rainy day."

Securing adequate operating capital to launch or grow a business is one of the biggest challenges a small business owner will face. In my view, capital markets offer great benefits, namely the option to work with somebody else's money rather than risking your own.

The first time I ever tried to get bank financing in Canada was for start-up capital for Café Saison. I approached all the big retail banks, and was flatly rejected by each of them. Not only was I frustrated but I was also very surprised that the loan officers did not recognize a solid business opportunity.

In retrospect, experience has taught me that I wasn't providing those loan officers a clear picture of the vision I had for my business or my ability to manage it. Investors—bankers, venture capitalists, angel investors, or rich uncles, for that matter—all want to know the same things in order to judge whether you are worthy of their money. They want to know about your experience, your customers, what distinguishes your business from others, how much skin you have in the game, and what return on investment your business will generate.

I was too inexperienced when applying for that first loan to see a key piece of the puzzle. Loan officers have a wealth of knowledge about business. They deal with a wide variety of business ventures and they know right away the key success factors to look for. In my case, it was the loan officers' knowledge of my industry that was working against me. Fifty percent of all new coffee shops and restaurants fail in their first year. I wasn't aware of that statistic, but those loan officers certainly were. In their eyes, there was a fifty percent chance that I would default on my loan.

I ended up scraping together a bit of money and starting the coffee shop without a bank loan. It was a shoestring operation at the beginning, but I managed my cash carefully. Café Saison came close to insolvency three times in the first two years, in spite of Judith's many great ideas. Without a line of credit to buffer my cash flow, I was forced to buy my equipment on credit from the manufacturers, who charge a much higher rate of interest than the banks. But with hard work and a creative approach to marketing, Café Saison became a success story.

After launching Café Saison, I sought financing to buy a commercial building to house Collage Tapis. I had been renting a retail location for Collage Tapis and found a great opportunity to purchase a location that I could finance for less than I was paying in rent. Given the experience I had gained in trying to get a loan for the coffee shop, and the fact that the building would provide the necessary collateral for the loan, I didn't anticipate having any trouble. But I encountered the same barriers all over again when I approached the banks. I could not fathom why it was so easy for people around me to get a mortgage, yet I was being denied again. Was I doing something wrong? I had been in Canada for three years by then and felt that I had a reasonable grasp of the business landscape. Were the bank managers discriminating against me as a new Canadian? Or was I simply making a glaring mistake in my loan applications that I simply did not see?

I vented my frustration and sought answers from almost every friend and business acquaintance I had at the time. I acted on one suggestion that a family friend made, which was to consult a mortgage broker that she and her husband had dealt with when arranging the financing on their home. She said that this broker had been dealing with banks and private investors for years, arranging personal home mortgages and multi-million dollar loans for commercial buildings. If anyone could provide me with useful insights, it would be him. His name was Richard Sommerville. She gave me his number.

I called him the next day and I was pleasantly surprised to find that he had been expecting my call.

"Hello Reza," he said. "Nice to hear from you. Lorrie telephoned me last night to say that you would likely call."

"Richard, I would be grateful if you could advise me on my current situation," I said. "I am interested in purchasing a building for my business but I am facing challenges with getting financing." I gave him a quick overview of my situation.

"Why don't we meet in person? Given what you have told me so far, I would be interested in learning more," he said. "I just might be able to help you out." I took him up on his offer to meet in my office two days later.

Richard arrived precisely on time, which impressed me. On the surface, he seemed quite polished and successful. He dressed well, drove a European luxury car, and was very respectful and polite. I welcomed him into my conference room and poured a cup of coffee for each of us.

After exchanging a bit of small talk about our mutual connections to Lorrie, we quickly got down to business.

"Richard," I said, "here is the building that I described to you over the phone." I showed him pictures from the real- estate listing. "The building was repossessed by the bank. I submitted a low-ball offer and the bank accepted it. To be honest, I can hardly believe they were willing to let it go for such a low price. But I have to remove the condition of financing to close the deal. I am having trouble lining up the financing."

He nodded while looking through the pictures. "Is the building vacant?" he asked.

"Yes it is. I want to locate my store there," I said. "What do you think?"

"It appears to be in good condition, but more importantly, it's in a fantastic location. You got an amazing deal from the bank," he said, nodding in agreement.

"But I need financing," I replied, shrugging my shoulders. "I really don't know why I am having difficulty getting a loan. I have good credit."

"I think I might be able to help you out, Reza," Richard said, lifting his coffee cup. Where did you go to get financing? Did you apply to financial institutions or did you approach private investors?"

"I went to three banks, but was rejected by all of them," I said.

"Which banks? It's important for me to know so I don't waste time."

I gave him the names of the banks and account managers I had approached.

"You probably didn't realize that each of these banks has preferences for the types of loans they issue," he said. "Actually, it's true for all banks. Some favour residential mortgages while others prefer to focus on commercial properties. I know one bank that works exclusively with large commercial high- rise buildings, like hotels. Each bank has its preferences."

"Really?" I replied in surprise. "I had no idea."

"It's true. So, first we have to identify the banks to which your building would be of strategic interest," Richard said.

"Do you think I am asking them for too much money?" I asked.

"No. The dollar amount is not the only deciding point for the banks," Richard said. "In theory, the more a financial institution gives you, the better it is for them. Look at it this way: issuing a thirty- thousand dollar loan takes the same amount of time and energy as a three- hundred- thousand- dollar loan. I don't need to tell you which one earns the bank more money. Larger loans are more appealing for any bank manager, as long as they are well supported."

I nodded as he spoke.

"Okay, Reza, if I understand correctly, you want to buy that building and move your store to that location," he said.

"Yes, that's correct."

"Then, I think I know a banker who might be interested in working with you."

I'm sure my eyes lit up. "Fantastic!"

"But I cannot absolutely guarantee that your mortgage application will be approved," he said.

"Don't you think that we should have more than one choice?" I asked. "Limiting ourselves to just one bank will reduce our chances, won't it?"

Richard shook his head. "I don't think in your case it would be a good idea. Every time you apply for any kind of loan, the institution checks with the credit bureau and verifies your personal credit rating. Through the credit check process, lenders can determine the other institutions to which you have been applying. Applying too often is a red flag that can weaken your rating, which is why I think that applying to more than one institution will not necessarily improve your chances—unless you apply for a loan through your company. Credit agencies do not cross-reference for corporations."

"You are more of an expert in this area than I am. I will follow your advice," I said.

"Thank you. We need to think like a banker, Reza," he said with a slight grin. "I'm going to need your personal financial statements, including income tax assessments."

"Sure, anything you require," I replied.

"The Business Development Bank of Canada offers business financing for property if it will be used to bring revenue to the business," Richard explained. "Although it charges a slightly higher interest rate, I think it might be a good potential financing vehicle for you. Working with the Business Development Bank of Canada is very convenient, since it is a crown corporation."

"What difference does that make?" I asked.

"BDC was established by the government to help entrepreneurs. In some cases, BDC might take on risk that the chartered banks would avoid. BDC can also offer entrepreneurs flexibility. For example, for businesses that are seasonal, BDC will allow their owners to adjust their monthly payments according to cash flow cycles, increasing them in the high season and decreasing them in the low season.

"Interesting," I said. "I've seen their logo before but didn't realize the specialized services they offer."

"I will need to present them with some key information about your business and why you think moving to that location would be better for you," Richard said. "You'll need to give a forecast of how your business would do in this new location, the amount by which you think you would increase your revenue, and the net impact of becoming your own landlord."

"Not a problem," I said. I had mapped out the financial benefits of purchasing the building in my mind long ago.

"While you compile that information, I will talk to an account manager I know at BDC to get his initial impression. I will get in touch with you again before the end of the week and we'll go from there," said Richard.

"By the way, where are you originally from, Reza?" Richard asked.

"Iran," I responded. "I've been in Canada for about three years."

"How does one get financing in Iran?" he asked.

"Well, there is not much of a credit system in Iran. If you have cash you can buy; if not, you rent," I said.

"Interesting," he said. "Well, I'll be on my way. I'll be in touch again by the end of the week." We shook hands and I showed him to the door.

That week, I worked on gathering the documents Richard had requested: some financial statements, the offer to purchase that had been accepted by the vendor, my personal tax return, and a couple spreadsheets detailing how the rental payments for my current location would be applied to mortgage payments and taxes, with a little extra left over each month to leave me further ahead.

As promised, Richard called me toward the end of the week to say that the BDC account manager reviewed my file with a great deal of interest. He wanted to drop by my office in the coming week to talk about the application. Despite the positive news, Richard was careful to point out that it wasn't a sure thing, and that it was too early to get my hopes up.

Wow. What a difference from all of the rejections I had gotten from the other banks. To be honest, I had been getting quite discouraged. Richard's news gave me a badly needed lift.

The BDC account manager's visit was anti-climactic. Given what I had experienced with the banks, I was honestly expecting to be treated indifferently, and my business plan to be criticized as being unworthy. The BDC manager asked a lot of important questions, congratulated me on recognizing a good business opportunity, and asked me to fill out some standard forms and pay a small application fee. I was impressed that he actually came to my office.

I was stunned to get Richard's call four days later to say that BDC had approved my loan. And thanks to Richard's advice and knowledge of the system, BDC actually gave me more money than I had initially requested. The loan increase was good for all three of us. Richard would get paid more money, as he was working on a percentage- based commission, the BDC account manager would get closer to his monthly quota, and I would get a boost to my cash flow, though it would cost me slightly more to service the loan than I had anticipated. Actually, for me it was a bit of a double-edged sword. I didn't want to come across to Richard as though I were looking a gift horse in the mouth, but I hadn't budgeted on the slightly higher costs of servicing the loan. I had told Richard that I wanted to negotiate the terms with BDC. Items like the administration fee, the interest rate, and the deposit (not to mention the mortgage- broker's fee) are all negotiable. He didn't disagree, but recommended doing so after receiving their official letter of intent. He pointed out that BDC likely knew that I had no other options.

Two weeks later, I received a ten-page letter of intent from BDC, which took me by surprise. I just knew that the process seemed too easy. I called Richard right away.

"Richard, what is going on?" I asked, without even saying "hello.".

"Good morning, Reza. What's wrong?"

"I just got the letter of intent from BDC. There are more than fifty clauses that will limit me and jeopardize me from finalizing this loan. One clause even says that they are under no obligation to give final approval to my application, and have sole discretion to reject me! Richard, I'm no further ahead than I was with the other banks!" I said.

"Reza, it is just a standard form that legally protects them. You remember how supportive the account manager was in your office. If you have received the letter of intent, the process is almost done."

"And what about all these new documents the bank is asking for?" I asked. They are requiring an environmental assessment, an appraisal and a building inspection. I didn't know about this. This is all going to cost me more money!"

"Look, Reza, you need those documents for your own good, anyway," he replied. "They should be part of your due diligence."

"But they're requesting other documents, too. Insurance policies, a title report, and we also have to have the deed signed by the bank's notary. I am the one who will be paying for the notary. I should be the one who can choose!"

"It's just the way it works, Reza. The bank has to ensure the title is clear, that there are no liens registered against the property, and that they are the first rank mortgage holder. The bank will only register deeds in a specific form. There are not many notaries who will draft a deed as the bank wants. They have to make sure their money is secure and are able to use any means to get their money back if you default."

I was ready to back away from BDC's loan offer, but Richard convinced me that it would have been no different with any of the other banks. He encouraged me to have my lawyer review it and note any modifications.

I thought I was being unfairly targeted, but after talking to Richard, I realized that BDC was treating me like any other client. I had my lawyer review their letter of intent. He proposed a few changes and I replied to BDC, noting my lawyer's comments. Richard negotiated with BDC on my behalf for about a week. That in itself was a surprise to me because I assumed that the terms presented by such big institutions were non-negotiable. But I guess anything in life is negotiable; you just have to ask.

In the end, it worked. BDC issued the loan about five weeks after the account manager had first visited me in my office. I was able to remove the condition of financing on my offer to purchase the building and complete the transaction.

As I mentioned earlier, I had started Café Saison with next to no start-up capital because I could not secure financing. Maintaining it was a financial struggle for the first two years, but careful management, creative marketing, and sheer determination led me to success. It became a very popular and trendy place. Two other coffee shops opened in the same area, trying to capitalize on the trend that I had created, but each one went out of business in less than a year.

The success of Café Saison was too compelling to limit to just one shop. I decided to open a second one just like it. This time around, I had more knowledge. Richard had taught me the importance of applying to a bank whose lending preferences were in line with my business. Finding a bank that would finance a retail start-up venture would be a challenge; especially a new coffee shop, given the high failure rate in the restaurant business.

In my research, I discovered a special government program to support small business start-ups. Through this program, the federal government would guarantee small business loans of up to two hundred and fifty thousand dollars. The loans had to be issued through a retail bank and registered against equipment. It sounded exactly like what I needed.

Reflecting on what I learned from working with Richard, I approached only two banks that I knew offered small business financing. Not only did I meticulously review the terms and conditions they were offering, but I carefully sized up the account managers. In actual fact, I was shopping for the right loan manager because a small business borrower must interact very closely with his or her loan manager. Life can be miserable if that relationship is not solid.

Gilles Fortier, the account manager at the second bank I visited, seemed very willing to give me his time to explain his company's loan products. He was also interested in hearing about my business idea and my past experience. Coincidentally, he had just recently provided financing to a similar business in the hospitality industry, which was very encouraging for me to hear.

Gilles made a positive impression on me. He was professional and respectful, and his bank's various business loan products seemed to be designed with small businesses in mind. It was a refreshing contrast to the indifferent attitudes I had encountered at other banks. By the end of that initial meeting with Gilles, I decided that he was the person I wanted to work with, although I did not let him know that I was ready to do business with him. I wanted him to understand that I was not willing to work with just anybody, and that a bank was going to have to earn my business. When I left his office, I gave no indication that I wanted another meeting with him.

I called Gilles two days later to follow up. He was by no means pushy, but he opened the door to future discussions. I really liked his style. I told him that I gave our discussion a lot of thought and that I would be interested in speaking to him in more detail about my business financing needs, and the possibility of working together. He welcomed a second meeting, but said it would have to wait until he returned from vacation in two weeks. He advised me that in our next meeting he would be looking for me to provide assurance that I was determined to create a successful business, and that I knew what I was talking about. He wasn't saying it to intimidate me. He was just giving me all the information I needed to be properly prepared.

While Gilles was on vacation, I approached my wife's niece to see if she would help me draw up a professional business plan. Her nickname was Rosie. She was in her final year of business school at Montréal's Concordia University. She had plenty of resources and, more importantly to me, a strong sense of determination. She jumped at the opportunity to work on a real-world business case.

Rosie spent a few days questioning me about my business and gathering the necessary information to write the plan. She sized up the task in front of her and asked to have four weeks to write it. I would have been shocked at her request had she not shown me three other business plans, one of which she wrote herself and the other two she used as guides. From them, I learned just how comprehensive a properly written business plan is. Having seen those plans, I gave her the time she requested. I would simply have to email Gilles and postpone our second meeting.

Hiring Rosie to write the business plan was one of the best decisions I have ever made. She brought to the task the youthful enthusiasm of a university student. She got excited about my business idea along with me, which was enormously motivating. Without her, I would not have had anyone to offer me a second opinion or to say to me, "Reza, what about doing this?" One set of eyes cannot possibly see everything. Without Rosie, I would have been doing a lot of talking and thinking to myself.

Rosie and I met regularly over those four weeks. She challenged my assumptions with impressive business insight. I spent at least six hours each week talking with her about the business and the details of the plan. She pushed me to articulate important details that I would have simply overlooked because they seemed obvious to me.

Four weeks to the day, as promised, Rosie presented me with two beautifully bound business plans. I knew exactly how much effort she put into the task. Her attention to detail was beyond description. Including exhibits, the plan was over seventy pages long.

The two of us sat down at my conference table, each with a copy of the plan. I had seen draft versions, but it was my first time to see the plan in its final form. I began flipping through the pages to look for items we had discussed and to make sure that all of the changes had been included. Everything was there and it was watertight. The plan addressed questions big and small about my new venture: the location of the new coffee shop, target customers, prices, the menu, equipment suppliers, opening hours, a detailed cash flow projection, and opening and closing balance sheets for the first year. The plan answered every possible question an investor could pose.

I invited Rosie to join me for lunch the following week at a nice restaurant in downtown Montréal, where I would present the plan to Gilles. I told her that she had impressed me so much throughout the plan writing process, I thought it would be good to have her present in this crucial meeting. I made it clear that I would be relying on her at times to speak to the plan. She was thrilled. It would be the first time she had ever dealt with a banker in a real-life, high-stakes business deal.

We all met at the restaurant and sat at a special table that I had reserved through the owner, whom I knew personally.

"Gilles Gervais, I would like you to meet Rosie Amin. Rosie is in her fourth year of business school at Concordia University. She helped me draft my business plan."

"Hello Mr. Gervais, it is a pleasure to meet you," Rosie said, shaking Gilles's hand with confidence. "Reza told me a lot of good things about you."

"I'm glad you're joining us, Rosie. Perhaps I will learn something from you today," he said warmly.

We got straight down to business. Rosie handed each of us a bound copy of the business plan and asked us to open it to the table of contents. She walked us through the various sections of the plan. "I researched the demographics of the area, and direct and indirect competitors. There is a section on Reza's past business experience. All the financial information you will need is in the last section," she said.

"Do you know how this government program works, Reza?" Gilles asked.

"Sort of," I replied, "but it would be helpful if you could elaborate on it."

"Well, we have to study your business plan. Judging by what I have seen at first glance, I don't doubt that it will be very comprehensive. I will also be sending you a form to fill out and sign, which will give the bank authorization to verify your company's credit history. If the bank is interested in this file, you will get a letter of intent in the mail, which outlines the terms upon which the bank would issue the loan."

"How long will it take?" I asked.

"Anywhere from four to six weeks after we have received all the necessary documentation," Gilles said.

Rosie was quiet. She was listening very carefully and taking notes.

"If everything is approved, the bank will lend seventy-five percent of what you have spent on equipment and leasehold improvements, up to a maximum of two hundred and fifty thousand dollars," Gilles said.

I nodded in agreement. I was familiar with the terms, and presented my financial projections accordingly in the business plan. The bank would not lend for intangible expenditures like marketing costs.

Gilles continued. "This loan, if it is approved, would be guaranteed in part by the federal government, but you are responsible to guarantee twenty-five percent of the total amount received by the bank. Any change to your business as it is represented in the articles of incorporation after the loan is issued would require the bank's agreement."

That was one point I was not aware of, but it seemed logical to me.

"How would the bank transfer the money to me?" I asked.

"When you order a piece of equipment, you pay a down payment of twenty-five percent to the supplier. When the merchandise is delivered, you will send us the invoice and the proof of payment for the deposit. The bank will then issue a cheque payable to that supplier for the difference. For small purchases, you should keep the receipt and proof of payment. We will then issue a cheque to you."

The waiter interrupted our conversation to ask for our order. I could see at that point that Gilles was enjoying everything. He was impressed by the restaurant and our presentation.

Throughout lunch he took the time to explain everything to me from A to Z about the loan program and his bank's policies. He had some tough questions for me to answer, even after just a cursory glance at my business plan. For example, he knew of two other coffee shops that had opened within blocks of my proposed location over the past year but went out of business, which I did not realize. Why would I succeed when they failed? He also noted that I was already running a carpet store and another coffee shop, and questioned whether I might be spreading myself too thin. But he didn't belabour any of these points. They were just simple questions gleaned from his first glance at the plan.

No question, he was sharp. I could tell that he wasn't trying to beat me down, but rather to draw my attention to things that might pose challenges to my success. I looked to Rosie for support, and she was outstanding. Her responses to his questions were reasoned and she presented them with a sense of authority and professionalism that was well beyond her young age. She and I made a great team.

Overall, the lunch became a casual conversation about my loan application. While Gilles seemed to be convinced of the potential for my second outlet of Café Saison, he was very non-committal. He said that he and his team at the bank would review the plan in depth by reviewing market factors and key financial ratios, and give me a preliminary response within seven days.

Gilles was true to his word. Early the following week he phoned me to say that the bank had approved my application in principle. Hallelujah! He said that the business plan reflected a perceptive understanding of the market, included a creative marketing strategy that had been proven by my first coffee shop, and demonstrated my solid understanding of the financial realities of running a start-up in this sector. He said that our conversation over lunch painted a picture that couldn't be captured in a business plan, namely my determination as an entrepreneur and my personal integrity. He said that I had addressed all of the factors the bank evaluates when analyzing a loan application, and that I had made it easy for them. The business case I had presented was sound.

The letter of intent arrived soon thereafter. That the bank required additional documentation was not a surprise to me this time around. Final approval for the loan took about eight weeks. The second location of Café Saison was about to become reality.

As a business person, I am always terrified and fascinated by the unexpected. What lies around that next corner can be lethal if your business is not on solid, competitive and financial ground. On the other hand, what can jump out from behind a corner is sometimes an opportunity that you simply did not see.

Just before I opened the doors to the second Café Saison, Rosie approached me to work behind the counter a few hours a week while she was finishing her program at Concordia. That decision was a no-brainer. She started in February. In May, after she finished her program, she started working full time for the summer as assistant manager. It was a great fit, for me and for her. Then, in mid-July, something popped out from around a corner that I was not expecting. After closing up one night, Rosie asked to sit down and talk.

"Uh-oh," I thought to myself, "what has happened?"

It was ten o'clock in the evening. Rosie poured two cups of Jamaican mountain roast coffee, and we sat down.

"So, what's up?" I asked.

"Reza, I want you to consider something. If you don't like the idea, there will be no hard feelings," she said. I could tell she was nervous.

"Of course, Rosie," I replied, with a warm smile to help her feel at ease.

"I know I am your wife's niece, and that it is not wise to mix business with family, but I would like to become your partner in this business," she said, looking me straight in the eye with a cute grin on her face.

I paused for a moment and could feel my shoulders fall in relief. "Oh," I said, "I thought there was a big problem you needed to talk to me about! Thank God!"

"I know this business inside out, especially since I started working here. I want the challenge of building up this business to the level of your other Café Saison. I can be here every minute of the day, whereas you have to manage your carpet stores."

"You're right, Rosie, I am not devoting the same time to this place that I was to the other Café Saison," I replied.

"I just finished university. I have the time. I can talk to people as a business owner when they come in, not just as an employee who is trying to make a few dollars in the short term. I can build this business!"

Even at ten o'clock at night after a full day's work, Rosie's enthusiasm was inspiring. She reminded me a lot of Judith at the other Café Saison.

"I've saved a bit of money, Reza. I would like to buy shares in Café Saison and become a partner. Think about it carefully. I don't expect you to give me an answer right away. I realize that this is your business and your vision. If you don't like the idea, I will have no hard feelings."

"Rosie," I said, "one of the best business decisions I have ever made was to hire you to write the business plan for this place. Let me give it some serious thought."

Rosie had impressed me from the moment I started working with her on the business plan. Most importantly she had strong leadership skills and was always respectful of the fact that I was in the driver's seat. Having a go-getter like her present at Café Saison on a regular basis would benefit me greatly.

I paused for a moment and felt myself nodding my head. I knew she had everything to take Café Saison to the next level.

I smiled at her and said, "Rosie, there's no doubt in my mind that you've got what it takes. Let me talk to my lawyer.

Instead of selling Rosie shares in the business, my lawyer recommended creating a new holding company with a shareholder agreement that gave Rosie minority ownership. Doing so required me to change all of the account information held at the bank. I had to provide the bank copies of the holding company's articles of incorporation and revise the existing bank accounts, including the pre-authorized payment details for the loan.

For six months, everything went extremely well with my new partnership with Rosie. Until, that is, I received a horrendous phone call at home early one morning from a very abrupt bank investigator.

"Is this Reza Sarshoghi?" the voice asked without any introduction.

"Yes it is." I replied, "May I ask who's calling?"

"What you have done with that coffee shop is fraud." He was speaking in a very forceful tone.

"Pardon? Fraud?" I asked.

"Yes, fraud," he replied. "We can refer you to a criminal court."

I figured it had to be a joke, so I didn't react strongly to him.

"Who is this?"

The man identified himself as a representative of the bank from which I had secured the start-up loan guarantee. He was accusing me of transferring ownership of Café Saison to a new company and maintaining the old one as a shell, which would allow me to easily walk away from the loan. Furthermore, I had not sought the bank's approval before changing the ownership structure.

I hadn't deliberately intended to create this scenario. Rosie and I were referred to a junior loan officer when we revised the ownership structure. He didn't recognize the legal implications of what we were doing, and how the move put the bank at risk.

"Sir," I said, "I have every intention to live up to my obligations to your bank. You have to keep in mind that I created this new corporate structure about six months ago with the full knowledge of one of your loan officers."

"Oh, yeah?" he said. "What was that person's name?"

I gave him all of the details.

"I need to talk with the bank manager to clear up this situation," I said.

"Yes, please do so tomorrow!" he ordered.

The next day I went to the branch to see what was going on. I usually had to make an appointment in advance, but this time I couldn't wait. I asked the receptionist for a meeting with Gilles, my loan officer, right away.

"I'm sorry Mr. Sarshoghi, but Gilles has been on sick leave for months now," she said. "I'm surprised that nobody informed you."

"Then I need to meet with the person who is replacing him," I said. "It's urgent."

"Yes, of course. His name is Matthew. He is with someone at the moment, but if you would just take a seat he should be free in about ten minutes."

Matthew soon came out and greeted me in the reception area. "Mr. Sarshoghi, it's a pleasure to meet you. I'm Matthew," he said, extending his hand. I stood up and introduced myself.

"My office is this way," he said, gesturing over to a wall of private offices on the opposite side of the bank.

"So, what can I do for you?" he asked.

"I own a coffee shop called Café Saison not far from here on Sherbrooke Street. I have a business loan with your bank," I said, and gave him the account number. "Yesterday I received a very rude phone call from one of your representatives accusing me of fraud."

"I see," he said. "What's the situation?"

I described the phone call and what had happened with the restructuring of the ownership.

"Matthew, I created this new legal structure based on the recommendation of my lawyer to accommodate my new partner. I'm not trying to commit fraud. One of your loan officers was fully involved from the beginning. I cannot understand why this move was approved without incident at the time, yet is causing such an alarm six months later."

Matthew entered my account number into his computer. "I don't know why, but I can't get full access to your file. Just give me one moment and I will talk to my manager to see what is going on," he said. He stepped out to find his manager. Although he was trying to be helpful, and his courtesy was quite a refreshing change from the man who berated me over the phone, I sensed that he didn't have much banking experience.

Matthew returned in about two minutes. "Sorry, Mr. Sarshoghi, but my manager is busy right now. Could I get your phone number and call you this afternoon when I have more information?"

I looked at him but remained silent for a moment in order to communicate my displeasure. "Okay," I finally said calmly, and gave him my cell phone number. "I'll be waiting for your call this afternoon."

Matthew returned my call as promised, late that afternoon. Apparently there had been some "miscommunication" between his branch and head office. Missing from the puzzle was a legal agreement that held the new holding company responsible for the loan. Without it, Rosie and I could default on the loan and the bank would be powerless to pursue my holding company. From a certain point of view, it could easily have looked like I was plotting a strategy to run away with the loan. But Matthew acknowledged that I had done everything above board with the junior loan officer, and that I would not be accused of fraud. He would work with his manager to solve the problem.

What I thought would take a few days ended up being dragged out over a few months. Negotiations went back and forth between the bank's legal team and my lawyer. The fact that I had a new minority partner in the corporation complicated things further. It ended up actually costing me a few thousand dollars in legal fees and what the bank described as "transfer fees," but the matter eventually got resolved from a legal standpoint. The holding company became the legal recipient of the funds. But more importantly, Rosie thrived as the managing partner of the second Café Saison.

My business group was growing. In addition to Collage Tapis, I had just opened two big-box floor covering stores,; I owned two coffee shops,; plus I owned commercial real estate. My two commercial buildings had mortgages on them held by the Business Development Bank of Canada. I hatched a new idea: refinance them, extract some of the capital, and purchase two more commercial buildings to house my retail carpet operations. It would be a large deal. The branch manager said that he would have to present it to the executive committee, but since they met every week, it would not take long to get a preliminary indication.

I was full of energy and vision, and had no intention of stopping. Moreover, economic conditions were quite favourable. There seemed to be no stopping the increase in real estate value. My ambition was to continue growing my businesses into the big leagues, especially my floor covering business. I wanted to own more locations rather than rent them from someone else. I happened to be talking about my ambitions with a real estate appraiser one day. He mentioned the name of an account manager at the National Bank of Greece, which had a branch in Montréal. He spoke highly of him and said that he would gladly check into this bank for me. He seemed sure that he would be interested in working with me on this financing idea.

It didn't take long for the NBG account manager to call and introduce himself to me. He was very pleasant over the phone and showed great interest in my business plans. He asked if I would be interested in meeting to discuss my financing needs.

What a change from my previous experience with the big retail banks! Maybe it was *too* easy; however I didn't think there was anything to lose by meeting him. I found out that the NBG officer was a newly promoted account manager and was in charge of loans of over half a million dollars. It was obvious from his call that he was very eager to bring new clients into the bank. So, I agreed to meet him at my office the following week.

Christophe, or Chris, as he liked to be called, was a first-generation Canadian. His parents had emigrated from Greece in the 1950s. His connections to Greece were nonetheless quite strong.

We sat at my conference table and Chris handed me some literature about NBG from his briefcase.

"You know, I have always passed by this building and noticed the beautiful windows," he said, looking around my office. "It's even more beautiful on the inside."

"It is a beautiful building, isn't it?" I replied. "It has a lot of historical character."

I described my business group to Chris. He spent quite a bit of time analyzing my business holdings and describing how his bank could likely meet my needs. I have to say that he impressed me.

After Chris left my office, I took a serious look at his information. His bank offered competitive rates, but more importantly, he was enthusiastic about the possibility of working together. In contrast, I seemed to have to push hard to get the banks to take an interest in me. Chris was very inviting.

I decided to explore the next step. I called Chris and asked for another meeting. There was potentially a lot at stake for both us. For Chris, it would mean landing a large portfolio early on in his new position. For me, I would finally work with a bank that was truly trying to help me reach my business goals, not pose barriers as the other banks (aside from BDC) seemed to be doing.

The next day, Chris called to let me know that the branch manager was interested in meeting me. He would be working directly with the two of us on the loan application. I was stunned by how quickly things had progressed.

I was surprised at how young the branch manager was. He could not have been forty years old. But he carried himself well and spoke with authority. I felt confident working with him.

I met with the manager on three separate occasions to provide details and to ensure that he clearly understood what I wanted to do. In yet another amazing reversal of fortune, I received a call from him to say that both the CEO and CFO wanted to invite me for lunch.

I wasn't sure what to make of all of this in the wake of my experiences with the other retail banks. Obviously NBG was interested in pursuing this loan agreement; but, being invited to meet the CEO and CFO? At the very least, it would be a good opportunity to expand my network. Although NBG was not a substantial player in the financial market, for the size of my operation, it was more than sufficient. I accepted their invitation to lunch.

We initially met at the branch. The branch manager and Chris introduced me to the CEO and CFO. They were both very gracious and made me feel like a member of a visiting royal family.

"Mr. Sarshoghi, it's a pleasure to meet you," said Nick Mavroudis, the CEO. "We will be having lunch just down the street. We can all walk there together.,"

We walked for about ten minutes and arrived at Club St. James, one of the most prestigious clubs in Montréal. "My God," I thought. "Am I dreaming? The CEO and CFO have personally asked me to Club St. James? They're actually courting me!"

After sitting down, the CEO said, "Mr. Sarshoghi, you have achieved an impressive level of success for a person of your age. How long have you been in Canada?"

"Thank you. I came to Canada from Iran a few years ago. Yes, I have accomplished a great deal in that time," I replied.

"This refinancing deal would represent a sizeable portfolio for us. Let me say that we are interested in exploring the possibility of handling all of your company's banking and financing needs," he continued.

We discussed my proposal to refinance my current buildings and take out an additional loan to fund the launch of big-box floor covering store. I brought a comprehensive business plan with me. They wanted to make sure that I knew what I was talking about, and had the skills to manage such a business. The group asked me a barrage of questions over lunch, including whether or not I was being advised by a team of experts.

During the conversation, one of them made a comment that has always stuck with me: "A loan should not only be safe but also sound." He was right. Their interest was to ensure their money would be returned within the stated period of the loan, with full interest and without any delays in monthly payments.

The meeting with the NBG senior management team went extremely well. They were supportive of my proposal. The CEO announced at the end of the three-hour lunch that I would receive a letter of intent within a week.

Indeed, I did. After reading it carefully, though, it dawned on me that I had made a mistake. At lunch, I had pitched my idea to simply refinance my two existing commercial buildings which were mortgaged through BDC. I would use the proceeds to purchase two more commercial buildings, but I did not commit to financing the new buildings through NBG. However, the letter stated that NBG would finance all four buildings in a package loan. It would treat all four buildings as one, meaning that I was putting all my eggs in NBG's basket. The deal would create restrictions in the event that I wanted to sell one of the buildings separately. The interest rate specified in the letter was very competitive, but it was conditional on the performance of my stores. NBG reserved the right to change the interest rate with thirty days' notice, which didn't sit well with me. I was concerned that the deal they were offering could be a bait and switch.

I gave the letter a lot of thought, weighed the pros and cons, and eventually decided to negotiate with NBG on the terms of the loan. Everything in life is negotiable. This financing deal was significant for both of us, well into seven figures. I pressed NBG to do better on the interest rate, which they lowered by a quarter of a percentage point. They were not willing to eliminate the clause about their right to change the rate any time with notice, but they did agree to restrict changes to only once per year if circumstances required an adjustment. There were other minor changes, but the NBG team negotiated in good faith. I felt comfortable proceeding with the loan package. Over the following six months, I purchased two more commercial buildings, which I used to expand Tapis en Gros.

Everything went smoothly with NBG for the first couple of years. I made all of my monthly payments on time. I got to know the executive team well. I could call Nick Mavroudis, the CEO, directly and meet with him any time I wished. We would have lunch together from time to time. I also received invitations to NBG social functions, where he would typically introduce me as one of NBG's most important clients.

It was 2001. All over North America, real estate was booming. I received an offer on one of my commercial properties outside of the NBG financing package that represented a five hundred percent premium over what I had paid for it just a couple of years before. It was the most profitable real estate transaction I had ever structured. Word of the selling price got out and became the talk of the town in many Montréal real-estate circles.

Three days after that deal was signed, I received a telephone call from a vice president at Royal Bank of Canada. The person who had purchased my property was financing it through RBC, where the deal attracted attention. The RBC executive who called me said that he was interested in offering the bank's services, and invited me to a business breakfast in the bank's executive dining room in Place Ville Marie, Montréal's premier corporate address. I figured there was nothing to lose, and at minimum, I could make a few new connections and enjoy a nice breakfast. I accepted his invitation.

I arrived at the office on the fourth floor of Place Ville Marie at eight o'clock in the morning of our appointment day. My host greeted me and then took me up to the dining room on the eighteenth floor. It was magnificent, one of the most luxurious places I had ever seen. We were led to a small private room that had an extraordinary view of downtown Montréal and the Saint Lawrence River.

What unfolded after we sat down for breakfast was entirely predictable. He had learned through a colleague about the real estate deal and the eye-popping amount for which I had sold my building, which was located just blocks from where we were sitting. He had heard that I was dealing with the National Bank of Greece and gently asked what had led me to such a fringe player in the Canadian financial industry. I told him that I had tried to deal with the big retail banks in the past but was flatly rejected by each of them. NBG treated me like a valued customer from the beginning. He countered by emphasizing the fact that Royal Bank was the largest bank in Canada, and that if I switched my business over, I would have a private wealth management representative at my service.

It was a cordial meeting. I didn't jump into RBC's arms, but left basking in the irony that an executive from one of the very banks that had closed the door on me just two years earlier was courting my business. My, how times had changed! The meeting was not a waste of time because if it ever reached the point where NBG was not able to serve my needs, I would have options with the Royal Bank.

I actually used some of the proceeds from the NBG refinancing deal to expand into the home furnishing business into Quebec City. It was my first business venture outside of Montréal. I had NBG's blessing, since it was part of the business plan I submitted when I started dealing with them.

Opening the Quebec City store took a gruelling amount of energy. I had to drive to Quebec from Montréal once a week, a five-hundred kilometre round trip. I was working flat out, seven days a week, a minimum of twelve hours per day, managing my real estate holdings, carpet outlets, and the coffee shops. On top of it all, my wife had just given birth to our first child, after a pregnancy fraught with serious complications. I was under a lot of pressure to devote the necessary time to my businesses and my family.

As with any new venture, cash flow for my Quebec City store following the launch was tight. To compound matters, I was experiencing problems getting the building owner to fund his portion of the leasehold improvements, which was a financial drain on my other operations. Given the relationship I was enjoying with NBG and the mutual trust that we had established with each other, I didn't think it would be a problem to delay one or two monthly instalments on my loan.

Three months after the launch in Quebec City, I was able to resume my payments on the NBG loan. Just then I received a letter from NBG notifying me that they would be increasing the interest rate on my loan package to compensate for the delay in payments over the last two months. NBG would be assessing a series of penalty fees as well. In stark contrast to the close working relationship I had developed with the bank, right up to its senior management team, the letter arrived, along with a stack of other mail, without a phone call or meeting to explain it.

Suddenly, the risk I had predicted when I received NBG's original letter of intent was materializing. My entire loan portfolio, which covered four different properties and capital financing within one single loan, was being affected by the Quebec City store. The impact would be huge, as each percentage increase in interest on my loan would cost over a hundred thousand dollars more in annual interest charges.

Naturally, I protested NBG's move, which I considered to be unreasonable. And there it started—arguing over the phone every day with Chris, the account manager. Day after day, Chris promised that this problem would soon be resolved, and that I would be getting the thousands of dollars in extra charges credited back to my account. I waited for months and nothing changed. I soon went above Chris's head and called the branch manager, but it was the same story with him. I felt that the only way I could get NBG's full attention was to simply stop making payments on the loan again.

It didn't take long to receive a strongly worded letter from an NBG lawyer demanding payment of all arrears, including the added interest charges and fees. The letter also threatened that NBG would not renew my loan when it came due.

I called Nick, the CEO, but for the first time, I was not able to get through to him. His secretary said that he would return my call right away. I called three more times over the next day but could never get through to him. I was being stonewalled. Ultimately, it would take weeks before Nick would return my call. So much for being able to call him up anytime and go out to lunch.

Somebody once said to me that in business you always have to be ready to jump. What an understatement, considering what I was now experiencing with NBG. In fact, I felt like I had been pushed off a cliff and was looking for a place to land. I thought it would be wise to start looking for a new financial institution to deal with. It would require transferring practically my entire business banking portfolio, so that I could pay off NBG and part ways with them.

I contacted the Royal Bank vice president who had eagerly courted my business over breakfast in Place Ville Marie. I had kept in touch with him since our meeting, so receiving my call did not take him off guard. He referred me to a senior commercial loans manager.

So, yet again I found myself in the position of applying for financing. As expected, I had to provide RBC with my business plan and reams of supporting documents, not to mention two personal interviews and an account of my personal credit history. It was tiring to say the least, but this time around I was much more prepared for the process. However, after two weeks, the commercial loans manager called me to say that, unfortunately, their risk management team would not approve my loan request. It was a devastating blow because I couldn't think of any other financing option. Furthermore, the clock was ticking.

NBG brought the matter to a head. They served legal notice that they were calling my loan and that the entire principal and all arrears, including a penalty, were due within sixty days.

All of my eggs were in NBG's basket. They were in a position to legally force the sale of all my properties to recover their loan, which would put my four floor covering stores and two coffee shops in jeopardy. I had spent years building up these businesses. All of it was now on the brink of tumbling down like a house of cards. NBG was well aware of the implications of calling the loan. I felt they were acting in bad faith.

There had to be a piece missing from this puzzle. I was an excellent customer. To be treated so punitively for missing just three payments was completely inappropriate, given the amount of business I was doing with them. (Remember, I had resumed my payments by the third month, but stopped them again because NBG was unwilling to reconsider the interest rate increase). Regardless, I was under pressure to basically pull a rabbit out of a hat within sixty days, by finding someone to refinance my entire operation or face foreclosure. The pressure on me was enormous.

I heard a saying once that has always stuck with me: "When you can't, you must; and when you must, you can." I held a personal bank account with another one of the big chartered banks. I had no choice but to approach them for a financing deal. So, yet again, for what seemed like the umpteenth time, I had to go through the process of gathering a mountain of documentation to make a business loan application. By now, I had become an expert, answering questions for their loan officer that she hadn't even thought of asking.

After a week of delicate negotiations, and perhaps a bit of divine intervention, they approved a refinancing package. I was able to pay off my entire debt to NBG and liberate myself from them.

But that wasn't sufficient. NBG had created unnecessary roadblocks to the growth of my business, not to mention the personal toll on me, and I was not going to accept their treatment lying down. I decided to sue them for damages. My lawyer sent notice to the CEO. Soon thereafter, I called him personally.

"Nick," I said, "I want to talk with you. The least you owe me is an hour to discuss everything. I know that there are missing pieces here."

He agreed to meet me for lunch, just as we had done on a regular basis when times were better. It would be an uncomfortable meeting, but one that I felt had to take place.

Remarkably, Nick expressed regret to me about the entire situation and took full responsibility. I found out from him that NBG was being considered for buy-out by another major Canadian bank, and that he was trying desperately to inflate NBG's holdings and income. As I suspected, they were not entirely justified in raising the interest rate on my loan. I had been an excellent client for three years before this episode began. They were under such pressure to raise their sale price that they unscrupulously looked at every possible way to inflate their earnings. I was one of many clients they had targeted.

I was shocked at what Nick was telling me, though not completely surprised. I knew there had to be something in the background that had suddenly changed their behaviour toward me. We talked about the potential for my lawsuit to distract both of us from our businesses. He agreed. By the end of lunch, Nick offered to pay back half of all the extra interest charges his bank had imposed, as well as the entire value of all the penalties I had been forced to pay. I, in return, agreed to cease legal action. It was a sensible solution to avoid another drawn-out round of legal wrangling and personal headaches that would, in the end, benefit our lawyers more than us. We agreed to simply bury the hatchet and go our separate ways.

Lessons Learned

Imagine trying to grow a business without access to capital. Modern financial systems offer business managers and entrepreneurs a remarkable resource; that is, the ability to borrow money to grow their business. Furthermore, the interest costs of a loan are tax deductible, which lowers the cost of borrowing. After getting approved for a loan, remember that it is not your money but somebody else's. Treat the money and the lender with respect by providing them with ongoing information about your business, in order to avoid surprises.

To secure a loan from a financial institution, it's important to think like a banker and understand how banks operate and make money. First, realize that the bank is not necessarily your friend. The bank, or any lender for that matter, is a business partner. So long as payments are flowing back to your partner and you keep him or her informed of your financial activities, your partner will be happy. The moment those payments or the information stops, you will realize that the bank will act quickly to protect its investment.

Consider that a loan is, in essence, a risk. Canadian banks, for example, didn't achieve their world renowned reputation for stability by taking on bad risks. Banks have a highly refined system for identifying risk. Certain banks tend to focus on a certain business sector because such focus allows them to gain knowledge about that sector, in order to better assess risk. So, one of the first lessons I would share with readers is before making a loan application is to determine the sector that a particular lending institution favours—commercial or residential real estate, industrial or service-oriented businesses, and so forth.

If you are successful in securing a bank loan, watch your fees very closely. Don't be intimidated by the institutional nature of a bank. Always negotiate the terms of a loan the same way you would the purchase price of a house or a car. Don't let a bank think that they are your only financing option.

I learned the hard way that it is important to diversify your sources of business financing. The National Bank of Greece tied all of my real estate loans into one package in order to maximize their interest payments. Ultimately, the shaky performance of my new Quebec City store in its first months of operation threatened to bring down the other parts of my business group that were legally separate. Never put all of your eggs in one loan basket.

One final word of advice: be careful not to over-leverage yourself, or borrow too much money in relation to your ability to pay the cost of the debt. Servicing debt requires real cash flow. The National Bank of Greece offered me more money than I actually needed. At the time, they were happy to provide me with the extra working capital as it increased their income off the loan. Taking more than I needed only compounded my troubles when my Quebec City store experienced a weaker than expected cash flow in the beginning. Borrow money, but do so prudently.

Chapter 5: Mind Your Pennies

Once up on a time, a king was walking across a bridge over the river that divides the city of Isfahan into two parts. He saw a local garment worker washing fabrics and laying them out on rocks to dry along the riverbank below the bridge. It was December and the winter wind was biting cold.

"What are you doing?" the King asked.

"I am washing my fabrics."

The King reacted emotionally. "You could not beat three with nine?"

"I'm not sure what you mean, Your Highness."

"Young man, you should have set aside enough money during the nine months of warm weather so that you would not have to work outside during the three cold months of winter!"

Walking through downtown Montréal early one morning, I popped into a bistro to grab a cup of coffee. I stood at the counter for a few moments without being served. A woman was kneeling down behind the counter arranging something that I couldn't see. After a few more moments of being ignored, I leaned over the counter and said, "Pardon me, but may I get a cup of coffee?"

The woman stood up. "Oh, hello," she said. "Usually, I do not serve customers, but what can I get you? A cappuccino or something?"

"Yes, that would be fine," I replied.

"Would you like to have something for breakfast too, sir?" she asked.

"No, I usually don't take breakfast," I replied.

"Perhaps I could make you something special," she said, with a slight twinkle in her eye.

I paused and shrugged my shoulders. "Sure, why not?"

"Okay, have a seat and I'll be right back."

She went downstairs and returned about five minutes later with a plate of fresh fruit and a croissant.

"Here you go. I hope you like it," she said.

She left me to eat my breakfast. Although I was busy talking on my cell phone while I ate, not paying attention to what was going on around me, I sensed that she was watching me to see whether I was enjoying her food.

After I finished my breakfast, I asked for the cheque. I left money on the table next to the bill, thanked her, and said goodbye. I quite enjoyed the breakfast and left her a nice tip.

One morning about a week later, I went back to the same bistro. The woman who had served me the week before wasn't in sight, so I asked a waiter if I could see the owner. He went over to the stairs that led to the basement and said, "Sara, there is a man up here asking for you."

When she came upstairs, I was sitting at a table and talking on my cell phone. I looked up, explained to the person I was speaking with that I suddenly had to go, and ended the call.

"Hello again," I said. "I am sorry to bother you. I was here last week."

"Yes, of course. I remember you," she said enthusiastically. "Nice to have you back."

"I would really like that same breakfast you made me last week, and a cup of your special coffee."

"Of course," she said. "Have a seat. How did you know last week that I was the owner?"

"I could tell by the way you tried to impress me to get me to come back."

"You are very perceptive," she said. She went away to prepare my breakfast, and returned about ten minutes later with a plate of fresh fruit and a croissant.

"How is business?" I asked.

She took a deep breath. "Well, we are busy. I start very early in the morning and I finish at around seven in the evening."

"Those are long hours," I replied, nodding my head in understanding. "Do you work weekends, too?

"Yes, of course."

"That is not good. Are you making money?"

She pursed her lips and gave me a vague gesture.

"What made you open a coffee shop?"

"It's a long story."

"If it would not be taking too much of your time, I'd like to hear it," I said. "But first, I don't even know your name. My name is Reza." I extended my hand to her.

"Pleased to meet you, Reza. I am Sara."

I sensed a spirit in Sara that jumped out at me. Here was a woman, similar in age to me, trying to make a go of running her own business. I could relate to the challenges she was facing. I had no romantic interest in Sara. I was a married man, after all. It was just so refreshing to talk with somebody who spoke the same language as me.

"Why don't you join me, Sara." I motioned for her to sit down with me. She looked around the restaurant and then took the empty seat across from me and began to recount her story.

"For almost five years I managed a restaurant in downtown Montréal. I loved my job. The owners were pleasant to work for and many of our customers were regulars, which allowed me to get to know my clientele. Quite unexpectedly, however, the owners decided to sell. The restaurant business is not an easy way to earn a living, and after about twenty years, they reached a point where they needed a change. There were only two months between their announcement to sell the restaurant and the new owners taking over. The speed at which it all happened shocked everyone on staff."

"Indeed," I said. "It sounds like they had a buyer lined up."

"You're probably right. Anyway, the first time I met the new owner, I came away feeling uneasy. I had grown comfortable working with the original owners. Change never comes easy. I prepared myself for a change, but I just could not get used to the new approach and working environment that came with the new owners. After a month, I resigned as manager."

"Wow," I said, raising my eyebrows.

"I spent three months searching for a suitable job, but to no avail. A few people suggested that I consider starting my own restaurant or bistro. I certainly had the knowledge, but I didn't have the money to get a restaurant up and running from scratch."

I nodded my head, listening closely.

"I bounced the idea off a number of people, one of whom was a friend who worked in the banking industry. He mentioned a type of small business loan available in conventional banks that might address my needs. There was nothing to lose in learning more about these loan packages, so I accepted his offer to have a bank manager whom he knew send me more information. A package arrived at my home three days later."

"Good move. I assume that decision helped change your life," I said.

"You're right. The more I read about this special loan for first-time entrepreneurs, the more I could envision the possibilities. I found myself asking why I hadn't considered going this route before. Business financing was not as daunting as I had imagined. There was no reason that I could not own and operate a profitable restaurant. Of course, there was financial risk, but all business involves a degree of risk."

"Absolutely. You can do anything you put your mind to, Sara."

"I was at a crossroads. I was thirty-one years old. If I were going to pursue something on my own, I knew that now was the time. It came down to a fundamental question about who I was and what I wanted out of life. Would I be content to allow somebody else to determine my professional destiny, or was I willing to take on the responsibility of charting my own path?"

"That's a realistic way of looking at things," I said.

"I woke up one morning and decided that I was going to go for it, with no looking back. If you throw yourself into the middle of the ocean, the only option you have for survival is to swim, right? And I wanted to swim."

I chuckled at her analogy.

"I found this location," she said, gesturing to the bistro around us, "which was a key consideration for the bank in determining whether or not my business proposal represented an acceptable degree of risk. I even hired a friend who had a degree in business to help me write a convincing business plan for the loan application.

"It took weeks of full-time work to prepare the documents for my loan application. The bank wanted to understand every possible cost associated with running the business, right down to taxes, advertising and electricity. But it was worth every bit of effort. The bank approved my loan."

"Congratulations," I said. "I know how difficult a new venture loan application can be. I have made many, many loan applications."

"I immediately put my plan into action. It took six months to get everything prepared the way I wanted it, which was exactly what I had anticipated in my business plan."

"Well, your bistro looks great," I said, looking around.

"Business was slow in the beginning, but over time I developed a core group of regular customers. I usually arrived here at about five o'clock in the morning to prepare bread and pastries for breakfast, and other menu items for lunch. I opened for breakfast at seven o'clock in the morning. I had two employees to take care of morning customers while I worked downstairs in the kitchen preparing the day's menu items. Each server took care of his or her own customer's bill at the cash register. Usually, just before noon, I would come upstairs to help serve lunchtime customers. After the lunchtime crowd had finished, usually by about two o'clock, I would spend the rest of the afternoon between the kitchen and upstairs, or out purchasing groceries and supplies. Not many customers would come in after five o'clock, so I closed the bistro at that time and spent another couple of hours cleaning up and managing my records. I put in those fourteen-hour days, seven days a week without a vacation for the first eleven months. It was exhausting. I would get home and go straight to bed."

"Believe me, Sara, I can relate to what you're saying. I have been through it all, too," I said.

"I was quite happy with the amount of traffic that was coming through the doors by the end of the first year. We always seemed to be busy. The problem was that I was not turning a profit."

"That is exactly what I thought," I replied, nodding. "Sometimes business managers forget that their primary objective is to make a dollar. Believe it or not, Sara, I used to run a bistro much like this one."

"Really?" she asked.

"Yes, and it was working very well." I was about to continue but she unintentionally cut me off.

"What do you do for a living, Reza?" she asked.

"I am an entrepreneur. I came to Canada from Iran. I run a few different businesses." I looked around her shop. "I have a lot of experience buying and selling businesses, Sara, and quite frankly, I don't think you are doing that well here.

"Are you thinking about buying my bistro, too?" she asked.

I chuckled. "You are very sharp." I looked around at the restaurant, nodded, and said, "Well, if I were looking to buy a distressed business then I would put your business on my list for consideration. However, I have no intention of buying your business."

"What makes you think I am not doing so well?" she asked.

"From what I have seen so far," I said, "most of the time you are working downstairs. You have no control over your inventory, nor do you have a strong connection to your customers. I am pretty sure that you do not know what your actual sales are because you don't have a clear sense of how much inventory you have sold at the end of each day."

"What do you mean?" she asked.

"Well, look at it this way…." My cell phone rang.

"Excuse me, I have to answer this call." I answered my phone, said a few words to the caller, and then looked up at her. "I have to go, but we'll talk again." I needed to meet somebody.

Just after stepping out the door, I realized that I hadn't paid for my food. I ran back into the restaurant. "I am sorry, I forgot to pay you!" I left a fifty dollar bill on the counter and rushed out again.

"Reza! Your change!" she cried. But I had to run.

It was two weeks before I could return to Sara's bistro. When I walked in, she was just coming up the stairs from the kitchen.

"Hi, Sara." I said.

Her eyes lit up and she gave me a big smile. "Reza!"

I responded with a smile. "Could I have something to eat and a cup of coffee?"

"Yes, of course!" she replied. "Have a seat and I'll be right back."

She went down to the kitchen and brought me back a wonderful breakfast and a cup of cappuccino.

"What kind of coffee is this, Sara?" I asked. "It has a wonderful aroma."

"This is one of the best coffees available, made from Jamaican Blue Mountain coffee beans. I would be happy to grind some for you to take home," she said.

"That would be great. I would love to take some home with me," I said.

"Reza, the last time you were here, we were talking about my business. Do you remember the conversation?" she asked.

"Quite clearly," I replied.

"I was amazed. What did you see in just a couple of short visits that told you I was not turning a profit here? I have a lot of experience in the restaurant business. I didn't have any problems getting financing and I have a great location. My restaurant is reasonably busy and I get a lot of compliments on the atmosphere and the food. The problems with my business are obvious to you. Why are they so difficult for me to see?" she asked.

"I manage some commercial property around here. That is why you see me around here from time to time. I think you could use my help. You are the owner of this business, but it appears that you spend a lot of your time in the basement. You told me that you work seven days a week. To me, that means you are working hard to cover your expenses."

"That's true," she said, looking around the room and nodding her head. "I am making a living." she said.

"Perhaps," I countered, "but would you be making more money if you worked for somebody else seven days a week?"

She shrugged her shoulders. "It depends on how you look at it. At least I am free."

"I don't think you are so free," I said, raising my eyebrows at her. "You work the entire week and you get no vacation. My guess is that you work about ten hours a day. At just ten dollars per hour, you should be making over forty thousand dollars per year. By working for someone else, you would probably earn much more than that and work less. Are you earning that much?" I asked.

"Not even close," she responded. I have worked hard this year. The restaurant is busy, but I don't know why it is not profitable. This is my second year in this location and I am barely making it."

I noticed that she kept glancing out the front window of the restaurant. "What are you looking at?" I asked.

I am parked on the street in front of the restaurant," she said. "I am watching for the parking enforcement officer. Would you excuse me for a moment?" she said. She walked over to the main counter, took some change from the cash register, and went outside to feed the parking meter.

She came back to my table. "Sorry about that. As I was saying, it is not easy to…"

I cut her off in the middle of her sentence. "How much money did you put in the parking meter?"

"Three dollars. It lasts for two hours," she replied. "In this area you can get a ticket very fast. I have to be on constant watch. But I only get about one or two tickets a month."

"Why in the world do you park on the street and not in a lot?" I asked her.

"Well, I have to unload supplies myself, so I park close to the building."

"I saw you take money from your cash register. Do you record it every time you do that?" I asked with a puzzled look on my face.

"No," she said. Why bother? It's only a few dollars. And it's my money. It's not a big deal."

"Sara, have a seat."

She sat down to listen to what I was about to say.

"A few dollars per day plus a parking ticket per month can add up to thousands of dollars a year. But more importantly, it's not your money until it is accounted for and it has been declared as a salary, benefit or dividend. Recording it that way, you will know if your business has actually made any profit or not."

"You're right. I managed a restaurant for five years, but the bookkeeping was the owner's responsibility," she said.

"I should ask you something else, Sara. If you don't track all of your cash in and out, how do you balance your cash at the end of each day?"

She didn't have a response.

"Why don't you just rent a monthly parking spot somewhere close by? It would cost you less than your parking tickets and you would be much less distracted. Sara, the first piece of advice I would give you is to focus on the details of your business. Every penny counts," I said.

"Reza, I know from the way you are talking to me that you care. And the more I listen to you, the more interested I become in your ideas. But I don't entirely agree with you. I always wanted to own a business so I could have more freedom over my spending. If I wanted to count every dollar, I could have worked for someone else for a salary."

"I wonder if that might have been a better choice for you," I said.

Ouch. She couldn't help but take that comment to heart. But it made her stop and think.

By then I had finished the coffee and fruit she had prepared for me. "Listen, I have to leave now, but I'll come back. I know you do not want to work for someone. But on the other hand, you want to have a profitable company. Why don't we arrange a schedule? I would be happy to come back and offer you some advice on managing your business. I believe your problems stem from how you are managing your cash," I said.

"I hope to see you again, Reza." she said.

I put some money on the table and left. I sensed she didn't want me to leave. I was the solution to her problems. Or at least she thought so.

A number of days passed and I just couldn't find any time to go back to Sara's bistro and follow up on our conversation. So I called her to make sure that she knew I hadn't forgotten about her. Over the phone, I asked her to try to keep tighter control by recording each time she spent money. It would be important to get into the habit of doing this twice a day. I also mentioned that she should stop taking money out of the register to pay for parking. That alone would save her an average of two hundred dollars every month, which she could hardly believe.

A couple more weeks passed before I found the time to pop in to Sara's bistro again. I wasn't sure if she was still on track. I called her to see if she had time to talk.

"Hi," I said. "This is Reza."

"Oh, hi!" she said enthusiastically. "It's been a while since I heard from you."

"Sorry, Sara, I have been busy. I promised to help you out with managing your cash. I was thinking of dropping by on Friday morning at around eight."

"I'll see you then," she replied.

"Could you gather some financial reports, like bank statements and a summary of your purchases? I would like to analyze your revenues and expenses to see how you are managing you your cash."

"Sure."

"I will see you on Friday," I said, and hung up.

I walked into Sara's bistro just before eight o'clock on Friday morning, as promised.

"Very punctual!" she said.

"Let's sit down, Sara," I said. She guided me over to the corner table and asked if I wanted something for breakfast.

"I would like to spend a bit of time looking over these statements. After that, I wouldn't mind having something to eat."

"Great. Have a seat and I'll get you a cup of coffee."

"How long did it take you to get all of these documents together?" I asked.

"Oh," she said, rolling her eyes, "all of Wednesday afternoon. I worked quite hard so that I could close up a bit earlier than usual the next day to get my hair done. It was the first time in a very long time that I had actually enjoyed myself outside of work. In addition to getting my hair cut, I also had a thirty-minute massage. But as relaxing as it was, I found myself getting anxious about the questions you might ask. What could you possibly see from bank statements or receipts from suppliers?"

She sat down with me as I started to look over her financial statements and take notes.

"What would the cost be, Reza?" she asked.

I looked up at her. "The cost of what?"

"Your time."

I laughed. "Sara, you don't have to pay me anything. Working on this project brings back memories of when I had a bistro. I am happy to do it for you. Nobody was there to help me when I was starting out, and I learned some very tough lessons along the way. My payment is the satisfaction in knowing that I am helping somebody else. But if you don't feel like continuing, just let me know," I said.

"No, no, no! I am grateful for your help!" she said.

In a few minutes, I had looked over most of her documents.

"May I see your lease?" I asked. She went to her office and grabbed the file. I carefully read the thirty-page lease, highlighting some of the points.

"I have never looked through it in detail," she said.

After I finished reading the lease, I put it aside and asked her if she had any bank loans.

"Let me bring you my loan agreement with the bank."

I spent about fifteen minutes going over her records and making notes, and then waved to get her attention from behind the counter. She came over and sat down in front of me.

"Okay, I've got some ideas. But first, may I have something to eat?" I asked.

"Sure!" she said. "I planned a nice breakfast for you. It is your favourite: a bagel with cream cheese and smoked salmon, fresh orange juice, and a cup of cappuccino. How is that?"

"Great." I said with a warm smile.

"You know, the first day I came in here I had a sense of what the problem was, but I couldn't be certain. Now, I am certain." I said. "We need to put something together to enable you to better manage your cash. Mind your pennies and the dollars will take care of themselves."

"I've heard the saying before."

"From what you have provided me, your revenue is strong, given the size of your restaurant. The interior design is very appealing and your location is very good to attract customers. You were also well capitalized by the bank at the beginning, but whether it was well spent or not, I don't know. At this point, I don't think it is relevant. I don't see much of an investment in advertising."

"There are a few things that I think you should start to work on, immediately. First and foremost, I want *you* to take care of your cash register. You should be the only person handling your cash, not your employees. Could you give me some numbers on the number of customers you get on a day-by-day basis, say for one

126

entire month? There are some other pieces of information I would be interested in knowing, too." I passed her a piece of paper with a list of what I wanted.

I stopped talking but she didn't say anything. There was an awkward pause. "Sara?" I said.

"I don't know what to say. I have been struggling with this business. With you here, now, the sun seems to be coming out from behind dark clouds. I'm really grateful," she said.

I smiled warmly at her and nodded. "May I see your kitchen, downstairs, sometime?" I asked.

"Do you want to see it now?"

"No," I said, "but I will be back next week. I will call you in advance and then we can continue. May I have my bill?" I asked.

"Absolutely not. You will never pay to eat in my bistro."

"No, I can't accept that. If you don't charge me, I will not come here anymore," I said.

She paused for a moment. "I guess I have no choice. I think you are the type of person who is used to getting what he wants."

I paid my bill, said goodbye, and left.

Another week passed before I telephoned to ask how she was doing.

"Fine, Reza. How about you?"

"Excellent, Sara. Excellent."

"You are always in such a positive mood. I'm not sure if your optimism is annoying or inspiring. Everything is always perfect to you," she said.

"Come to think of it, you are right. But believe me, I have my fair share of frustrations, too," I said, and laughed.

I asked her if she had prepared the information I had asked for the previous week. "Yes, I have it," she replied.

"Did you take over your cash register this week, Sara?"

"Yes," she said. "But why do you want me to be on the cash? It prevents me from taking care of other more important tasks."

"For two reasons, Sara. I want to see if you have found less discrepancy in your cash. It also will force you to meet your customers in person. You will get to know them, build important relationships with them, and understand their needs. Could I pop by tomorrow at the same time to talk about some new things?"

"Of course," she said.

"Then, see you tomorrow."

The next day, at five minutes to eight, I walked in and found a seat off to the side. Sara came over to the table to greet me.

"Good morning. I can spend about an hour here today, but I won't have breakfast. I have an appointment with someone else for breakfast. I'll have a cup of that wonderful Jamaican coffee, though."

She brought me a cappuccino and sat down. "Well, Reza, as you know, I have been taking care of the cash register myself, as you suggested."

"Did you notice any difference in sales?" I replied.

"No, not much," she said. "Perhaps an increase of about ten dollars per day, on average."

I shook my head. "Sara! How can you say it that way? Right now you are barely making ends meet, so any increase is a step in the right direction."

"But we are only talking about a few dollars," she said.

I began to write something on a scrap piece of paper. "You have found ten dollars per day from not mixing company money with your personal parking money. You have found an additional ten dollars per day, on average, by operating your cash register by yourself. Even if you just stop there, you are making around twenty dollars more per day, on average, which gives you about six hundred dollars more per month. That's over seven thousand dollars a year!"

Sara was doing the math in her head and nodding.

"On the other hand, I see your cost of goods is very high, around thirty-five percent of your sales. Your cost should be less than twenty-five percent. There is a variety of possible causes behind this problem." I then wrote down the following points for her on a piece of paper:

- High-quality recipe items, yet low prices charged to customers
- Suppliers: too many, and not the right ones
- Too much waste out the back door and front door
- Inadequate cash flow

"The first thing I can tell you is that each and every penny counts. I know you don't like the word "'penny".' But consider this story: A long time ago I had a supplier, — an older man who built up his business after the war. One time I got an invoice from him. I tried to negotiate with him a bit by rounding off the pennies to the nearest dollar. 'Hey, what's a few cents?' I asked him.

"He was a wealthy man. But he became quite offended with me.

'Reza, those pennies are my profit. You should pay me the pennies before anything else. If I give you a one-penny discount today, tomorrow you will ask for a dollar and the next day for ten dollars. Business is business.'"

"I see your point," Sara said.

I turned the focus back to her.

"To begin to identify your problem, we should break down the cost of each meal on your menu and compare it with your selling price. If your cost is twenty-five percent or less, we will go to the next step. If it is higher, you should look for a new supplier or try to concentrate your orders with fewer suppliers in order to get a volume discount. You will save money because you will have fewer cheques to mail and you'll spend less time on bookkeeping. You might also be able to get a term payment from them, which will help you with your cash flow."

She sat there nodding at what I was saying. "It makes complete sense to me."

"If your cost of goods is at a reasonable level, then you must watch your back and front doors for waste. For example, I knew a restaurant owner who, at the end of each day, would look in the garbage bin to see if his kitchen staff was wasting too much food."

"I am listening to what you are saying, but I don't understand what you mean by front door and back door waste."

"Sara," I said, "some of your waste will go out to the garbage through the back door and some will leave your restaurant through the front door, unpaid for. My grandfather used to say that whenever you plant seeds, you should plant extra, knowing that the birds will take some."

I looked down at my watch. An hour had gone by. "Wow! Sara, I have to leave or else I will be late. I will call you. I want you to think about what I have told you this morning." With that, I got up, gave her a reassuring look, and rushed out the door.

That day, I had given her some practical information to manage her cash. I was sure she could follow my lead on most of the points, but on some, she didn't have any direction. I knew she really wanted to learn more from me. For the most part I had talked about how to save money. She also needed to know how to increase her sales.

I telephoned her about a week later.

"Reza! How are you?"

"Excellent, Sara. Excellent! I am calling to see if we can meet tomorrow to continue our discussion."

"Yes, of course! Can you spend more time here? It seems that as soon as you start to give me some hints about what I have to change, you have to leave."

I paused for a second. "Let me see if I can arrange my schedule tomorrow. I'll do what I can to stay there for the better part of the day. I will call back to confirm."

"Can I ask you something?" she asked.

"Sure."

"Why do you believe that if someone asks you how you are doing, you should always say 'excellent'?"

"Well, I simply believe that a positive attitude is infectious, and that it will help attract good people to you."

I paused to let her think about it.

"I have to let you go, Sara. I will call you later to confirm, okay?" As promised, I called her later that day and confirmed that I would spend the entire next day with her.

I showed up at eight o'clock.

"Right on time again," she said.

I was carrying a bunch of files and had a computer bag on my shoulder. "I think we will have a productive day today."

"Did you just say what I think you said?" she asked with a surprised look on her face. "Reza, I want to be straightforward with you. I was thinking that today would be an opportunity to…add a personal dimension to our conversations. I probably should see if you are involved with someone, and if you are not, maybe we could go out sometime on a date."

I cut her off. "Whoa, whoa, whoa. I am flattered, Sara, but I think we should focus on fixing your business," I said, looking her in the eye. "I should have been more up front with you from the beginning. I am quite happily married."

A look of embarrassment washed over her face and her shoulders began to droop. I felt bad, but it was important to draw that line.

"I have made up some forms that will help you with managing your cash, your capital, your inventory and your employees," I said.

She didn't reply, and just nodded her head. I felt bad for her and tried to shift her focus.

"I want you to put these forms on your freezer, refrigerator and in your back storage area. Record every change in your inventory in detail: product, quantity, date in, date out, and by whom. At the end of the day you should verify that your physical inventory matches the information on the form."

She interrupted me in a subtle attempt to get more information about me. "You told me that you had a coffee shop. What made you decide to open it, and what happened to it? Do you still have it?"

"I have commercial property not far from here. I also own a carpet store in which I sell exclusive high-end Persian carpets. Typically I get a customer or two per day, which is enough. However, at certain times of the year it is even quieter. My employee and I used to sit down behind the piles of Persian carpets waiting for customers. Without having much to do, we had a lot of time to just talk. One day, my employee had a friend visit from California. He asked me if the store was always so quiet. I said that the winter period was always quieter, but yes, it was a quiet business. He then asked me why I did not do something else."

"Like what?" I asked.

"Something like a restaurant," he said. He then spent some time talking about the restaurant business, and how I could operate both businesses at the same time. To make a long story short, I opened a coffee shop exactly one year later."

"Interesting," she replied, nodding her head in understanding.

"Do you still have it?" she asked.

"Not any more. Let's finish these forms, Sara. I pointed to a form. "This one is used to calculate how you pay a bonus to your employees. I strongly recommend it. It will give them an incentive to produce more for you."

She looked at the various forms that I had laid out in front of her. "If I have to track every movement or change in this restaurant, then how will I have time to do other tasks, like cooking?" she asked.

"Perhaps it would be better to leave those jobs to someone else. On the other hand, if your strength lies in cooking, then you should hire an assistant manager to manage. In any case, with you working such long hours every day, you need more time off. You will find that with more time away, you will be more productive."

"Reza, what cologne are you wearing?" she asked me.

I paused. "I can't remember the name." Her question caught me off guard and made me slightly uncomfortable. I steered the conversation back towards business.

"Sara, let me show you how to use these forms for inventory control. Why don't we go downstairs to your kitchen?"

Walking downstairs she asked me, "Do you always work or do you take time off for yourself? What do you do for fun?"

"I used to work seven days a week. I took great pride and satisfaction from working. But I came to realize that I wanted more from life than just running businesses. A friend once said to me that one should work to live, not live to work. I thought about it and began to look at work differently. Besides, I have a young family."

The basement covered a large area. A corridor at the bottom of the stairs had doors to a small office and a washroom. The entrance to the kitchen area was at the end of the corridor.

We walked into the kitchen. It contained a walk-in refrigerator and freezer.

"I am impressed!" I said. "Alright, I think we can put one form here beside your freezer, and another one next to the refrigerator."

After pointing out the specific places I wanted to hang the forms, I said with a bit of hesitation, "You do know there is special software for controlling restaurant inventory, don't you?"

Sara shrugged.

"Look around, Sara, your money is spread all over this room. Everywhere you look in this kitchen, and upstairs for that matter, you have money. You should watch it like a hawk. You have to think beyond the cash that your customers pay you. My father used to say, 'if you leave the lid off the pan, the cat will come and eat the meat.'"

"I see what you are saying. I thought my experience managing a restaurant for five years had taught me everything I needed to know. I was making sure that the restaurant was operating smoothly on the surface, but I failed to realize that the owner was doing so much behind the scenes, including managing the restaurant's capital."

"All right, Sara, let's focus on your suppliers. You should be trying to get every possible kind of discount, promotion and freebie from them. But there's a fine line. You don't want to squeeze your suppliers to the point where you are putting unnecessary pressure on them. You want them to serve you well. In short, you should be striving for ways to reduce the cost of your supplies."

"You can think of it this way: Your problem is like a chain. If you sell more, you will buy more; and the more you buy, the lower your per-unit costs will be. So maybe we should come up with a marketing strategy to see how you can sell more of the same thing. I think we can have a whole discussion around this idea."

"Now you're speaking my language," she said. "But I didn't ignore your observations about the need to manage my costs better."

"After looking at your inventory, cost of goods, and your selling price, I would look at your overheads. We should look at ways to control your electricity, gas, telephone and any other similar costs. They are a direct bleed on your profits."

I started sifting through some bills that she had gathered.

"We will look at government programs and also energy providers and see if we can get bundle deals for your phone, fax and debit card machine. You can reduce the cost of your energy by using a programmable thermostat. With your phone, we can explore the option of single or multiple lines."

"I was aware of these options but I have to admit that I took a rather carefree approach to them. I was not maximizing all possible cost savings from them," she said.

I didn't stop. I was searching through the cost base very meticulously looking for savings.

"I am not sure of the arrangement you have with your credit card companies. Do you push them to get any special discounts? Alternatively, by becoming a member of a business association you can sometimes get favourable credit terms."

It was now one o'clock in the afternoon. We had been talking business for almost five hours. She asked if I wished to take a break and have lunch.

"Great idea," I replied, and put the forms down on the table in front of me.

I had frequented her restaurant so often that she already knew my favourite pasta dish. We went upstairs and sat at a quiet table in the corner. One of her servers soon brought us lunch. I looked at it with a an approving smile.

"So, Reza, tell me, what do you do with your life?" she asked.

"I work," I replied with a slight grin, looking down at the pasta I was twirling in my spoon. "No, I am kidding. I enjoy my life. I treasure my time with my family. Kids grow too fast."

I turned the question back to her. "What do you do, Sara? You devote a lot of time to your work, too. Let's fix your business so that you have more time to enjoy the fruits of your labour in this wonderful country." I steered the conversation back to business. "You should try to practice what we discussed this morning. Record the information and analyse it week by week to determine if there is anything you should change about your operations.

"You're right," she said.

We finished lunch and called it a day.

"Remember, Sara, if you're not measuring something, you can't manage it."

She smiled and nodded.

"I will see you soon," I said, and went out the door.

Lessons Learned

One should always watch his or her business like a hawk. Every detail in business is important—particularly financial planning and financial management.

Since small businesses, especially in the beginning, mostly depend on cash (capital is the lifeline of any business),). An entrepreneur should identify ways to minimize costs and increase profits.

In any business, every penny counts.

To have a strong foundation for any business, you need financial sustainability.

Trusting your people is the best thing you can do. But do not turn a blind eye to what is happening around you.

Collect information, analyze it and use it to your best advantage.

If the information you're collecting has no effect on your bottom line, stop collecting it. Concentrate on what helps drive profitability and growth.

Chapter 6: Hitch Your Wagon to a Trusted Horse

A man named Mustafa approached his friend, Amir, to borrow some money. When Amir requested to have the details of the loan stipulated in a written agreement, Mustafa insisted that, because they were friends, his word was better than any contract. Amir raised concerns that if—God forbid—something happened to Mustafa, nobody would know about their agreement, and he could be left in a situation where recovering the debt would be difficult. Mustafa relented, and agreed to go along with Amir's wish. He signed a contract with Amir, to put his friend at ease. The contract stated that Mustafa had to repay Amir the loan in one year's time.

When the loan came due the next year, Mustafa refused to pay Amir a cent. When Amir reminded him of the contract, and about "his word," Mustafa's response was, "Well, I will still tell you the same thing: I am not going to pay you anything. That is my word and my word is better than any contract."

Early one evening, Charles, my real estate broker, dropped by my office. Charles was a consummate salesman, always telling people what they wanted to hear, but I knew him well enough to distinguish facts from fiction. I just accepted Charles for who he was. When it came to doing real estate transactions, he was a good person to have on my side. He had an eye for a deal, and when an opportunity presented itself, I was often the first person he would call.

Charles came by to ask if I would like to go out for dinner. We sometimes talked business over meals. Interestingly, whenever we did, I was left to pick up the cheque.

"Okay," I said. "Just let me finish and we'll go. What's up?" I asked.

"I want to show you an office building that just went on the market in Old Montréal. It's a bank foreclosure. They're letting it go for a song."

"How much are they asking for it?" I asked.

"Well, commercial space in that area is going for about a hundred and ten dollars," Charles said, referring to the value per square foot. "I think we could get this building for about thirty."

"Is it fully rented?" I asked. I knew that the building could not have had a tenant. The bank had obviously taken it over because the owner couldn't honour the mortgage payments.

"No," he said. "But that's why you can get a good deal. That's what you want, isn't it?"

"Let's discuss it." I turned out the lights, set the alarm and locked the door.

"Where do you want to go?"

"Let's go to see the building, and afterward we can go for dinner on Saint Denis."

"All right," I said.

We took my car and drove to the building in Old Montréal. It was a beautiful old grey stone building. From the outside, it looked like it had been recently renovated.

I looked up at the building. "How big is it?"

"Twenty-eight thousand square feet over five floors," he said, barely able to contain his excitement.

I nodded and didn't say anything. I took another long look up at the building and drove away. "What do you want to eat?" I asked.

Do you feel like Japanese tonight? I know of a great restaurant called Soto, a sushi bar. I know the owner."

"Sure, why not?"

We pulled up to the parking lot of the restaurant. The valets knew Charles. One of them rushed toward us and Charles rolled down the passenger side window.

"Good evening Mr. Sauvet," the valet said.

Charles replied to him by name. "Hi Marc. We will be having dinner tonight."

The valet bent down to make eye contact with me in the driver's seat. "You can park your car there, sir," motioning to an empty spot on the street beside the main entrance. I was driving an expensive European car back then. There were more cars like it parked outside the entrance. It appeared that the owner of Soto wanted to make a statement.

Soto was on the second floor. Charles and I walked upstairs and were greeted by a well-dressed man standing in the entrance.

"Hello Tony!" Charles said to the man.

"Charles! Welcome! How are you?"

Charles introduced me to the man at the door. "Reza, this is Tony Faso, the owner of Soto."

I shook his hand politely.

"How are you, Reza? Welcome to Soto," Tony said. "It is a pleasure to meet you." He then led us into the restaurant.

The decor was absolutely exquisite, designed with the discerning customer in mind. While walking over to our table, I just about stopped dead in my tracks, when I saw what I thought was a famous face.

"Charles, is that who I think it is?" I whispered.

He looked at me, raised his eyebrows, and nodded. It was Denzel Washington, the famous Hollywood actor.

"This is our best table. Sit down, please," Tony said. In the tradition of an authentic Japanese restaurant, our view was obstructed from other guests to ensure privacy. Japanese shamisen music was playing quietly in the background.

After sitting down, Tony motioned for a waiter, who was Japanese, to come over to our table. He continued to do all of the talking.

"We will start you off with some warm sake. I have asked our chef to prepare something special for you tonight, compliments of Soto. Tonight, you are my guests.

"Hmmm," I thought to myself. Obviously there was more to this evening than met the eye.

Charles and I spent the next two hours discussing the building: it's physical condition, potential tenants, annual taxes and rent, among other things. It seemed like an incredible opportunity. Of course, to a real estate broker, every potential sale is an incredible opportunity. But I believed that this opportunity was, indeed, genuine.

We were mid-way through our dessert when Charles brought it all home. "Reza, the building on its own represents a once-in-a-lifetime opportunity. And, Tony would like to be your first tenant." he said.

"Ah," I thought to myself. There was a method to his madness.

"Soto is doing extremely well. Tony has plans to open two more restaurants and develop sixteen Japanese take-out counters called Soto Express. He wants to locate a restaurant in this building. I have shown it to him and he thinks it would be perfect. He loves the location. He would be willing to sign an agreement with you right away.

Obviously Charles had been concocting this plan for a while.

I had to admit, though, that the building was too good of an opportunity to pass up. The price was cheap because it wasn't in a particularly trendy area. I had a hunch, however, that the area was on the verge of gentrification. Real estate values in a number of blocks surrounding the building were much, much higher.

I gave Charles a verbal indication that I was willing to proceed to the next step, to thoroughly inspect the building and do a financial analysis.

At around midnight, I asked for the bill, despite Tony stating earlier that we were his guests. The waiter insisted that Tony had taken care of our table, but I really wanted to pay. I didn't want to have any reason to be indebted to him in the future. I wanted to make sure that any potential contract negotiations between us would be impartial. I left a couple hundred dollars in cash on the table, and told the waiter to thank Tony for the beautiful meal and to explain that I just felt more comfortable paying for it.

On the way home, Charles started to praise Tony and his success in positioning Soto as one of Montréal's top-tier restaurants in a relatively short time. The two had known each other for a couple of years through a past real estate deal. I was wise to Charles' motive, however. He stood to earn an impressive commission from the bank by selling the building, and then from me by renting it to Tony for a restaurant.

It was no doubt an impressive opportunity; a distressed building with an anchor tenant waiting in the wings to occupy it.

An opportunity like this one would not last long on the market. Within ten days, after discussing some particulars with Tony and doing a close inspection of the building, Charles and I met with the bank official in charge of foreclosed properties to submit an offer. The bank had its own pre-written offer-to-purchase agreement, which was the only form they would accept. Purchasers of foreclosed properties were given no latitude to stipulate conditions in their offers. The only blank space on the bank's form was that in which the offer price was indicated. Everything was standardized.

Through Charles, I submitted a low-ball offer that represented less than twenty-five percent of the building's previous selling price. My reasoning to the bank official was that it was located in a nondescript area of downtown Montréal, there were no tenants, and that the cost of carrying the building would be quite high. The official faxed my offer to head office and Charles and I left. It was eleven o'clock in the morning.

Just after four o'clock that afternoon I received a call from the bank. My offer had been accepted by their head office. I was in shock. I was excited for sure, but part of me was sceptical. Why was the bank letting it go so cheaply?

The next step was to firm up the terms on which Tony and I had verbally agreed. Charles assisted me in designing a lease agreement. I didn't have a great deal of experience in this field, and Charles was, after all, a real estate broker. He used what he said was an excellent piece of software, purchased from a legal services Internet company, to write the lease agreement. After entering the financial terms and specific conditions, we printed and signed a lease agreement. It took less than an hour.

Tony and I got to know each other well over the following months. As entrepreneurs, we both spoke the same language and were motivated by the hard work of chasing dreams. One day, I mentioned that I was planning on attending a large trade show in China. I described the show to him, and the incredible deals that could be found there. He was quite enthusiastic about it, and asked if he could join me, as he was interested in sourcing restaurant equipment. I happily agreed and, three months later, we were sitting on a plane together for the sixteen-hour trip from Montréal to Guangzhou.

Early into the flight, I raised the question of how his business expansion plans were proceeding. He was just preparing to open a Soto Express take-out restaurant.

"I have found a fantastic location and I should be able to sign the lease within two weeks," he said.

"But hasn't it been about four months since you started negotiating with the owner?" I asked.

"Yes, but you know these big corporations. Every imaginable detail has to be covered. So far, the lease is more than one hundred pages long. It has already cost me thousands of dollars in legal fees and we are not even done yet!"

"What? One hundred pages?" I exclaimed, my eyes bulging, I'm sure.

"And that does not even include the exhibits," Tony replied, shaking his head.

What details could there possibly be to fill one hundred pages of a lease agreement?" I asked incredulously.

"Well, for example, the first few pages alone are taken up with definitions of the language that is used throughout the lease. But I am not worried. I am working with one of the best law firms in the city to make sure that my interests are protected."

Tony spoke at length about the details of the agreement. I listened carefully and nodded. But the more he spoke, the more I felt like sinking into my seat. My lease agreement with him, the one that Charles printed using a standardized template downloaded from the Internet was only three pages. Was I putting myself at risk, out of pure naiveté? I couldn't stop thinking about it throughout the entire flight. I concluded that since Tony had become such a close business acquaintance over these past few months, I should trust him. We had easily worked out a minor disagreement not long after he assumed the lease, so there was little to worry about. I didn't want to tip my hand and indicate that I was nervous.

Our trip to China was fruitful from both business and personal points of view. My respect for Tony continued to grow. There was no question that he was ambitious and highly skilled. Within a period of just months, he opened sixteen Soto Express outlets, —take-out sushi restaurants that drew on the formula of the original Soto restaurant's revered reputation. He registered each one separately, so as to limit the exposure of the whole restaurant group if one of them ran into difficulty.

Our business relationship continued to grow, too. Tony and I struck a deal for him to rent space that had freed up in another one of my commercial buildings for his expanding chain of regular Soto restaurants. His plans were to completely gut and remodel the building's interior to fit his vision for the restaurant. We anticipated construction to take about six months. Tony said he would cover the cost of the renovation while construction was underway, in exchange for a slight reduction in rent. I didn't have a problem with that idea.

Time ticked away. A year passed with no movement on construction, although he did pay me rent during that period. The building just sat empty. We met regularly throughout that period, and he assured me that everything was on track. Apparently, the delays were due to his contractor. Charles, meanwhile, started alluding to the notion that Tony had encountered financial difficulties due to the withdrawal of an investing partner. It was the first time I had ever been informed that Tony was working with anyone else.

More weeks passed without any progress on the building renovations. I was growing concerned because I had planned on subsidizing his rent for only six months. Something was not right and I wanted to hear the truth of the situation. Over the phone one day, I called his bluff. I wasn't confrontational about it. I simply wanted to know the truth of the situation.

We met in a small family restaurant in downtown Montréal. As always, he started by flattering me, complimenting me on how understanding and cooperative I had been. He then confessed his financial troubles. In addition to the sixteen Soto Express take-out locations, he was carrying leases on two other regular Soto restaurants besides the two leases he held with me. Those locations also needed to be renovated, but he was having difficulty proceeding because his existing restaurants were not running as profitably as he needed them to be. He was in a financial bind, for sure. The irony was that he was actually looking to me to come up with a solution for him! I was floored.

Someone once said to me that, if something goes wrong with a hundred- thousand -dollar mortgage, it is the homeowner's problem. When something goes wrong with a hundred- million-dollar mortgage, it is the bank's problem. While I was certainly not dealing with such large figures, I certainly felt like the bank.

In the end, I made a verbal promise to continue subsidizing his rent on the building on the condition that he would find a way to get his investors back on track and to start the renovations. We both knew that he needed that restaurant to be operating and generating revenue. He appreciated the gesture.

Then came *the call*. It was a crisp mid-January morning. I was driving through downtown Montréal when my wife called me on my cell phone. She asked if I had heard the news about what had just happened on Saint Jacques Street.

"No," I said. "What's going on?"

"I just saw a news report on television. The fire department has closed the street because the roof of our building has caved in!"

"Oh, my God," I said out loud. I rushed right over to the building. It was the second commercial building that Tony had rented from me, the one that he was supposed to renovate but with which he had experienced delays.

My wife was right. The street was closed and there were fire trucks and police cars everywhere. The media were present, too.

I parked on the next block and walked. I found the fire chief and explained that I was the owner of the building. He gestured to the roof, four floors up. A sprinkler pipe had frozen and burst open. Being January, the water spraying from the pipe eventually froze into a massive block of ice. Its weight cracked the roof's main supporting beam. The roof caved in and damaged the exterior wall on the top floor. The wall threatened to come crashing down onto the sidewalk. The fire chief had closed the street.

Without consulting me, Tony had already given the city officials on the scene permission take matters into their own hands. Just before I arrived, they had wrapped cables through the window openings and yanked the damaged portion of the wall from the building with a crane, leaving a gaping hole on the top floor exterior wall. Tony was not concerned in the least. Then again, he didn't own the building. The way he was talking, we didn't have a thing to worry about because the insurance company would simply write a cheque for the damage and everything would be rebuilt. But the media became suspicious. Reporters who were hounding the scene for a scoop knew that the building was designated a heritage property, and somehow came under the impression that a couple of Iranian and Italian business partners had sought permission to renovate, but were refused by the city on the basis of heritage property by-laws. True, Tony and I had, at one point, been denied permission by the Montréal city heritage board to alter the building's façade, and the media was aware of the case. But we had accepted the board's decision and moved on. But the story spun by the media was that Tony and I, in retribution, had sabotaged the building in order to set the stage for a clean renovation. Nothing could be further from the truth.

So there I was, owner of a five-storey building in downtown Montréal, with a caved-in roof. I couldn't begin to imagine the headaches I would be facing in the coming months to clean up this situation.

Tony and I went to see our respective lawyers to review our insurance policies. My lawyer advised me that Tony's insurance company would likely be required to deal with the situation, as he was the legal tenant and he ordered the roof to be demolished. But his insurance company denied the claim because Tony was not occupying the building. The onus was back on me as the owner of the property.

Meanwhile, I consulted many people about the situation I was facing. Charles actually had the gall to point the finger at me for not insisting that a real estate lawyer draft the lease and include the appropriate clauses to protect myself. My lawyer, naturally, blamed me and Charles for not discussing the implications of a generic lease agreement with him. He said quite bluntly that my awkward situation was a result of not wanting to spend money on hiring a lawyer to draft a comprehensive legal agreement. "In the end," he said, "you always end up paying more." He was right.

Save for turning back time, there was nothing I could do but pursue the matter in court.

For three months after the accident, Tony did not pay me any rent nor return any of my calls. Then, out of the blue one day, he contacted me and asked if we could have lunch together. I suggested we meet at my office the next morning, instead.

He was normally late for our meetings, but that day he arrived on time. I was standing next to the reception desk when he walked in. The air between us was filled with tension. He greeted me with a friendly "Hello, Reza!" and extended his hand. I shook it cordially and we went to my office.

"Reza," he said, "I have talked to my business partner. We have decided to go ahead and start the renovation. All the plans are ready and I have my partner's commitment, too. Here you go." He handed me a cheque for the three months' rent he owed me. "I want to resolve our issues."

"Oh, sure, that's fine because your restaurant will be on the first floor, but what about the roof?" I said.

"It still has to be resolved between our insurance companies. I really don't know, Reza."

I was happy to hear the news, but I honestly did not have much faith in his word. Tony was a great talker. However, time would tell. I told him that I would have to discuss the matter with my lawyer.

My lawyer said that since Tony had paid his arrears, he wouldn't be in default anymore. It would not affect the ongoing legal case surrounding the roof. My lawyer's analysis was that Tony's decision to proceed, if indeed he would follow through on his word, brought us both one step closer to a restaurant, and generating more revenue from the space.

This new development with Tony came as positive news to Charles, my broker. According to the terms of my agreement with him, if I had lost Tony as a tenant, he would be required to either partially refund his commission or find me a replacement tenant.

Meanwhile, as if my saga with Tony was not enough, I found myself tangled in yet another major financial problem, this time with a person named Kevin Bronson, whom I had met through a cousin a couple of years before. Kevin was a carpet retailer in the United States who bought a significant amount of merchandise from me on credit. He seemed trustworthy, but he simply could not live up to his word. Unfortunately, my efforts to recover the money from him had deteriorated to the point where I had to launch legal proceedings. Kevin had commercial properties in Montréal, so my lawyer advised me to register a lien against them to secure what he owed me. Kevin's equity in those properties would cover his debt to me.

I took my lawyer's advice and told him to proceed with registering the lien. To make a long story short, Kevin agreed, after much negotiation, to transfer the title of three commercial buildings over to me to cover his debt.

On the surface, my problems with Kevin appeared to be over, but little did I know that I was walking into a legal hornet's nest. Learning from my experience with Charles and Tony, I worked closely with my lawyer and a notary to ensure that my proceedings against Kevin were legally sound. An array of comprehensive legal documentation was prepared and registered. Having spent a great deal of money this time on professional help, I felt secure. However, my optimism did not last long.

Soon after the transfer of title, I found out that Kevin was being sued in New York City by Credit Swiss First Boston, a powerful global investment bank. For whatever reason, Kevin had had a trading account with them, which had fallen into arrears. CSFB placed a margin call on Kevin and he didn't have the money to cover it, so the firm launched legal proceedings against him. He had declared his Montréal commercial buildings as collateral when he first established his account at CSFB.

I found out that Kevin had declared personal bankruptcy. It couldn't have been better for CSFB and their case against him. CSFB was represented by Ogilvy Renault, one of the most powerful law firms in Montréal. The file was referred to their bankruptcy division, which requested the bankruptcy court to cancel all of my proceedings against Kevin, and for legal permission to take possession of the buildings that Kevin declared as collateral to CSFB. So, that left CSFB and me to struggle over who had the rightful title to Kevin's assets.

After two years of expensive legal wrangling between our respective lawyers, CSFB and I finally went in front of a judge. The judge opened by declaring a potential conflict of interest. Her daughter-in-law was employed by Ogilvy Renault, CSFB's legal counsel. But since I always believed that judges served justice blindly, I said that I didn't feel disadvantaged by her family connection, and welcomed her to proceed with the case.

The judge made her ruling after considering arguments from both sides. Not only did she rule in CSFB's favour, she awarded them *more* than what they were seeking by giving me no right of appeal. She awarded CSFB two of Kevin's three Montréal properties. I was granted title only to the third property, which I was eventually able to sell and recover most of the losses and legal costs that I had incurred through my dealings with Kevin. The personal toll on me over those two years was significant. It was a long and expensive legal struggle.

Meanwhile, the renovations that Tony had started on my St. Jacques Street building ground to a halt after only six weeks. His contractor had stopped work because Tony had stopped paying him.

After learning this news, I went home, made myself a drink, and sat down to reflect on all the challenges I had endured with Tony, Kevin, and CSFB. There was a beautiful full moon that evening that cast a warm glow on the garden in my back yard. A beautiful sense of serenity was just outside my window, but my world, inside the window, seemed to be in turmoil. Where did it all go wrong? I thought about the contracts I had signed with Tony. In hindsight, my lease with him should have been much better grounded, from a legal point of view, and shaped by a professional with appropriate expertise. As for Kevin, I should definitely have had a comprehensive loan agreement in place before giving him credit. I trusted him because of his connection to my cousin. My experience with Kevin reinforced the importance of a solidly worded agreement, especially when working through a family member. On the other hand, even if I had protected myself with professionally crafted loan agreements, I still don't think I would have been completely protected, at the end of the day. No agreement would have uncovered the fact that Kevin had previous undisclosed obligations to CSFB.

The stress I endured while juggling two legal cases at once, on top of running my existing businesses, was numbing. I remember early one morning, near the latter part of my legal dealings with CSFB, seeing a young student mowing a golf course fairway. I envied his seemingly peaceful and uncomplicated life, and pondered whether my business pursuits were truly worth the stress. No matter, I had to push forward. I had made choices, and could not simply abandon them just because the going got tough. Standing inside my home looking outside at the moonlit garden, I felt like I was still caught in a web. It was time to break free and make a fresh start.

The next morning I went to my office and called Tony.

"Hi Tony," I said. "I'm calling to get the latest news on the renovation."

"Reza, why don't we have lunch together?" Tony asked.

"I just want to know what is happening with your contractor."

"Look, Reza, I would like to come and explain to you in person what is happening."

"All right. I am in my office. You come here and we will go somewhere for lunch," I said.

Tony came by my office at around noon that day. He walked in and greeted me with great trepidation. I walked toward him and reassuringly shook his hand. We went to an Italian restaurant where the owner knew us both. He offered us a table next to the window.

After ordering, I asked about his contractor. "What's happening, Tony? Why did you stop work on my building? You need to finish that renovation to open your restaurant and start generating income."

"Well, I talked to my partner. He feels that this project is too costly. He is not prepared to support me on it," he replied, looking down at the table. He paused until the waiter was out of earshot. He then continued.

"My partner says that it is your building, and is challenging me as to why he should have to pay for the cost of renovations."

"Look, Tony, you are the one who ordered the roof to be demolished, not me. Besides, your rent is too low to begin with. If you are ready to renegotiate your contract, I would be ready to help you out with the cost of rebuilding."

The conversation seemed to go nowhere. The more we talked, the further away I got from reaching any reasonable agreement with him. We left the restaurant without a clear resolution.

I went back to my office and called my lawyer to inform him of every detail of our conversation. In sum, I explained how I saw the hole that we had dug ourselves into with Tony simply getting deeper and deeper, and that I didn't see the situation reversing itself anytime soon. Despite the huge losses I would incur, it was time to liberate myself from Tony and move on. I told him that, in order to cut my losses, we should just finish this saga with Tony and rid myself of the nonsense. He didn't disagree.

I informed Tony that I wished to have him out of my properties immediately, and that we should simply go our separate ways. I was quite willing to tear up our agreement if he was, too. Judging from the ease with which he accepted my offer, he felt the same way. He agreed to vacate the first building within six months and abandon his plans for my second building.

For the first time in a very long time, I felt like I had my life back and that I could face each day without a ball and chain around my ankle.

I enjoyed a couple of blissful months of relief. Incredibly, though, I found myself thrust into yet another situation in which somebody threatened to destabilize the world that I had worked so hard to build up. Thus began another saga.

I have never liked accounting, so I hired a part-time bookkeeper, who would come once or twice a week to maintain the books for Tapis en Gros, the five big-box floor covering stores I was running at the time (more on that saga, later). His name was John Ryan. He was in his forties, not very tall, and had a really bad comb-over to cover his baldness. But he was polite and always punctual. John worked primarily with one of my managers, Gail Sauvé.

Gail was not a fan of John. A few times, she mentioned that if she were me, she would have fired him long ago. But John seemed to do a reasonably good job; enough for me to trust him.

Back then, I would not get too concerned with details, in part because I didn't understand the world of accounting. I didn't understand debits and credits, journal entries, and the trial balance. But I would never forget the details of any payment. I could remember the date, amount and even the cheque number of any payment my company issued. In stark contrast, John couldn't seem to remember the details about any accounting entry. He always had to refer to the computer to be able to answer my questions.

A couple of years after opening the first Tapis en Gros outlet, I received a call from the Canada Revenue Agency, the arm of government responsible for tax collection and enforcing tax policy. They wanted to audit my books. The CRA official asked to meet me in my office on the following Monday. I asked John to be there, too, and for him to work closely with Gail in advance to ensure that our records were solid.

I arrived at my office at seven o'clock that morning, two hours earlier than usual. John arrived a few minutes after me. I had also asked Gail to be there at the same time, but she called me early that morning to say that she would be a few minutes late, which wasn't like her. She was always a few minutes early.

"Hi sir," John said.

"Good morning, John. I want to make sure that we have properly reported everything to the government."

"Don't worry," John replied.

"I know you are confident, but I want you to verify one last time before the auditor comes." We sat down and went through the files together. Everything was balanced, but I happened to notice that a large amount had been debited from my equity account and credited to the company, when I glanced at the shareholder equity line.

When I opened the first outlet of Tapis en Gros, John had entered the financial details of my lease agreement into the accounting system, making sure that everything from leasehold improvements to depreciation and rental payments followed the proper accounting procedures.

"John, what is this entry?" I asked, pointing to it.

"Let's see."

"John, what is going on? Where is this amount coming from?" I asked, referring to an entry of tens of thousands of dollars.

"That's the money you transferred to your company. It is the shareholder loan," he said.

"John, I have never transferred such an amount to the company. Let's go back and see where the entries are coming from."

Gail walked in. "Good morning, guys. Sorry I am a bit late."

"Is everything alright, Gail?" I asked.

"Yes, yes," Gail answered. "I was just trying to put together all my notes since the beginning of operation."

"Gail, would you take a look at this?" I said to her. "Do you know where this entry came from?"

She looked at the computer screen for a moment. "I am pretty sure that was the money that came from the landlord for leasehold improvements. But let me look back in my notes."

In a few seconds she said, "That's right. It refers to the last time we sat down with the landlord to summarize the lease."

After verifying the detail, we found out that John had allocated the tenant allowance that I received from the landlord to shareholder equity. This entry changed what would have been a profit that year to a loss, and reduced the tax my company paid.

Gail looked at me sternly and, without saying anything, motioned that she wanted to talk to me privately in my office. We calmly stepped away for a moment and shut the door behind us.

"Look, Reza, I have told you more than once that he is not the right person to do the accounting. I am sure that, even if everything goes fine today, other problems will surface later on."

"What do you think I should do? Get rid of him?" I asked, shrugging my shoulders.

"Just let him go!"

"I can't do that, Gail. He has been working for me for almost three years. He is part of our family."

Gail was frustrated, but she was respectful. With a calm voice she continued. "What about me, Reza? What about the other employees? Aren't we your family? He is only here once a week for a few hours."

"Let's just finish with the auditor and then we will see."

"All right, all right. But I will tell you that it is going to be very hard to continue working with him. Don't feel like you owe him something, Reza. You're not his only client."

"Anybody can make a mistake, Gail. I will look at it."

"Okay. But Reza, look at it from another perspective. Letting him go might just be good for him, too."

The auditor came, as scheduled. I was very up front about the mistake we had just discovered. He was understanding, and allowed us to report it as a voluntary disclosure. I wasn't penalized. Aside from that issue, the audit went smoothly. But the whole episode prompted me to reflect on Gail's sentiments toward John. I respected her judgment on many fronts. In the end, I knew she was right, and that I was sticking with John for the wrong reasons. This time, we were able to catch his mistake before it became a real problem. But who knows what the future would bring?

My dealings with Tony and Kevin had taught me the supreme importance of being able to trust the people you work with or must rely on. John parachuted in and out of my office once a week. I appreciated that he had a number of different clients. That he had to rely on his computer each time to understand a transaction, said to me that his heart was not in my business, which presented a potential liability to me. I knew Gail was right.

Dream Beyond Borders

It was awkward, but I soon told John that I would no longer be requiring his services. Surprisingly to me, he didn't give much of a reaction. It proved to me that he did not have the same degree of loyalty to me or my business that I, perhaps, had for him. We parted ways and I assigned his responsibilities to Gail.

Lessons Learned

I have recounted in this chapter some of the most trying situations I have ever faced in business, ones which I had never imagined when I first started out. The root of the problem in each of these situations was the person I had chosen to deal with, or rather, the horse to which I hitched my wagon. Business success comes down to people.

While contracts are essential to guide expectations between individuals or parties, if one party reneges on an agreement, no lawyer or court can get blood from a stone. I have fought cases in court, both as a plaintiff and as a defendant, more times than I wish to remember. Sometimes, I feel like I could have bought a small city on the amount of money I have spent on legal fees. But each case taught me a little more about the essence of doing business. The most valuable lesson I learned from all of these challenges was the paramount importance of knowing the people you work with or rely on: their integrity as individuals and their loyalty to your relationship.

I knew from the beginning that there was something about Charles, my real estate broker, that I did not completely trust. But I was neither experienced enough to recognize the true risk to which he exposed me, nor honest enough with myself about my ability to manage that risk. Charles led me down the garden path by introducing me to Tony, the owner of Soto. Sure, I was aware that his true interest was in setting up a deal to make a commission. But a combination of ego, naiveté, and failure to

160

think critically about what was lying around each corner of that relationship made me vulnerable.

Survival in business means making smart decisions, not emotional ones. It is important to trust somebody enough to do business with them, but not enough to let them threaten your destiny. I agreed to use the generic contract that Charles provided for Tony's lease agreement because I believed that our relationship would be enough to see me through any potential difficulties. I was so wrong. The business potential of the building, combined with the aura of success that Tony radiated through Soto, blinded me. Always dig deep beneath the surface.

My experience with Kevin was another painful lesson in trusting a friend of a friend. My experience with Kevin taught me to check, and double check, my assumptions, in order to guarantee that they reflect the facts. When Kevin transferred title of his buildings to me in lieu of payment, I took it at face value that there were no liens registered on them. I felt I had no reason to be sceptical of Kevin. He was a friend of a family member, after all. Big mistake. I should have made an effort to do a conclusive search on the title on his properties. By assuming ownership of the buildings, I inadvertently entangled myself in legal action with one of the world's biggest investment banks, whose corporate legal team was determined to make an example of me. Always try to understand your assumptions and confirm facts before diving into a transaction.

Be selective about the people you choose to deal with. People are the essence of business. A firm's operations, be it those of a small coffee shop or a large corporation, are only as good as the values and integrity of the employees. As a business person, the most important thing you can do is to surround yourself with honest, intelligent, loyal people whom you can trust. People like Charles, Tony, and John can land you in trouble without any bad intention. In my case, it was the courtroom. I trusted them when I should not have.

At the outset of any business relationship, set your standards high and don't relent. Scrutinize people's values and integrity. Check references, and in the process, ask relevant, hard questions. And always keep a professional distance from people to maintain objectivity in your decision making. Running a business is like driving a school bus: all it takes is one wrong passenger to spoil the ride or cause a serious accident. So, be highly selective about the people you hire and deal with. They are your lifeblood.

Chapter 7: Mind the Tax Man

Once upon a time there lived a poor shepherd, named Borzou. Having just a few sheep, it took him months to collect enough wool to make a scarf, mittens, a sweater and a blanket. By late fall, when he had saved enough wool to meet his goal, he felt secure knowing that he would be warm for the coming winter.

Borzou took the wool to the local spinner. Because he had no cash, he offered to pay the spinner for his work by giving him one-eighth of his wool. The spinner agreed, and the next day he produced eight rolls of yarn for Borzou. Borzou left one ball for the spinner and then proceeded to the village dyer's shop.

"Would you dye these balls of yarn for me?" Borzou asked the dyer.

"Of course," the master dyer said. "I can dye them today and they will be dry by tomorrow evening."

When Borzou asked if he could pay him for his services with a ball of yarn, the dyer said that he would require two balls for payment. Borzou agreed, and two days later he had seven balls of yarn in the most extraordinary colours he could imagine. He was very happy, but after giving two balls to the dyer in exchange for his services, he was left with only five of his original eight balls. He had enough yarn now to make only a scarf, mittens and a sweater. There was no longer enough for a blanket.

His next stop was the village tailor. "Master tailor," Borzou said, "I would like you to knit me a pair of mittens, a scarf and a sweater. But in return, I can only pay you with wool. Would you be willing to make such an exchange?"

The tailor looked at Borzou's wool. "These colours are magnificent, Borzou. I would do it for two balls of yarn. There would only be enough left for me to knit you a sweater."

Borzou agreed to the tailor's offer. Five days later, he returned to pick up a beautiful wool sweater. He wore it with pride.

With only a sweater and no blanket, mittens, or scarf, Borzou suffered through the cold of winter. Every time he wore the sweater, he was reminded of the importance of carefully planning his wool supply. In order to pay for all the services he received from other people, he would need to collect double the wool he actually needed for himself.

Many business people view the government negatively: an immovable bureaucracy that takes away their hard-earned money. In my opinion, this view is somewhat skewed. I believe business people should view government as their business partner, not their competitor. The harder you work, the happier your partner is. Just be ready to answer to your partner whenever necessary. A gap in your financial records, or an inadvertent mistake in the way you file your taxes, can make you a target of the tax authority. Take it from me, undergoing an audit is not a nice experience.

The story I relate in this chapter is about my experience of being audited. It is not about tax planning strategies or interpretations of tax law. Rather, I am sharing this story to illustrate what can go wrong if you don't keep solid records.

At one point, I held a number of separate corporations: Collage Tapis, the high-end Persian carpet business; Tapis en Gros, the big- box floor covering chain; two furniture stores, a gift shop, two coffee shops, and my real estate holdings. In the summer of 2004, I decided to close one of those companies. When you close a company, the government will want to confirm that you have done everything according to the law. My journey with them began with an inadvertent error they discovered on the financial statements for the company I closed.

The audit of that one company was very quick. The government cleared me of the mistake without charging me a penalty. But three weeks later, they notified me that they would be auditing not only all of the other business entities I held at the time, but my personal finances too. Little did I know how exhausting and nerve wracking the process would be.

Simply establishing a date for an auditor to come to my office and start reviewing my records took almost an entire year. The revenue agency was undergoing a departmental restructuring at the time, and it was proving very difficult just to establish the initial appointment. Finally, they were able to assign a young woman in her early thirties to my case file. Her name was Catherine Belanger.

I arrived at work one Monday morning at around nine, my usual time. Catherine had already arrived and was waiting on the street in front of my office building. From the point at which I greeted her and shook her hand, I sensed that it was going to be a chilly journey.

At the time, I had two bookkeepers working for me, Sue and Ellen. I had asked Sue in advance to be in the office while the auditor was present, in order to ensure full and speedy access to my financial records.

I had offices on two floors of the building. Previous years' financial records were in a storage room on the first floor, and the current year's files and staff offices were on the second floor.

The four of us walked upstairs from the lobby. Catherine asked if I could provide her with a desk, which indicated she was going to be with us for a while. I provided her with a nice desk and a telephone, and gave her free access to the cabinets in which all financial records were stored. She used her own computer.

She was very focused and professional. Once she began her work, there was absolutely no small talk with her. Behind the scenes, I made a special point of telling staff to treat her well and not to disturb her work.

After a few hours on her first day in the office, Catherine asked if she could have a few minutes of my time for a meeting. We sat down in my office and she handed me a five-page list. "These are the documents I will need from you. Because there is quite a bit of overlap between your personal and corporate financial activities, I am going to audit your corporate tax returns from the last five years as well. But I will start with your personal records."

Yeeeeeeeesh.

She handed me the list and I took a moment to absorb it all. She wanted me to produce all the invoices for which I had received payments, and proof of all my expenses for the past five years. She said that any expense for which I could not produce a receipt would have to be reclassified as revenue, which in turn would increase net earnings for those years and, potentially, my tax

166

liability. On top of that, there would be penalties and interest accrued over those years.

"How much time will you need to provide me with these documents?" she asked.

"I don't know," I replied, a bit bewildered. "I will have to dig pretty deep. Here, for example, you're asking for the deed of sale for this property and for documentation supporting all of the capital investment I have made since then. This is going back a long, long time."

"That's correct," Catherine replied. I will need all those documents to be able to have a full picture. Do you think you could pull them all together in two weeks?" she asked.

"I will need *at least* two weeks," I replied. It was difficult to hide my desperation.

Sue and I worked every single day, digging through piles and piles of documents. My mother always complained about my habit of never throwing anything away. An old toy, slips of paper, even a piece of wood can have sentimental value for me. I have always believed that even though I don't need something today, it might be important tomorrow. There is a price to being a collector, in terms of clutter and the cost of storage space. But being able to locate something from the past when you really need it is priceless.

We ended up requiring about three weeks to compile the documentation that Catherine requested. During that time, I was completely consumed with obtaining all of the items she identified on that list. Even among friends, it was all I could seem to talk about. Catherine's List became barbecue and water-cooler conversation. It made me rather insecure because she was asking for very personal financial information. It felt as though she was violating my privacy, but I knew she had the authority to request the information.

Three days before the date we had both agreed on, Catherine called to confirm whether the list of documents would be ready. She was clearly under pressure to finish this audit because Canadian tax law requires the government to issue a judgment within a certain period of time from the date on which the tax dispute was filed. A lot of valuable time was lost at the beginning, just in trying to arrange the initial appointment for Catherine to start her work. She was under pressure to meet a legally defined deadline.

The day before the scheduled meeting with Catherine, Sue and I meticulously organized all the documents to ensure everything was well prepared for the audit. I believed that if the files were presented to Catherine in a well-organized way, she would see that I was not trying to hide anything.

"I honestly get the feeling that she is going to want to come to my home and search through my closets," I said to Sue. "I just can't believe the level of detail she is requesting."

"But why is she looking through your personal information?" Sue asked. "I thought she was focusing now on your corporate information."

"Well, most of my capital is registered under my personal name," I replied.

"I remember once, Reza, you said that keeping property in your personal name raises the risk of liability. Isn't it better if you have everything registered under a company?" Sue asked.

"It might be better, but sole proprietors of a business can be held personally liable. There are pros and cons to each approach. On one hand, it is better from the perspective of capital gains taxes to operate under a company. However, individuals pay a lower rate of tax on pure capital."

Finally, the day arrived for Catherine's follow-up visit. When I arrived, she was waiting on the street outside the office, carrying a bulky briefcase in one hand and a computer bag in the other. After opening the door and turning on the lights, I invited her inside. Before walking upstairs to the second floor, I offered to help her with her bags. She gave me a curt smile and said, "No thanks."

"They look heavy," I said.

"I am used to them."

Sue happened to walk in just then. "Good morning, Reza. I am going to make some coffee. Would you like some when it is ready?"

"Sure," I replied.

"What about the lady from the government?" she asked. Sue never referred to Catherine by her name.

"Would you like a cup of coffee?" I asked Catherine. With the same ambiguous smile, she responded, "No thanks." Sue nodded and went to prepare the coffee.

Catherine and I walked upstairs. She placed her bags next to the desk, set up her laptop computer, and got straight to work. She wasted no time with casual conversation. I tried very hard to break the ice, but got nowhere. The most I could get out of her were one-word responses like "yes" or "no." After walking her through all the documents, I decided to take a step back.

"I will start with the bank statements, Mr. Reza, and then I will let you know if I need anything else," she said.

She once tried to call me by my last name, but it was difficult for her to pronounce. I asked her to just call me "Reza." From that point, she insisted on calling me "Mr. Reza."

She worked through the morning nonstop, like a machine. At exactly noon, she packed her bags and told me that she was going for lunch, and would be back in an hour.

"You can leave your bags here, if you wish," I said.

"No thank you, I will take them with me."

I was amazed at her focus on work. She didn't waste one minute that morning. She wouldn't accept anything from me, not even a cup of coffee. All the staff in the office felt uneasy about her, but I felt that she was an honest, hard-working person, doing only what she was supposed to do. Perhaps she was a bit extreme in her approach, but that was alright with me.

After two days, she asked to have a meeting with me. She gathered some papers from her portable printer and joined me in my office.

"Mr. Reza," she said, "I have calculated all your deposits against your withdrawals." She pointed to two different figures. "This is the income that you reported for this period, and this is the figure that I arrived at," she said, comparing two separate numbers. Her figure was much, much higher than I had reported, suggesting that I was not disclosing income.

"Huh?" I asked, picking up the paper and studying the two figures.

"My calculation is based on all the deposits in your accounts minus all the withdrawals you made, and factoring in various deductions like allowable depreciation, deferred revenue, and other expenses, according to Canadian tax law."

"That's not how it works," I said, puzzled. "There are likely deposits in there you have misinterpreted. For example, if somebody gave me payments on a loan, or if I had sold a property bought years ago without any profit..."

"In that case, it is your obligation to prove it," she said.

I was careful not to say anything. My father always told me that if you don't know what to say, it is better to say nothing.

"All right," I said. "Can you give me a few days to try to locate these documents?"

"Sure. I will give you a call in the middle of next week to schedule our next appointment.

"That would be fine," I said, nodding.

She went back to her desk, packed up and left. I was in shock. I didn't know where to begin. Using her calculations for income, I was potentially facing a six-figure tax bill. For some reason, I couldn't help but feel that she was biased against me.

The next day, I called Catherine's supervisor. I didn't think Catherine was being entirely neutral, and I wanted to respectfully make this information known to her superiors. I had to leave a message, but was pleasantly surprised when my call was returned later the same day. The woman on the other end was very calm, and listened to me with patience about my experience dealing with Catherine. At the end of conversation, she said that assigning a different person to my file was not an option. She assured me that, as long as I had documents to prove everything, Catherine would be reasonable with me.

I was able to dig out a number of other documents related to Catherine's calculation of income. I summarized them on a spreadsheet and provided explanations where necessary. I was extremely confident that everything was in order, and that there was nothing I could not substantiate. I reviewed everything with Sue to double check my work before meeting Catherine.

The day before Catherine was scheduled to return to my office, I arrived early. Sue arrived before me and had two cups of Starbucks coffee ready for us to start the day. Sometimes I brought the coffee in the morning, sometimes she did. Sometimes one of us would just make a pot of coffee after arriving at the office. Coffee was an essential part of the morning for each of us.

"Thanks Sue," I said. "Let's go up and finish preparing the documents for tomorrow's meeting with Catherine."

Ellen, my other bookkeeper, happened to arrive at the same time. I asked if she would join us to provide another critical eye for this important task. The three of us sat at a table and went over the work that had consumed Sue and me for the past month.

I went through the receipts one by one, piecing together a financial picture that was tied off to the balances quoted on the bank statements.

"This is the numbered list of deposits," I said to my colleagues. "Each number corresponds with a supporting document."

"Let's look at the first one," Sue said.

"It shows a deposit of twelve thousand four hundred dollars, which comes from my line of credit," I explained. And if you look at the line of credit statement, the amount was not paid back till a year later. I have all the account statements for that year. We can see the transaction here.

"The next deposit is the mortgage I got from the bank. I have a copy of the cheque from the notary."

"Reza, I think you should also get a copy of the deed. It indicates exactly the terms and conditions," Sue said.

"Yes, yes, that is a good idea," Ellen said. "Which year was it for?" She got up and went to look for the file.

"It was three or four years ago," I said.

The next document was regarding the proceeds of the sale. "Sue, do you think there is sufficient explanation for this?" I asked, handing her the documents.

"What do we need here?" she asked.

"Well, every deposit to my account is considered pure revenue unless there is an expense to balance it. It can be deferred revenue from any previous year. We just have to document the terms of that deposit."

"Reza, I am pretty sure that the original cost of this property was less than what you show it to be here," Sue said. She handed me a document and pointed it out on the spreadsheet summary.

"Let me take a look," I said. She was right. "But what about the transfer tax?" I asked. "We have to add it to capital."

"Then, you need to produce a copy of that tax bill from the city," Sue said.

Ellen was still up looking for the deed. "Ellen, could you look for the transfer tax invoice for the property on Notre Dame Avenue?" I asked.

The three of us spent the entire morning reviewing the documents. Everything was in order. I took Sue and Ellen for lunch to show them my appreciation for their effort, but also to get more feedback from them about how I should handle my next meeting with Catherine. The anxiety of not knowing whether Catherine would accept the documents was overwhelming. I was facing a potential tax bill, and penalties, of over six figures.

The next day, Catherine arrived before everyone else, as usual. Before taking her up to her desk on the second floor, I made sure that she was aware of the effort we had all made to ensure that nothing was missing. Upstairs, I sat down with her and walked her through all of the new documents that Sue, Ellen and I had compiled, as per her request. It took me about half an hour to get through everything.

"Okay. I will need to review them," she said. "It might take a few days. I will then let you know what I conclude.

From that point, it actually took Catherine about two weeks to sort through everything and conduct her analysis. She was like one of my employees, arriving every morning precisely on time and working with very few breaks. On occasion, when she had to be absent from my office, she would tell me in advance. I think she had to attend a training program once a week, and she also had to keep her supervisor abreast of her findings.

It was during those two weeks that I got a call from my mother in Iran. My father had suffered a severe asthma attack. On one hand, she tried to tell me not to worry. He had experienced such attacks many times before, and that everything seemed to be okay. But the tone of her voice was much more serious than her actual words. I knew beyond a doubt that the situation was serious. Without hesitating, I told her that I would drop everything and be there as soon as possible. That she didn't try to dissuade me confirmed that the situation back home was serious.

I purchased a plane ticket for Iran right away, and departed two days later. From Montréal, the trip to Isfahan, took thirty-six hours, including the stop-over in Europe and the five-hour bus ride from Tehran to Isfahan. I arrived at my parents' home at around nine o'clock in the morning, after waiting much of the night at the airport for a bus.

My father was very sick. He was struggling to breathe. He had been to see a respirologist at the hospital just the day before, who recommended putting him on oxygen to ease his breathing until the medication took full effect. Since my mother did not have the opportunity to do so, I set out to find a medical supply company.

I was amazed at the changes in Isfahan. There seemed to be twice as many cars on the street compared to when I lived there. Then there was the interesting experience of shopping. I knew I had lost a bit of my Iranian heritage during my years of living in Canada as the experience of buying something at the market seemed so complex. To begin with, when one asks for the price of something, a merchant will typically offer a polite reply like, "This is not well suited to you. I wouldn't want to sell you this piece." One then has to say something like, "I thank you, but I am really interested in this product, and in knowing how much it costs." After gauging your true desire for the product, the merchant will then offer it at a very high price. From there, the negotiations begin. The whole process is a dance.

After five hours of searching around Isfahan, I finally found a personal oxygen supply system. I purchased it and headed back home. The door was locked when I arrived, so I rang the doorbell a few times. Nobody answered. It was very strange. My mother had given me no indication that she was going to leave the house. I went over to their next-door neighbour's home and knocked on the door. Our two families were very close.

"They went to the hospital, Reza," Mr. Daraby replied. Your father had another serious asthma attack and had to be rushed to the hospital."

I froze, fearing the worst.

"Wait here, Reza," he said. "I will take you. You will need somebody with you." He ran back into his house and came back with car keys and a jacket. "I will drive," he said.

I was terrified, but Mr. Daraby tried to keep me calm by talking to me along the way. I appreciated his intent, but I honestly did not hear a word he said while I was in the car with him.

"How is life in Canada? I am sure you have much better services than we have here. You will see that the hospitals here are of low quality. Nobody cares if you are sick."

That was not very comforting to hear. My mind wandered back to Canada for a moment, to Catherine's audit. I leaned my head back in the seat and closed my eyes. The stress of the ongoing audit on one hand, combined with my father's health on the other, was taking its toll on me. On top of the stress, I was still fighting jet lag from my long trip from Canada.

The drive to the hospital took about fifteen minutes. I got out right away and left Mr. Daraby to park the car. The attendant at the main reception desk confirmed that my father had been admitted to the emergency department, and he pointed the way. I ran in the direction he pointed and found my mother. She saw me and started sobbing. "There, there he is!"

The asthma attack left my father unconscious. A doctor and three nurses were trying to recover a heartbeat with defibrillator paddles. It was an intense scene. I rushed up to his bed but one of the nurses gently pulled me away and asked me to give the doctor space to work.

It took a few minutes before he regained a normal heartbeat. The doctor yelled, "He's back.."

I was so relieved. I hugged my mother and assured her that everything was going to be alright. The doctor approached me. I shook her hand and thanked her.

"You had better take him to another hospital after he regains consciousness," the doctor said to me. We were in a private hospital. She said that public hospitals were better equipped to treat severe respiratory problems.

My father regained consciousness about three hours later. The following day I had to arrange for an ambulance to transfer him to another hospital. The woman responsible for coordinating the ambulances gave me an invoice. I had to pay the fee in another section of the hospital and then bring back proof of payment. I did, and she directed me to wait nearby for the ambulance to pick him up. Meanwhile, the nurses prepared my father to be transported.

What appeared to be a cargo truck drove up to the exit door where I was waiting. The driver got out and walked toward me.

"Are you the one who called for an ambulance?" he asked.

My jaw dropped. Not knowing whether he was a cargo truck driver or an ambulance attendant, I wasn't sure what to say. I nodded to him and then called to the orderlies inside to bring my father to the door. They did, but they actually asked him to walk to the truck while they loaded his wheelchair. I was stunned. Barely twenty-four hours had passed since he had gone into shock!

The weather was chilly. I sat inside next to my dad, since that was really the only place for me to sit in the back of the truck. My mother drove behind us in her car. My father and I bounced violently for the entire twenty-minute journey to the public hospital. My father began to feel cold, so I took off my jacket and covered him up. I kept talking to him to help draw his attention away from the bouncy ride.

The public hospital was much larger than the private one, but had many more patients, too. I got out first and found a security guard at the front entrance. I explained the situation, and he offered me a wheelchair. I got my father to step out of the truck and I wheeled him in to the emergency department. It cost me a bit of money to help speed the process, but it succeeded in getting him admitted immediately. The "tips" I paid along the way were to front-line hospital staff. Despite their lower-level positions of responsibility, they controlled access to the doctors. A non-Iranian might interpret these tips to the hospital workers as bribes, but in Iran they are considered no different than paying a little bit extra to a restaurant server or hotel attendant to reward good service.

The chief resident was very compassionate. He asked me to wheel my father to the radiology department, located in another building, for an X-ray. We would have to go outside again. This time, an orderly wheeled my father for me and I walked alongside.

Along the way, I noticed a few portable X-ray machines in the corridors, so I asked the orderly why we could not use one of them, instead of trekking outside to another building.

"They have all been broken for a while. Nobody knows how to fix them," he said. I nodded, and reminded myself that I had to adjust my expectations after living in Canada.

In ten minutes, we arrived at the radiology department. The radiologist took my father into the X-ray room right away to examine his lungs.

I found a waiting room where I could sit down. I slid into an old, discoloured chair and tried to relax, comforted a bit by realizing that both the chief resident and radiologist were not alarmed at my father's condition. One of the many things that went through my mind was the differences I had experienced between Canada and Iran. Given what I was going through back home with the government audit, I had taxes on my mind. In Iran, people pay very little tax, which was reflected in the quality of their public services. But then again, I was looking at the situation through a

Canadian lens. I wondered if it was because Iranians paid relatively little tax that they were not so demanding of their government. I dozed off with an endless stream of thoughts circling around in my mind.

"Hello again," the doctor said, touching my arm to wake me. "Your father is going to be okay. His lungs are clear, aside from his asthma. You can take him home."

I was not comforted by his assessment. "Doctor," I said, "just yesterday my father was unconscious and his heart stopped beating. He had to be resuscitated with defibrillator paddles. He is in a very delicate condition! I would like him to remain here under observation. My family is not equipped to take proper care of him!"

I explained how I had dropped everything in Canada and traveled half-way around the world when I first learned of my father's condition. I pressed pretty hard for the doctor to allow my father to stay for at least a couple more days. With reluctance, he finally agreed. "Okay. Two days, maximum," he said.

My mother and I stayed at my father's bed-side that night. Despite the exhaustion and jet -lag from my trip, I couldn't get to sleep. My father's health and the business issues back home in Canada were weighing heavily on my mind. I wanted desperately to stay with my parents, but had no choice but to return to Montréal two days later to tend to the audit . With my father in this condition, the thought of leaving was agonizing. The audit just compounded my stress. But as difficult as it was, I absolutely had to return to Canada. The next day, I consulted with the doctor again, and he assured me that my father's condition had stabilized. I spent my remaining few hours in Isfahan with my father and mother in the hospital.

When it came time to leave, saying good-bye to them was one of the most heart-wrenching experiences I have ever had. It was especially difficult for my mother. I knew that my presence gave her strength. My father showed less emotion, but I could tell that he was devastated to see his son leave Iran, yet again. But I had to go.

Thirty-six hours of bus rides, waiting in airports and gazing out over the clouds from an airplane window gave me a lot of time for solemn reflection. I vowed on that return trip to do everything in my power to bring my parents to Canada, so that I would never again have to experience the pain of leaving them half a world behind. My parents would be more secure near me, and their quality of life would improve in Canada.

I went to my office the morning after arriving in Montréal. As usual, Catherine was waiting outside for someone to open the door. I greeted her and started to describe the adventure I had just had over the past ten days. She showed no interest in my circumstances, so I abruptly changed the subject. While walking upstairs, I asked if she had everything she needed, and if she had any questions.

"I will be finishing your personal tax assessment this week. Let's meet at the end of the day on Friday," she said. "After that, I will start to focus on your corporate tax assessment." She gave no indication as to whether there were any problems. But I was confident that things were on the right track.

"All right, we'll talk on Friday," I said.

First thing Friday morning, I went to Catherine's desk to let her know that I would be free to talk at any time that day. She proposed to meet at three o'clock. Although I was hoping to talk earlier, I didn't want to do anything that might disturb her. At three o'clock, the two of us sat down at my conference table to review her work.

"Well, Mr. Reza, I accepted almost all of your documents," she said. I held my breath. "But there are three issues I need to discuss with you."

I should have assumed from the beginning that she was going to discover problems.

"First, you indicated that this deposit relates to an item you sold. I have to consider the total amount as income. If you can find me the receipt that details the original purchase price, then I will consider the difference.

I told myself to stop and count to five, so as not to burst out. "But I made that purchase more than ten years ago," I said. "How do you expect me to find it?"

"That is your challenge to solve, not mine," she said.

I saw very quickly that she was not willing to veer from the policy book one tiny bit. There would be no mercy.

"Next are these expenses you claimed on your Sherbrooke Street property." I cannot see any documentation to back those expenses up. So, this amount must be considered as income, too. And because of the rule of double taxation, you can't claim it as a capital expense," she said.

"What does that mean?" I asked.

"Well, I know it doesn't sound logical, but if you make a mistake, you can't go back and correct it."

I was puzzled by her response, but she didn't elaborate.

"The third issue is your automobile expense. It is too high and I can't accept it."

"Really? Why not?" I was being very careful not to come across as aggressive or defensive. "I have my own car and I have another car that I use for my business," I said.

She paused for a moment and nodded ever so slightly. "I see. If you can substantiate it, your automobile expense will be all right. If not, I will have to revise your taxation," she said.

She continued without letting me respond. "I will come back on Monday to do some more work. Based on what you have provided me, I am finished with your personal taxes. But I still cannot draw a final conclusion because there is quite a bit of overlap between your personal and corporate finances. There is still more work to be done on your corporate tax filings. But could you please sign these forms to show that I have completed your personal reassessment?" she asked.

I took the forms out of her hand and glanced through them. I was reluctant to sign something on the spot that had so much small print.

"I would prefer to read through them carefully this weekend before I sign them," I said.

Catherine nodded indifferently. "Okay, but whether you sign them or not, it won't change much. It is up to you," she said.

As soon as Catherine left the office, Sue and Ellen rushed to my desk. Sue asked me what happened. I explained what Catherine had determined so far.

"That's ridiculous! After all this time, that is all she found?!" Sue exclaimed.

"Aren't we only required to keep documents for five years?" Ellen asked.

"Yes," I said, "but any documentation related to capital should be kept forever," I said.

We chatted a bit about Catherine's big discovery, and laughed at how the government spends so much to find so little. All in all, the day of reckoning didn't end badly. "If worse comes to worse, I will have to pay," I told myself, and shrugged it off.

The next day, I called my father in Iran. I could hear in his voice that his condition was improving. At the end of the conversation, I asked my mother to try to locate an invoice for the item Catherine had identified, which I had actually bought ten years earlier in Iran and had shipped to Canada. Later that day, it also occurred to me that the receipts for the expenses Catherine said she would have to restate as revenue were actually in my home office. It took quite a bit of digging, but I soon located them.

On Monday morning, Catherine called me to say that she would not be coming that day, and that she would instead be coming over to my office on Wednesday to continue the corporate audit. It was a bit of a relief that I would not see her for two days, but a big part of me just wanted this whole episode to be finished.

Armed now with a bit more experience, I took some time with Ellen to go through different scenarios. We wanted to make sure the audit of my businesses would continue smoothly. I wasn't exactly sure what Catherine would look for, but I wanted to avoid making assumptions. Ellen helped me organize literally a suitcase full of personal financial documents.

Catherine arrived on Wednesday morning as scheduled. I returned the papers she had asked me to sign the previous week, and provided documents that showed rental income on my Sherbrooke Street property. It was the same story. She glanced at them and asked me to give her some time to analyze them.

Another couple days of waiting ensued while Catherine worked quietly among my other staff. She finally came to my office to discuss some key points of her analysis. I set aside what I was doing and welcomed her to sit down at the conference table. She put all her papers on the table and started to explain her conclusions.

"I took all your expenses and deducted them from all the deposits," she said. "Doing this is a clear way of showing income."

"Okay, that's good," I said. "Then we are done. You have what you were looking for."

"Well, yes and no," she replied. "Now I would like to see invoices for these expenses that you reported over here, as well as sales reports for the periods those expenses were incurred."

I nodded at her and said, "No problem. All the suppliers' invoices are in the same filing cabinet over there." She knew where my filing room was. "Take anything you need, and help yourself to the photocopier if necessary."

"Thank you," she replied. "Could you please prepare copies of the following invoices for me?" she asked, handing me a list four pages long. "I will call you later this week to see if you have all the documents ready, and then I will come back," she said. "And, by the way, we have only till the end of this month to finish your entire file."

I was floored by her comment, and lost a bit of the composure I had so carefully maintained in my dealings with her to that point. The end of the month was just two weeks away.

"But, Catherine, the delay at the beginning was not my fault," I said. "Your department delayed the start of this audit by a year!"

"There is nothing I can do. I will finish my report, and if it is not to your satisfaction, you can always file an objection," she said.

I didn't want to argue with her. She had a job to do, which was to determine whether my tax filings fairly represented my business dealings. I really wanted to avoid making an objection to her analysis further down the road, because it could further drag this stressful exercise out for months. Seen from a different angle, the audit actually jeopardized my business growth plans, because the information it uncovered – revenue, expenses and income – could affect future loan applications. The government, however, would demonstrate little empathy for me on that level.

Over the next few days, Ellen prepared copies of all the suppliers' invoices. She asked me a lot of questions along the way, which was helpful in that they refreshed my memory.

"Why would you have some of your investments under your personal name, and others under the company name?" Ellen asked.

"It is mainly to avoid paying a higher rate of tax on capital," I replied. "A company has to pay tax on any capital that it borrows from a third party. It's different than the tax on capital gains."

"I see," she said. "So, why would you not just have everything under your personal name?"

"Listing anything under my personal name creates liability issues. If I deal with somebody through my company, and there is a problem, I am not personally liable since the customer is dealing with a legal entity that is separate from my personal affairs," I said.

"Are there any other taxation benefits in this approach?" Ellen asked.

"Well, you should know better than me, since you are an accountant," I said, trying to end the conversation and organize the documents.

"But I am just a bookkeeper," Ellen responded.

She was right.

"Look here," Ellen said, "she wants to know about this big deposit."

I looked at the list that Catherine had drawn up. A very large deposit made into one of my accounts caught her eye. I looked at it for a moment and tried to recall the specific transaction in my mind, rather than find the corresponding receipt in the mountain of documentation. Then it dawned on me.

"Ah....yes. That transaction was a rollover that I did that year," I said to Ellen. You can probably look for a deed of sale in the filing cabinet over there."

"What is a rollover?"

I explained it to her. "A rollover is when you have a property under your personal name and sell it to a company in which you hold more than ninety-five percent of the shares, without paying a transfer tax. The selling price can be less than market value. This way, you can avoid paying tax on capital gains. "There are other important considerations, but the accountant will take care of them," I said.

All of the documents were ready by the end of the third day. I called Catherine and made arrangements for her to come to my office the following Monday.

In the meantime, I was thinking more and more about a strategy to have ready when Catherine revealed her findings. I telephoned my accountant for advice, one of many recent phone calls I had placed to him. He assured me again that there was nothing to worry about. He oversaw all of my tax filings, and was confident that everything had been done with proper diligence. He told me that I should not accept any of the government's findings before talking to him. We decided not to meet until I knew the conclusions of Catherine's audit.

On Monday morning, I was surprised to see that Catherine had brought a colleague with her.

"Mr. Reza, this is my supervisor Marie-José Martin," she said, gesturing toward her.

I shook Marie-José's hand. She had a warm smile, which put me at ease. She seemed to have a better sense of humour than Catherine. I hoped it would last.

"You are much younger than I expected," she said. "You have built a sizeable business group in a short time, Mr. Sarshoghi."

I walked them up to the second floor.

"Do you need a desk too?" I asked Marie-José. She laughed and said that just a chair would be fine. "I will be sitting next to Catherine today to provide guidance on a few points."

I had a pleasant chat with Marie-José. She gave me assurance that they were not there to convict me of any wrongdoing. The reason she had joined Catherine that morning was simply to provide support in interpreting certain tax rules. When it comes to complex transactions, many tax laws require interpretation. Catherine had encountered a few such transactions in my records, and sought guidance from Marie-José.

It took Catherine another week and a half to assess my corporate files. She was cutting it very, very close. The government was required by law to officially accept or reject my original tax filings in three days. We sat down late one afternoon to discuss her conclusions.

She opened the discussion by saying that she had to reject a few of my expense figures, since I couldn't give her the necessary supporting documents to match them with revenue. It was not a big issue at all. However, she quickly moved the discussion to a major problem she claimed to have discovered. A few years prior, I started a new business line in Montréal and rented one of my personal properties to the business. In the beginning, I didn't personally receive any rental payments in order to help the company conserve cash. Her dispute was with the expenses that I had claimed on a personal building that was not generating revenue.

In fact, such an arrangement is legal if it involves a third party. When signing a long-term lease, you can get a discount for a number of months. But, since there was no third party involved in this transaction, I was not allowed to give a discount to my own company. In Catherine's opinion, that discount decreased my reported income, by a few hundred thousand dollars.

If she was right—and I was not convinced she was—the expenses I claimed for the building that year were not eligible, meaning that I should have paid significantly more tax, plus a penalty and accumulated interest for the three years that had elapsed since filing. I have to say, though, that she was absolutely correct on one aspect of her conclusion. There should always be a clear line between a company and any other related party.

After spending about ten weeks auditing my business and personal transactions, those two discrepancies were the only ones that she found. Without emotion or any undue pressure, she simply gave me the choice to either accept or reject her assessment. As soon as I started to provide explanations for those transactions, she said that I had the right to refute her claim.

Weeks and weeks of auditing work ended that day with me signing an objection to Catherine's conclusion. Her job was done. She cleaned her desk, packed her bags and left. It was an odd feeling to have worked with a person for such a long time on such an important matter, yet feel no personal connection to her. Regardless, Catherine's work was done. My work, however, was not.

Soon thereafter I received a revised tax assessment. It indicated that I owed about three hundred thousand dollars in adjustments, penalties, and interest. Although I had the right to wait for the revenue agency to make a decision on my objection, I ran the risk of further increases if my objection was overruled, because interest on the outstanding amount would accumulate each day the balance was outstanding.

I arranged a meeting with my accountant and one of his colleagues, a tax specialist. They advised me not to pay, and to wait for the ruling from the objections department. Their opinion was that while Catherine could be right, my tax filings were not necessarily wrong, and that in certain situations my filing would be acceptable.

Two years passed before I heard from the revenue agency's objections department. That is to say, I lived for the next two years with the question of a huge tax liability hanging over my head. First, I received a letter informing me that someone had been assigned to my file, and that she would be in touch with me regarding the objection. Meanwhile, I had gathered the other missing documents to respond to the first discrepancy Catherine had identified.

Incredibly, the revenue agency ordered an entirely new audit. The thought of enduring such prolonged scrutiny was crushing, but I knew I had to look at it from the positive side. They obviously saw merit in my argument, and needed a second review. As all of the necessary documentation was already in order, the subsequent audit was much less demanding on me. Furthermore, the transactions were fresh in my mind, so I could speak to them with confidence to the new auditor. But this audit took even longer to complete, about six months. While I was confident that I had done nothing wrong in my original tax filings, they were six stress-filled months.

The revised audit upheld my objection. While I was liable for a few thousand dollars in adjustments, Catherine's assessment, arguing that I owed hundreds of thousands of dollars in unpaid taxes, was dismissed.

Case closed. After more than two full years of stressful government scrutiny, I could once again face every morning without feeling as though I had a gun pointing at me.

Lessons Learned

I have experienced challenges in running my businesses that have shaken me to the core. I have argued cases in court more times than I wish to remember, sued tenants and landlords, and dealt with rogue employees, miserable customers, and blood-thirsty competitors. But I can say without hesitation that those experiences paled in comparison to the intense scrutiny brought on by the government audits of my finances.

As I noted at the beginning of this chapter, I do not believe that the government is your enemy. Nor do I think it is your true friend, either. The government is your business partner. It provides infrastructure that enables you to conduct business— streets, traffic lights, airports, an education system, and the power grid, among many other essential public services–that enable our economy to function. All you have to do is pay the government your fair share for providing that infrastructure. My trip to Iran to tend to my ill father taught me the consequences of a thin tax base. I feel happy to pay my fair share of taxes in Canada because, as a Canadian, I enjoy some of the best public services in the world. As a small business owner, you must always be conscious of keeping your partner happy by making sure you follow the rules.

The excruciating pressure that weighed on me those years of the audit was not from feeling targeted by Catherine. Quite the contrary. Although she was rather cold and distant, she was highly professional. The stress was from not knowing if I could substantiate the financial picture I had presented in my tax claims. While I knew that I was required to keep financial records, I didn't maintain them in earnest. When the revenue agency came knocking and forced me to prove my financial picture, it was an enormous challenge to gather and organize the reams of documents necessary to back up my tax claims. Hundreds of thousands of dollars were in potential jeopardy.

I cannot overstate how important it is to have fully complete, organized records of each transaction you make, no matter how small. In Canada, the burden of proof is with the individual. Businesses are required by law to maintain records of all transactions for five years; however, records related to capital investment or borrowing must be kept forever. The lesson I learned was to be highly disciplined about maintaining detailed records. If your documents are organized and easy to follow, it will be easy to get along with the tax man.

Always maintain a distinction between your company and your personal financial affairs. The owner, shareholders and administrators of a company should understand that a company is like an employee to the owner. One should not withdraw money or get financial assistance from a company without full documentation, even if they are the sole shareholder. Any personal financial transaction with the company should be considered a repayable loan. If a company in any way facilitates a service to its owner, it is seen by the revenue agency as a taxable benefit to the owner. On the other hand, any service rendered to the company by its owner creates financial benefits for the company, which must be reported at market value. It is of monumental importance to keep all personal financial transactions at arms-length from your company.

Before you get into business, learn at least some of the basics about tax law and tax planning strategy. Ideally, you should consult a tax professional. It will save you money in the long run. Governments make a surprising amount of information about tax policy available on their websites. Take advantage of it. Drop in to your local municipal office. Arm yourself with a bit of knowledge.

The bottom line is to keep solid records. You never know when the tax man is going to come knocking.

Chapter 8: Expand With Caution

Once upon a time, a shepherd lugged a large jug of goat's milk to market. Along the way, he mused about how, with just a bit of extra effort, he could milk his goats a couple of extra times per week, which would increase his production and his earnings. He imagined how he could save the extra money and, within one year, have enough to buy five more goats, and produce five times the milk he was currently selling. With that extra money he could buy even more goats and sell more milk! He would no longer have to live the humble life of a peasant.

The long road to the market gave him plenty of time to think hard about his idea. Of course, more goats would mean that he would have to spend more time growing food to feed them. And it would be impossible to carry all that milk to market by hand; he would need to have the tinsmith make new buckets to hold the extra milk, and a carpenter to make a special cart to haul them. He would eventually need a mule, which would cost him more money to feed. And what about all the extra money he would have to carry home from the market? He would need a safe box, for security.

The shepherd came to realize that most of the extra money he would earn in the beginning would be consumed by the added costs of increasing his milk production. Considering all of the extra work, would it really be worth it? He contemplated this question and decided that, indeed, it would be worth it. He wanted to be able to provide more for his family than just a basic subsistence.

As he made his way toward the market, he became lost in his dream of a brighter future. So focused was he on the idea of increasing milk production that he did not pay attention to what was going on around him. Another farmer, hauling many buckets of goat's milk on a mule-drawn cart, came down the path toward him and knocked him over as he passed by. The poor shepherd tried to hold on to his bucket as he fell, but it hit the ground and rolled into the ditch. The milk splashed across the dusty path and, with it, the shepherd's earnings for the entire week. The shepherd was not badly hurt, but the incident sent a clear message to him about the potential fallout of not identifying hidden risks when considering a business expansion.

In my early days of running Collage Tapis, Fred, my salesman, and I would commonly go for an entire day without a customer walking into the store. But since I was selling high-end silk carpets, which had very good profit margins, just a few sales per week were enough to comfortably sustain the business. Fred and I had a lot of time to chat about how we would solve the world's problems. It also gave us time to muse about ways I could expand my business, to increase revenue and fill our spare time.

One afternoon, Fred started musing out loud about how I could expand beyond ultra-high- end carpets, down into the higher volume segments of the market. I was quite intrigued by the idea. Fred and I talked about the possibilities for days. The more we talked, the more interested and motivated I became in pursuing the idea.

Our ideas made a great deal of sense. I understood the market extremely well. Expanding beyond my narrow market niche would not be diversifying away from my core business. It would actually boost my purchasing power with my suppliers, giving me more control over the market. Furthermore, Fred had been working for me for over ten years. Expanding my business would give him an opportunity to challenge his potential as a manager, and would boost his morale. It would be a shame to limit Fred to just selling carpets in a small store. I honestly believed he had the skills to manage a team of salespeople.

Fred and I both saw an opportunity in the market for a store that offered a variety of low- and medium-grade floor coverings beyond silk carpets, such as tile, vinyl flooring and hardwood. Securing financing would not be an issue. Plus, I worked with an excellent team of professionals, including a lawyer, an accountant, and a designer, who could provide me with good guidance.

Within days of our initial brainstorming session, I found myself starting to put together the necessary pieces to expand my business. I knew the market well, and could see a gap that was begging to be filled. I knew that if I didn't seize the opportunity, somebody else certainly would. There was no defining moment at which I made a decision to start. It just seemed to happen. I only came to realize it myself when Fred said to me, "So, Reza, based on the way you're now talking, and all of the phone calls you have been making, I take it that you are moving ahead with the idea of starting a new floor covering store."

I stopped for a moment, looked at Fred, looked around the store, and said, "I guess you're right!"

There was a huge amount of planning involved, such as further market research, identifying a sound retail location, establishing terms with suppliers, designing all aspects of the store's design and visual identity, and hiring good staff. I didn't anticipate that the planning stage would take so long, but I wanted everything to be absolutely perfect.

From those initial conversations with Fred at Collage Tapis, it took me two years to put all the pieces in place to open my first big-box floor covering store. I called it Tapis en Gros, which, loosely translated, is French for Carpet Depot. It was a one-stop retail concept, with about twenty thousand square feet of every imaginable type of household flooring, installation materials, and floor cleaning supplies. The store's motto was, "You Have the Floor. We Can Cover It."

Tapis en Gros was a smashing success. I brought it to full profitability in a bit more than a year, which is very quick for a retail business. Referrals from Tapis en Gros actually helped grow revenue at Collage Tapis by fifteen percent. Previously, I was turning customers away from Collage Tapis, but Tapis en Gros enabled me to meet a wider array of customer needs. I was amazed at how well the two stores complemented each other. Together they offered something that fit everyone's floor covering budget.

I spent practically all of my time at the new Tapis en Gros store, which was located in a Montréal suburb. Fred, meanwhile, managed Collage Tapis in downtown Montréal. After opening the new store, he and I went from spending ten hours a day with each other, to only meeting once or twice a week. He did extremely well managing the store on his own, but with this transition, I lost an extraordinary salesperson who was impossible to replace.

The new Tapis on Gros store brought on a huge amount of work for both me and Fred. Whereas, before, I was able to close

Collage Tapis on Sundays, Tapis en Gros had to stay open seven days a week, a standard practice for any mass market retail store. So, while Fred was able to free himself from Collage Tapis on Sundays, I desperately needed his help on Sundays at Tapis en Gros. Neither one of us was able to take a day off for the first year. Sure, we both enjoyed our work, and the satisfaction of watching our business idea take shape, but the commitment to managing the expansion put a great deal of pressure on our family lives. We both had young families, and we each felt like we were missing out on watching them grow up. Fred and I agreed that we needed support.

Managing such a high volume of inventory presented an unforeseen challenge. When I made a sale at Collage Tapis, I would simply hand-write a receipt. With a weekly volume of a couple of dozen carpets, I had memorized my entire stock of inventory. I only had to physically count my inventory twice a year. In contrast, Tapis en Gros was operating at the other end of the spectrum. Its volume was one hundred times greater than that of Collage Tapis, requiring a much more sophisticated inventory control system. If a customer placed an order for a product, we would then have to place a purchase order with one of a few different suppliers. We had to register to receive the merchandise, and from there, register with another supplier for installation. Only after an installation was complete would we issue the final invoice to the customer. This whole process would occur a dozen times each day. I underestimated the accounting system required to control my inventory, as well as the computer system to run it. In the beginning, controlling such a large volume of inventory was a huge challenge for me. I soon had to hire a new employee to develop and operate an inventory management system.

A year and a half after launching Tapis en Gros, I was feeling invincible. The store had already become profitable, and my personal income had soared. To look back and realize that I had successfully achieved an ambitious business goal was quite empowering. Of course, Fred was a key player in this achievement. We hatched the idea together. But in essence, I was the one who pulled it off. So, I asked myself: *Why stop here?*

One day, I presented Fred the idea of expanding Tapis en Gros by four more stores. It would position Tapis en Gros out of the reach of any of its competitors, by boosting its purchasing power and distributing its marketing costs among more stores. It would be the largest floor covering chain in Quebec. Fred was in total agreement. Although we were well aware of the challenges, not the least of which was the time commitment away from our families, the thought of building the largest chain of retail floor covering stores in Quebec, and for him to share in a piece of that growth, was very enticing.

I hired a small firm to conduct a thorough market study, and began discussions with a financial institution to secure the necessary capital.

After gathering all the information, I sat down with Fred and the new assistant manager I had hired, to assess the data and evaluate the viability of expanding Tapis en Gros by four more stores throughout Montréal and Quebec City. The success of the first Tapis en Gros, the pilot store, was proof that the concept was solid. They both encouraged me to realize the full potential of Tapis en Gros through further expansion.

Many factors pointed to the potential of the idea. The market opportunity was wide open. Much of the conceptual work had already been addressed in establishing the first store. The next four stores would simply copy the first one in design, product line-up, and marketing, and could share the IT and inventory management systems that were already in place. I maintained excellent relations with my suppliers and financial institution. Most importantly, I had a strong and loyal management team, whom I trusted.

Still, there were many questions surrounding the expansion that Fred and I knew we could not answer, which created uncertainty. But in life, the people who cannot tolerate a certain amount of ambiguity tend to get left behind by those who can. Instinctively, I knew the expansion was viable. If I wasn't going to take advantage of this unexploited market opportunity, somebody else would. There was no time to hesitate. With support from my management team, I decided to go for it.

We set about to identify appropriate areas throughout suburban Montréal for two of the four new stores. I was able to use two of my existing commercial properties for the other two stores. We looked all around the Montréal metropolitan area for high- traffic areas with large-scale retailers in the vicinity. The age-old mantra "location, location, location" played over and over in my mind while I searched. But there always seemed to be something about a building that made it an awkward fit for our particular needs. At one location, I remember having to negotiate with three neighbouring tenants simultaneously over changes I proposed for the store's entrance. Those negotiations dragged on for weeks, causing delays to my plans. In another location, everything was picture perfect, save for the lack of a loading dock, which was a necessity for this type of operation. Again and again, I ran into frustrating dead -ends like that one.

It took months and months of searching, and iron-clad perseverance , to finalize the additional locations for Tapis en Gros. I was never willing to settle for a second-class location for these new stores. The eventual success of the chain would be a tribute to that discipline.

I have to say that the four new Tapis en Gros stores got off to a great start. I learned lessons with the first Tapis en Gros outlet about the local floor covering market, and about dealing with suppliers, that saved me a lot of headaches in the expansion phase. Without the experience of the pilot store, I would most definitely have failed in my attempt to open the other four stores at once.

Sales were actually stronger than I had forecast. But I underestimated the need for administrative personnel. It was impossible for Fred and me to keep up with everything, even with an assistant manager to help oversee the entire operation. In addition to two full-time bookkeepers, a human resources manager to coordinate over one hundred employees, and a marketing manager, I had to hire a team of people to coordinate the independent contractors who installed the flooring. Admittedly, I did not properly anticipate the costs of so many administrative positions.

The biggest unanticipated threat I encountered with the new Tapis en Gros stores was competition. I had wrongly assumed that the size of the new chain would make it untouchable. But practically all of the existing players in the local floor covering market turned against me. I had disrupted what had been a stable market, and created a very real threat for them. The smaller, independent retailers around Montréal formed an association and excluded me. The association targeted Tapis en Gros through negative advertising, suggesting that it was a big company that could not offer the same level of personal service as the smaller, family-owned stores. The advertising didn't have a dramatic effect. If anything, I think it benefited Tapis en Gros by drawing attention to its size and, inadvertently, its selection and better prices. But the campaign took me by surprise. In expanding Tapis en Gros, I did not anticipate my competitors becoming outright enemies. The landscape had changed.

With five big- box stores, I was now playing in the big leagues. I had to focus on remaining competitive with even larger national retailers, who posed the same threat to me that perhaps I was posing to the smaller local retailers. Then, about a year after completing the expansion, The Home Depot made their Quebec debut in suburban Montréal. Their floor covering section was practically identical in concept to Tapis en Gros. Despite my careful attention to planning, I was blindsided by them. Nor did I anticipate the competitive threat they would pose.

One might think that The Home Depot's advantage would be to draw customers away from the other local retailers. In fact, their truly debilitating threat was their ability to control the supply chain. In launching Tapis en Gros, I enjoyed the benefits of being the largest floor covering chain in Quebec. It allowed me to strike a private label arrangement with Beaulieu Canada, a major manufacturer, which gave me a significant competitive price and quality advantage over my competition. But when The Home Depot moved into Montréal, Beaulieu stopped supplying me, due to an exclusive agreement they forged with The Home Depot. It was just one example of how I suddenly became a second- choice retailer in the eyes of my key suppliers.

Manufacturers tripped over themselves to forge agreements with The Home Depot. I remember one time visiting another supplier's vice president with Fred, to negotiate a new pricing agreement. Whereas a year earlier he would have bent over backwards to lower his prices and renew his agreement with me, after The Home Depot came to Montréal, I was no longer a favoured customer. I had to make the effort to actually visit his office, where the conversation lasted barely fifteen minutes. "Reza, that's our best price. Take it or leave it." It is a common saying that the customer is always right. In truth, I have learned that only important customers are right.

Experienced managers know that competitive forces are not only on the outside, but inside your company, too. As your business grows, it becomes a bigger target for everyone, including your own employees. Aside from the predatory behaviour of the local flooring retailers, another unexpected aspect of expanding Tapis en Gros was encountering competition from one of my own managers. He surmised that if I could be successful in the flooring business, he could be, too. He learned everything about the retail floor covering landscape while working for me. He soon jumped ship, opening his own store nearby taking all my business secrets with him. Eventually, I found out that he had been talked into opening a new store in partnership with one of my competitors, who had promised to provide him with all the necessary support to maintain a stable supply chain. But it would seem I knew something they didn't. He went out of business in less than a year.

Perhaps this incident was a reflection of the challenge of building loyalty among your employees when your business reaches a certain size. Fred and I were like brothers, given the time we spent working so closely together at Collage Tapis. But when you employ one hundred people across five locations, it is impossible to develop that same trusting bond with everyone. After the expansion, I often reminisced about the good old days, when Fred and I used to sit together at Collage Tapis on slow afternoons and solve the world's problems. Although this rogue manager did not harm my business, it taught me the importance of not only keeping customers satisfied, but employees, too.

I began to sense that Fred was becoming increasingly withdrawn. He wasn't asserting himself in management meetings, and he often seemed to stare off into nowhere, even in the middle of important discussions. I invited him for lunch one day to see if there was a problem. Perhaps Fred had a job offer or wanted to open a store of his own. If that was the case, I wanted to hear it straight from him.

We went to one of our regular spots just around the corner from Collage Tapis. I got to the point, right away.

"Fred, how are things going?" I asked.

"Sales are strong," he said, "but aside from minor issues in the stores, I think things are going as well as expected."

"No, Fred, I mean how are things going with *you*? We don't get time to chat anymore."

He knew where I was taking the conversation, but tried to steer it away from his personal troubles.

"Everything is fine, Reza. I love my job."

"Fred," I said, putting my coffee down on the table and looking him straight in the eye, "We have known each other for over ten years. I can recognize the signs. Something is wrong."

He took a deep breath, and let out what seemed to be a sigh of relief and nodded at me, his eyes welling up slightly.

"You know Reza, you are like my brother. Over the last ten years, our families have gotten to be quite close...."He looked down at the table.

"What's wrong, Fred?" I asked. "Is there anything I can do to help?

"Reza, I think Leanne is having an affair."

Leanne was his wife.

At first, I couldn't believe it. I thought he was trying to cover up something else, but Fred would never joke with me about these sorts of things. I had known Fred and his wife for more than a decade. I was in their home when their son took his first steps.

"What?!?" I exclaimed in disbelief. Fred was very loyal to his wife and very dedicated to his family.

"Yes," he said, nodding in disbelief. "I think she is having an affair with one of her co-workers."

"How do you know? It just doesn't seem possible that she would do something like that."

"I actually overheard one of their phone conversations. Reza, I have never laid an eye on another woman. Leanne and I have been married for more than fifteen years. I never believed that I would face a situation like this in my life." He was almost in tears.

Things got worse for Fred over the coming months. The situation was indeed true, and he eventually filed for separation from his wife. His performance at work suffered, as he was preoccupied with the legal proceedings and the painful impact of the situation on his kids. Had Fred been just any other employee, I would have relieved him of his key responsibility in my company. But he was like a brother to me. I couldn't just let him go.

Separating from his wife allowed Fred to escape a tension-filled existence at home. He and his wife made every effort to maintain a cordial relationship and a stable environment in the interests of their children. In my opinion, their separation seemed to help the entire family.

The problems I was experiencing with my suppliers and the competition seemed trivial in comparison to the ones Fred was facing in his personal life. Nevertheless, my problems were serious . One thing that continued to puzzle me was that, overall, the annual sales volume for Tapis en Gros had increased by the end of the second year, but the net earnings per store, in particular the first store, had dropped significantly.

After a few meetings with Fred and the manager of the first store, and also with help from Johanna, the controller, we identified the problem by analyzing the addresses on customer invoices. We discovered that a surprising number of customers on the east side of Montréal were traveling to other Tapis en Gros stores across the city. After more digging, Fred revealed that some salespeople, willing to do anything to make a sale, were competing against salespeople at my other stores, by reducing prices and drawing customers from one store to another. My company was actually cannibalizing itself, eating away at its own profits for lack of a sound set of management policies.

We brainstormed to find a solution. Fred was totally against the idea of paying higher commissions to the sales staff. He argued that if money was the only thing motivating them, they wouldn't relate effectively to customers. He thought it would be in the company's best interest to have a performance evaluation system in place. But Johanna questioned how we could effectively measure performance in a carpet store. I found the idea appealing, but had no clue as to how we could put a performance plan together. In my estimation, two main factors drove salespeople to perform better: commission and the potential to be considered for a promotion. The company was growing, and many people aspired to management positions. But I could see very clearly that if anything went wrong with the company, many salespeople would leave, and take their client relationships with them.

Johanna talked about merging two stores. That way, we could consolidate those customers and reduce overhead. I was reluctant to do anything without proper planning. Often, the smallest action on my part would easily be misinterpreted by the employees.

The assistant manager raised an interesting point that seemed to be fuelling this problem. Since we had different market dynamics in each location, each store carried slightly different products. Even though the product line differences were not significant, he suggested that they might have been enough to attract customers from store to store in search of exactly what they were looking for. I was worried that having the same products in all the stores might increase the carrying costs.

The management team analyzed the problem in depth. In the end, we agreed that a pay-for-performance program would serve everyone's interests most effectively. It took time to develop a reasonable policy that served everybody well, and it produced very good results. To reduce cannibalization, we created a referral system, in which two salespeople could share a commission. Furthermore, we standardized the design of all the stores, to reduce people's perception that different stores were offering different products. The product lines themselves were standardized as much as possible, but we were still careful to give priority to local demand.

While the management team was analyzing this debilitating problem for Tapis en Gros, Johanna proposed an idea to resolve another issue that was affecting the company. Remember, Tapis en Gros sold everything under the sun related to floor covering, like carpet, tile, hardwood, and vinyl flooring, as well as accessories and other complimentary products like brooms, cleaners, and flooring installation tools. If anything, I didn't anticipate just how successful the concept would be, and how quickly it would take off. Inventory in each store was turning over quickly, which is a retailer's dream. The problem was that we could not balance out suppliers' inventory shipments with customer demand. I had to place large orders to ensure that the shelves were always stocked. Each store then had to warehouse the inventory that would not fit on the shelves. When I selected the stores, I focused mainly on the location and the appeal of the retail space itself, but the stores did not have enough storage space. Inventory was getting buried in piles at the back of each store, which made it frustrating for staff to locate inventory and keep the shelves fully stocked at all times. Johanna argued that we desperately needed a central distribution centre to smoothly manage inventory. She was right, but it was another administrative expense that I had not anticipated in my business planning.

After studying the proposal, I concluded that the benefits of a distribution centre would outweigh the costs. I went ahead and leased forty thousand square feet of warehouse space. Including the shelving, inventory management software, and forklift I had to purchase, the distribution centre cost just as much as launching a new store.

I was blessed to find the perfect person to run the warehouse. He was in his early fifties, punctual, easy to work with, and had years of warehousing experience. He did an excellent job of receiving and cataloguing shipments, and fulfilling the individual stores' orders, but needed the help of a full-time driver to deliver the products to the stores. I calculated that I would need to increase gross sales by a million dollars per year just to cover the added cost of the distribution centre.

The distribution centre succeeded in smoothing out the ebbs and flows of my internal supply chain, but a new inventory problem emerged: unsold merchandise. When I worked as a carpet flipper for Marta after first arriving in Canada, I saw her experiencing the same problem, albeit on a much smaller scale. Every retailer makes a bet when placing orders with suppliers. Order too little inventory and customers simply walk away with their money. Order too much, or something that does not align with customer tastes, and you will be forced to write it off as a loss.

I had accumulated a small mountain of inventory that I just could not move. The problem wasn't going away, either. Every retailer is forced to write off a certain portion of their inventory, but I wanted a solution to minimize the waste. One of the employees from the purchasing department came up with a simple solution. Obviously, the large build -up of unwanted inventory was a reflection of a disconnect between the products we were ordering and customers' needs and tastes.

We needed an experienced buyer. With the help of another employee from my human resources department, we found a very interesting character, who had actually sent us his resume, unsolicited, months earlier. He was originally from India, but had been in Canada for many years working in the carpet business. He went by the nickname Sunny.

Sunny had an extraordinary memory. He could recall a customer's name and exactly what they purchased, years after the fact. He was remarkable. Sunny also had an uncanny knack with colors and design. We decided to give him an opportunity as a purchaser and customer relations representative for Tapis en Gros.

The strategy actually worked. We put Sunny, like all employees, on the performance management plan, and he thrived. He reduced the cost of unwanted inventory by almost one million dollars at the end of his first year with the company.

The challenges I faced seemed to grow along with the business. Sales grew each month, but the overhead costs of maintaining those sales were really dragging down the bottom -line performance of the business. I didn't anticipate the number of people it would take to support the operation. Back when I was running just Collage Tapis and the first Tapis en Gros outlet, all it took was Fred and me to keep things running smoothly. But expanding to five busy retail stores, which turned over some fifty shipping containers of inventory a year, required a lot of specialized help. I needed a human resources manager, a marketing manager, and a small team to coordinate installations with local contractors. Plus, each manager needed an assistant. Without boosting sales to cover these costs, Tapis en Gros would not be generating an acceptable return on capital. All of the work, stress, and risk I was undertaking was hardly worthwhile.

After evaluating the options, I decided to add some low- cost furniture and home accessories to my product line-up. It would enable Tapis en Gros to offer customers added selection without increasing my fixed costs. It was a turning point for my business strategy. The concept firmly took root and exceeded my expectations. In the first year, I sold about twenty shipping containers of furniture and accessories. I was riding a wave. It seemed like everything that I touched turned to gold.

Seeing the success of the new furniture line, my real estate broker approached me one day with the idea of opening a new carpet and furniture store in Quebec City. He knew of an ideal location that could help me expand my operation beyond Montréal. It could be my key to the big leagues. Even with running five busy floor covering stores, I still felt that I had not reached my personal potential.

My wife, Azita, and I were living a lavish lifestyle, but we were working seven days a week. Just as I was considering opening the Quebec City location, we found out that she was pregnant. Complications soon emerged with the pregnancy that posed dangers for her and the baby. We were referred to an obstetrician, who painted a rather grave picture of the risk, and strongly suggested that we terminate the pregnancy.

Azita and I were absolutely distraught. I decided to talk with her obstetrician myself, to explore the idea of getting a second opinion. She referred us to another doctor who specialized in high risk pregnancies.

The new specialist saw us in a matter of days. She was extremely calm and understanding. She thoroughly examined Azita and concluded that, although the risks were indeed elevated, there was no need for extreme measures. She assured us that everything would go smoothly, and agreed to take Azita on as her patient. I asked her, bluntly, if she held pro-life views, and was simply trying to save the baby. She looked at me and said in a calm, reassuring voice, that if she believed there was a reasonable threat to my wife or the baby, she would have suggested a different course of action. I trusted her opinion.

Time passed slowly. My wife and I lived on edge for her entire pregnancy. After months of specialized medical care, Azita gave birth to a beautiful, healthy baby boy.

Meanwhile, the idea of opening a store in Quebec City was still tempting me. It would raise my profile to the next level. The space in Quebec City that my broker had brought to my attention was still on the market. On the other hand, the prospect of regularly making the six-hour round trip was daunting. My broker kept pushing. The landlord's offer was attractive. It took two months of negotiations, but I sealed a lease agreement on the Quebec City location.

On September 11, 2001, following three months of renovations, the entire staff—more than two dozen people—reported to the store at eight thirty in the morning to put the finishing touches in place for the grand opening, which was scheduled for the following day. Needless to say, we all quickly became preoccupied with watching the terrorist attacks unfold in the United States.

Nobody could have predicted the events that shook the world that day, and the short- term economic crisis they would spawn. Personally, it left me with the difficult decision of whether or not to proceed with the grand opening as scheduled on Wednesday, September 12. But the publicity had been arranged. Newspaper advertising had been published long ago, and a television and a radio station were scheduled to cover the event. There was no way to pull it all back in.

I decided to proceed. It was a very difficult decision, but it turned out to be the right one. Everything went as well as could be expected. The grand opening of Titish attracted about three hundred people.

As I anticipated before opening the store, traveling to and from Quebec City once a week, on top of overseeing my five Tapis en Gros stores, Collage Tapis and real estate holdings in Montréal, quickly began to take its toll. I was working about ninety hours a week. I was under constant stress, my temper had grown short, and I was literally living on fast food. My son was eight months old. One night I suddenly woke and sat bolt upright in bed. I came to the painful realization that I was failing to grasp what was truly important to me: my family. In reality, I didn't know my family. I was a visitor in my own home. I was not being fair to them or to myself.

In an effort to spend more time with my infant son, one day, I decided to take him along with me to Quebec City. I talked to him the entire trip, as though he could understand every word I said. Coming back to Montréal, I reached behind my seat and held his hand the entire way. The way he squeezed my finger and made gentle cooing sounds, were new sensations for me. It was the first time I felt like a parent. Actually, it was the first time that I had taken on the full responsibility of being a parent. It taught me a great deal about the essence of life. I was denying myself by not spending time with my son and my wife. Things had to change.

It was on that drive home to Montréal from Quebec City that I vowed to stop working on Sundays, and to start consolidating my business. I had bitten off a little bit more than I could chew.

Lessons Learned

From one point of view, I experienced great success from expanding my business. I capitalized on a market opportunity that no other business was satisfying. But what I didn't properly anticipate in taking my business to the next level (or, rather, in reaching high to achieve my dream) was all of the new forces that come into play as a business grows.

Collage Tapis was a niche player in the market that attracted only a small number of customers per week. While other carpet retailers knew me, they did not regard me as a threat. Suddenly, when I broke out of my position in the market, I became a bigger target. I was naïve to just how ruthless competitors can be to protect their turf. In opening Tapis en Gros, I was aiming for the mass market. I wish I had realized just how fiercely other floor covering retailers were going to fight back. But business is not necessarily a gentleman's game. In the end, it came full circle. The competitive threat that I posed to the small retailers in opening Tapis en Gros was no different than that posed to me by The Home Depot, when they moved into Montréal.

Expansion should be judged and planned very carefully. In theory, I thought that expanding from one Tapis en Gros store to five would increase my bottom line profits fivefold. It didn't. As I described earlier in this chapter, overhead costs like the distribution centre, the people to run it, and administrative positions like human resources and marketing managers, were absolutely necessary, because Fred and I just could not manage the added workload ourselves. In effect, it took gross sales produced by two Tapis en Gros stores to cover the administrative overhead costs of the chain. Profitability increases in steps. The message that I want to leave readers on this front is be sure you carefully identify the added overhead costs of expansion, and don't assume that your cost structure will grow proportionally.

Recognize that you can't do it all, and that growth requires more people to help you. Every person you hire is a new person you have to trust, and whose trust you must earn. Remember, as your business becomes more successful, it becomes a bigger target. One of the most defeating aspects of expanding Tapis en Gros was teaching one of my employees everything about the floor covering business, only later to have him take what I had taught him and use it to compete against me. It's a fact of life in business; a risk that every business owner takes. To maintain employees' loyalty, I believe that you must have incentives in place that give them a personal stake in the business. Strategies include company stock plans, pay-for-performance schemes, and simply consulting employees for their advice. I have always believed that front-line employees have insights into the business that top management does not. It is crucial to treat employees as part of your team. In my experience, the true key to business growth is retaining satisfied employees, who do their best to act in the interests of the business. Treating employees like they are expendable is a sure-fire way to disengage them and get low performance from them. A big business needs every single one of its employees towing the line.

Consider, also, that your competitors' strength derives not only from their ability to attract customers away from you, but also on their ability to influence your supply chain. Perhaps I was too confident as the owner of a growing business, feeling invincible, and forgetting to watch my back. To that end, it is important to properly secure strong agreements with your suppliers, especially your most strategic ones.

I grew my business to the point where it was too big to be considered small, yet far too small to be able to compete in the big leagues. I didn't have the market reach to command supply chains the way The Home Depot or Wal-Mart or any other national retailer does. I was extremely proud to execute a growth strategy and strive for my dream. However, in the twenty-first century, I believe that being a mid-market player is an extremely challenging competitive position to play.

Finally, I want to draw your attention to last part of the story. One of the first full days I spent with my infant son was almost a year after his birth. I was so consumed by my expanding business, and driven by the opportunity to make it even bigger, that I lost sight of my true objective, which was to provide a stable life for my family. The drive home from Quebec City, with my son clutching my finger, made me realize that I was going down the wrong path. The added returns from expanding my business were negative. I learned an important lesson: instead of working to live, I was living to work, and my family was paying a dear price. Carefully reflect on just how big you want your business to grow, why, and what price you are willing to pay in order to achieve your goals.

Chapter 9: Look Before You Leap

A man named Harun bargained vigorously when negotiating the purchase price of a house. Malik, the owner, finally relented, and accepted an offer that was significantly lower than his original asking price. However, he stipulated an unusual condition to the deal. There was a nail sticking out from the rear wall of the house. Malik accepted the offer under the condition that the nail would remain his property.

Harun felt a rush knowing that he would be getting the house at an incredibly good price. He thought to himself, "What could be so important about a simple nail? After all, he will likely soon forget about it. But even if he doesn't, it wouldn't be a big issue. It is only a nail."

"I agree to your condition." Harun said. They shook hands and sealed the deal.

Three weeks later, after the legal procedures had been drawn up to outline this strange agreement, the two men met to hand over the keys to Harun. Just as he was about to leave his house for the last time, Malik stopped and turned to Harun. "I had better check my nail before I leave." Harun happily obliged him, and they both went inside and to the back of the house.

"I need to hang this bag on my nail," Malik said.

Harun was puzzled. "A bag?"

"Yes, but there is nothing in it you should be concerned about."
Malik took the bag from his shoulder, hung it on the nail, politely
thanked Harun, the new owner, and left.

Harun shrugged it off. He quickly got to work moving into his
beautiful new home. It was the bargain of the century.

Or was it?

At about five thirty the next morning, Harun was awakened by the
sound of someone knocking on his door. Having worked late into
the night moving in his possessions, it was not a pleasant sound
to hear at such an early hour. The knocking would not stop. He
got up and lumbered to the door. It was Malik.

"Sorry to bother you," Malik said, "but yesterday I forgot
something in my bag, which is hanging on my nail. I just came
over to get it."

Harun was not impressed. "Couldn't it wait?"

"Not really. It is very important."

Harun motioned for Malik to come in. Malik entered, got what he
needed from his bag, and left right away.

Harun went back to bed but couldn't fall back to sleep. He was
wondering whether the deal of a lifetime might actually turn out
to be the mistake of a lifetime. But it was just a nail.

A couple of hours later, while getting ready leave, there was
another knock on the front door. It was Malik again.

Harun opened the door and made no effort to mask his
frustrations with a smile. "Is it about your nail?" he asked.

"Yes and no," Malik said. "I am here to get my bag."

"Sure."

Malik went in, took his bag, and left.

It was not an easy day for Harun. His muscles ached from all the heavy lifting, and he was grumpy from lack of sleep. That evening, as he walked up to his driveway after a stroll around the neighbourhood, his excitement quickly turned to shock and frustration. There was Malik, sitting on the front step with another man. "I don't have the energy to deal with this," he thought to himself.

"Malik, it has been a long and tiring day for me. What can I do for you?"

"Yes Harun, I know you must be tired. It is not going to take long. I am just going to show my nail to this gentleman."

"But why now?" asked Harun, raising his hands and shrugging his shoulders.

"Well, since I do not have much time to check on my nail, I decided to rent it out."

"What?!" Harun said, his eyes bulging in disbelief. "You're going to rent your nail to someone?" It sounded ludicrous.

"Yes," said Malik, in all seriousness. "Do you think it would be all right according to our contract?"

Harun paused for a moment, and thought about the terms of their agreement.

"Well, it doesn't seem to contradict the agreement," Harun said, hesitating. "But it doesn't make any sense to rent a nail!"

Malik lifted his eyebrows and with a rather patronizing tone said, "But it is my nail, no?"

As crazy as it sounded, Harun could not argue the point.

"Harun, I have already made arrangements to rent my nail to this person for one week. I will return after a week to take back possession," Malik said. Then he left, leaving the stranger on Harun's front doorstep.

217

Without saying anything, Harun opened the door and grudgingly showed the man into his house. The man spent ten minutes thoroughly inspecting and admiring the small, nondescript piece of steel sticking out of the wall.

Later on that evening, Harun stepped outside to enjoy the peaceful night air. And sure enough, when he stepped out of his front door, the new "nail tenant" was sitting on his front step.

"What are you doing here?" Again, Harun made no effort to hide his irritation.

Very assured, the man answered, "I am here to watch over my nail."

"Your nail?" Harun responded, his face turning red. "What do you think is going to happen to your bloody nail? It's sticking in the wall. And by the way, that nail is not yours. You are just renting it!"

The man was surprisingly calm. "All the more reason to watch it. If anything happens to it, I will be in a deep trouble."

When I was first establishing myself in business, I typically worked six days a week, and a half -day on Sundays. Sunday was my day to sleep late. Early one Sunday morning, the phone rang. It was a friend of mine from Dubai, whom I had known for years. His name was Walid. He rarely called me, unless he needed something. Amidst the obligatory small talk at the beginning of our conversation, I could tell that this was one of those times.

"Walid, do you need anything?" I asked, trying to be non-confrontational.

"No," he said. "I just called to see how you are doing."

"So what's new with you, Walid?" I asked.

"Nothing, really... Actually, I have this friend here in Dubai who has been granted permanent residency in Canada, and wants to move there."

I knew he was looking for something.

"What would you like me to do?"

"Since you manage real estate on behalf of some of your investor clients, I thought I could refer him to you as a client. He is very wealthy, but he doesn't know much about the business landscape in North America."

By this point, in addition to managing my own real estate holdings, I was providing consulting services to manage other people's real estate investments, too. I focused mainly on commercial real estate around Montréal.

I wasn't sure what to make of Walid's call about this complete stranger, but I am not the type of person to turn something down just because I don't understand the details. After getting some information about this person from Dubai coming to invest money in Canadian real estate, I agreed to meet him at the Montréal airport upon his arrival the following Monday. His name was Rasheed.

I waited forty minutes in the arrivals area for a person I had never met, I saw a man who seemed to fit Walid's description, but with one glaring difference. This person was being pushed in a wheelchair by an airport staff member. Walid didn't say anything about a wheelchair.

I started walking toward the man, wondering what might have happened to him. "Excuse me, sir, are you Rasheed?" I asked.

"Yes," he replied.

"I am Reza Sarshoghi. Welcome to Canada," I said, extending my hand to greet him. "Are you all right? Have you had an accident?"

"No, no," he said. "I am okay." Then he looked up at the airport attendant behind him and said, "No more. You stop here." He motioned with his hand for the airport employee to leave. I nodded to the attendant and said that I would take him from there.

As soon as the attendant was out of sight, Rasheed stood up, grabbed a baggage cart, and started to walk with me. He grinned and said, "I always ask for a wheelchair in airport. I go faster through customs. No waiting in line."

I was shocked, but didn't let it show. Obviously, this was a man who knew how to get what he wanted.

After getting his bags in the car, I drove him to his hotel, which, incidentally, I had reserved for him. Along the way, he tried to get as much as information as he could get from me about doing business in Canada, and whether I knew of any business bargains for sale.

Before leaving him at the hotel, he made sure that I would come back the next morning to see if we could start looking at potential deals right away. I assured him that I would be there to pick him up at eight o'clock.

I was impressed by his focus and tenacity. There was no small talk, no pleasantries between us in the car; just straight business. On the other hand, he seemed to be a little bit *too* focused. I wasn't quite sure what to make of him.

The next morning, I met Rasheed at his hotel and took him to a coffee shop en route to my office in downtown Montréal. I could barely get a word in throughout the trip. He had many questions about doing business in Canada. After sitting down in a coffee shop and ordering our breakfast, I took the driver's seat and began to ask him some questions in return.

"So, what kind of investment you are looking for, Rasheed?"

"I think real estate," he replied. His English was choppy. "However, if I find a good business, I might be interested."

"How much you are willing to invest?"

"You don't worry about money if the investment is good," he replied, shaking his head and looking me directly in the eye.

"Rasheed, I need a more specific number to know what type of an investment opportunity I should look for."

My cell phone rang. It was Marc Bouvier, a real estate broker. I had long since parted ways with Charles, the broker who connected me with the owner of Soto restaurants. I excused myself and answered the phone.

Marc called to say that he had a signed offer to present on one of my other client's buildings, and that he wanted to drop it off in person. Thinking quickly, I thought it would be wise to introduce Marc to Rasheed. Marc would be an ideal person to look for a potential real estate investment for Rasheed. I told Marc about Rasheed, and his interest in investing in Montréal commercial real estate, and asked if he would be interested in talking further with him in person. Marc jumped at the opportunity, and offered to meet us in an hour's time.

I closed the phone and continued my discussion with Rasheed. But try as I might, I couldn't get him to specify the amount of capital he was willing to invest. I hoped he was not going to make me look foolish in front of Marc.

I had a clear view of the coffee shop's entrance from where I was sitting. I saw Marc come in, and waved to get his attention. Rasheed and I stood as he approached our table.

"Marc, I would like you to meet Rasheed Bishara. The two men shook hands, exchanged pleasantries, and then sat down. Marc handed me an envelope containing the offer he had told me about earlier on the phone.

Rasheed started a conversation with Marc right away, telling him the same things he had told me. "We look for a building. I want to make investment in Canada. Yesterday I come here for permanent resident," he said in his broken English. I filled in the gaps whenever Marc looked puzzled by Rasheed's English.

The three of us spent about forty-five minutes chatting in the coffee shop about doing business in Canada. The conversation did not end with any tangible outcome beyond Marc promising that if he encountered a good real estate investment opportunity, he would let me know.

After a number of days of touring around Montréal to get a feel for the city, Rasheed went back to Dubai. He planned on coming back to Montréal in two months, during which time I was to look for some real estate or business opportunities for him to evaluate. But it would be an awkward search. He wouldn't give me any indication of the type of investment he was seeking, the amount of capital he had to invest, or his timeline. The only guidance he gave me was that it should be a good investment, and "big is okay."

Over the next two months, I uncovered a few different opportunities that I guessed would appeal to Rasheed. They each involved businesses that included ownership of their buildings. Marc also gave me a file on a huge building that housed a family entertainment centre operation. I wasn't overly impressed by it, but Marc insisted that it represented a great deal. The owner was asking for a fraction of its potential market value.

"Why do you think he is giving it away?" I asked.

Marc shrugged. "I have no idea."

"I don't think this would be a good fit for Rasheed. I don't see him as the owner of a family gaming centre." I paused and thought about it a bit more. "But the asking price is very low."

"The vendor is willing to negotiate, too," Marc said. "He built up this business himself. His primary interest is in seeing the centre continue to grow. Price is not the important thing for him."

I skimmed over the listing again. It was eight pages long. "Marc, this is a complicated operation. It wouldn't be easy for Rasheed to run that place. The chances for failure are huge. I don't want to show him this one."

A week before returning to Canada, Rasheed called me to see if I could pick him up at the airport. Even though it would not be improper for me to send him a cab, I told him that I would be there.

That Saturday, I went to the airport. Rasheed appeared out of the arrivals gate, once again being pushed in a wheelchair. He located me right away. I shook hands with him and asked about his stay in Dubai, but he immediately changed the subject and asked me if I had found him anything. He offered no greeting at all beyond a simple "hello." I had never dealt with anyone like him before.

"How is business?" he asked.

We walked out to my car and headed for his hotel. I tried very hard to bring out some casual conversation, but he always went back to the same subject.

"Rasheed, I have some projects for you to see, but I would rather talk about them on Monday in my office."

"Why Monday? What are they, buildings or businesses? How much money?"

"I don't remember all the details, but I promise you will see everything on Monday," This guy was intense.

"What about tomorrow? You not work Sunday?"

"No, I spend time with my family on Sundays."

Rasheed pushed to arrange a meeting with me the following day, but I stood firm. Sundays were now sacred for me. I convinced him that he needed a day's rest after the fourteen-hour flight from Dubai. I dropped him off at the hotel and headed home.

I was in front of the hotel on Monday morning at eight, as promised. He was standing there waiting for me. I picked him up and we drove to my office, which was only a few blocks away. My office was located on the third floor of the building, and there was no elevator. He started to complain after the first floor.

"You are only fifty percent of the way up. Don't quit yet!" I said.

He was clearly not impressed at having to climb stairs. This was a man who was used to his creature comforts.

We walked into my conference room and I invited him to make himself comfortable. "I will be with you in a minute," I said, and went to the next room to get the files I had prepared for him. I returned and put them on the table across from him, then sat down to open them. "Okay, here is the first…"

Rasheed cut me off. "Reza, are these business or real estate?"

"Well, I have both, but I think the best choice for you would be real estate," I replied. "Since you are not going to stay in Canada, owning a business operation would not be a wise choice."

He gave no reaction.

"Right now, I only have files for real estate. Jonathan, my assistant, has a couple of other files that include combinations of business and real estate. He usually starts at nine. Why don't we start with these ones? As soon as Jonathan is in, I will get those files from him."

Rasheed waved his hand at me and closed his eyes, as if to say "as you wish." He sat across the table from me, waiting for an opportunity to leap off the page at him.

"Look at this one, Rasheed. This is a nice residential property that's producing about an eight percent return. Keep in mind that residential properties are extremely easy to finance."

"What is different in Canada between residential and commercial property, concerning financing?" Rasheed asked.

"Well, financial institutions are willing to take a bigger risk on residential properties. For one, residential properties have much lower vacancy rates than commercial, and they don't need major renovations with every change of occupancy. Operating costs are much lower, compared to commercial properties. On the other hand, if you have a triple-A tenant and a very good lease, a commercial property would not be difficult to finance, either."

"What is triple-A tenant?'" he asked.

"It is a tenant who is unlikely to default…"

"Reza?" It was Marc, calling over from the entrance. I had no idea that he was going to drop in.

"Yes, Marc? Come in. We are in here."

As he got closer, he called out, "Who is 'we'?" Marc didn't know that Rasheed was in my office. He walked in.

"Marc," I said, "Rasheed just came in from Dubai." I offered him a chair.

Marc sat down and started to talk to Rasheed. "How are you?" he said with a big smile, extending his hand.

Rasheed was very coy. "I am fine," he said.

"How was Dubai?" Marc asked.

"Okay," Rasheed said. The one-word answers made Marc feel awkward. "I think it was two months ago when we last met," Marc said.

Rasheed got straight down to business. "Did you find anything for me?" Rasheed asked.

"I was not sure what you were looking for," Marc said.

"An investment," Rasheed replied.

"Well, I don't know any specifics of what you are looking for, but if you are looking for property, I know of an interesting opportunity," Marc said. "I already gave the information to Reza."

I went to my desk to fetch the file on the family entertainment centre. Marc described it in detail while Rasheed skimmed over the pictures. It was a two-hundred-thousand-square-foot building.

"What you think, Reza?" Rasheed asked.

"I don't think it is a very good investment for you," I said bluntly. "They want to sell the building and the business as a package. It is a very complex business with different sections, including alcohol sales and gambling, which you don't like. I have no experience in this area, and I am not sure if you have, either. The facility is very old and it hasn't been renovated for a long time. So, my recommendation is to stay away from it.

Rasheed nodded quietly to himself as I talked, his hands clasped beneath his chin. "What about from real estate perspective?" he asked. As soon as I started to respond, Marc cut me off.

"It is a great real estate opportunity! It is very well located, and the owner is asking only a fraction of the market price for a building like this."

"Why the owner wants to sell it?" Rasheed asked Marc.

"He is a big developer, and this is too small a project for him to keep. He built this business himself and he is very sentimental about it. He just wants to see somebody continue the business."

"How much money he asks for it?" Rasheed asked.

Marc responded without hesitation.

Rasheed continued. "What is the market…"

I didn't wait for Rasheed to finish his sentence, since I knew Marc would come up with a tempting reply. "Well," I said, "it depends on if you look at the building or if you look at the business."

"What is the difference? They are together," Rasheed said.

It was nine o'clock, and the phone began to ring nonstop. "Where is Jonathan?" I asked out loud. "Excuse me for a second," I said, and went over to answer one of the calls.

I really didn't want to leave Marc alone with Rasheed. This deal could mean a big commission for Marc. But if there were problems down the road, they would land on my lap.

I went over to the phone. "Hi Reza. It's Jonathan."

"Jonathan, where are you?"

"I don't think I can come in today."

"What? You're kidding!"

"My son has the day off school. It's a professional development day for teachers. I can't come in."

"Not today, Jonathan! You know I have a client today."

"Oh, Reza, I'm sorry! I forgot about your client from Dubai." He was clearly upset with himself. "I'll see if my mother can take my son today. I'll call you back."

"Thanks, Jonathan." I hung up the phone and ran back to the conference room.

There was not much discussion between Marc and Rasheed. I think Marc understood that I was not in favour of the deal.

"Sorry about that," I said. "It was Jonathan, my assistant. Anyway, as I was saying, I think the building alone is worth about twice the asking price. Of course, that is if it were occupied by a good tenant. We would have to look very closely at what value the business adds to the building. I don't think it is a very profitable business. We would have to analyze the financial statements and all its other activities."

"What we need to analyze the company?" Rasheed asked.

"You would have to make a conditional offer first. With an offer, you can then ask to see all sorts of documents. Then you could verify the information during the due diligence period," Marc said.

Amazingly, Rasheed seemed to have already made up his mind. He believed he was on the trail of an unbeatable bargain. I could sense that there was no turning back from here.

"Let us make offer," Rasheed said.

"Whoa, whoa, whoa! Not that fast," I said. "Marc should gather some documentation about the property."

"Like what?" Rasheed asked.

"Marc knows," I responded. "A survey, recent tax bills, insurance information, and some utility bills," I said.

"Yes, yes," Marc said, nodding in agreement.

"If all those factors are sound, then I will get my lawyer to draft an offer. We will review it, and if everything is alright, you can sign it, and Marc will present it to the owner," I said.

"That might take a while," Rasheed said. He was a very impatient person. He wanted everything to be done yesterday. But Marc was ready to move. We agreed to meet the next day to go over the related property documents that Marc would gather.

We met in my office the following morning at eleven. Marc took a file out of his bag and put it on the conference table. The file contained copies of the tax bill, the survey, and a spreadsheet showing the building's basic operating expenses. He started with the tax bill.

"Usually the city's assessment of the building value is around thirty percent less than market value. Here you can see that their assessment is almost the same as the asking price."

"What you think, Reza?" Rasheed asked.

I started looking through the documents and, after some simple calculations, looked up at him and suggested that the asking price was a pretty good deal. Of course, I didn't have any idea about the family entertainment business attached to it.

"Just for the building alone, I have to say that this represents a good deal. But I think it would be very important to draft a conditional offer, and get the documents to conduct a thorough analysis of the building and the business. But that might be costly."

"What should we do regarding due diligence?" Rasheed asked.

"We need to list all of the documents necessary to verify the performance of the business," Marc said.

"What things?" Rasheed asked.

I started listing them.

"We need to get documentation about the local zoning bylaws, and meet with city authorities to see what new projects are being planned in the area. We should ask for an environmental study from the vendor. If he doesn't have one, we must hire a firm to carry one out. The third item would be an inspection report from an engineering firm, to make sure the building is sound,; and if it is not, to determine what kind of renovations would be required. At the same time, we had better get the building and the business appraised by a certified professional. We need to get the plans from the owner, including structural, mechanical, architectural, and any other plans available. Sometimes those plans are available from the city, too.

Marc jumped in at this point. "Don't forget to ask for all existing contracts, including any outstanding loan agreements.

"There might be more items, but I can't remember them now," I said. I am sure my lawyer has a list of them."

"Lawyer?" Rasheed asked.

"Yes, lawyer. The list would only be for the property itself. The business operation would require a different set of eyes," I said.

"Yes, like financial statements," Marc said.

"Yes, but much more than that," I replied. "We should start with the financials. From there, we will be able to see what else to look for. We will need three to four years of financial statements, plus an interim statement for this year."

Even though I was still not enthusiastic about Rasheed buying this business, I was hoping to answer all of his questions, and to make sure he understood that the value of any business was determined primarily by the income it generates plus its future potential. I had to clearly understand the business myself in order to counsel him on its value.

It was October by the time Rasheed decided to make an offer on the whole package—the building and the business. I asked Marc to forward the documents to my lawyer, to enable him to draft the offer to purchase. A couple of days later, my lawyer forwarded the draft to me by email and asked me to review it.

By then, Rasheed had rented a palatial apartment in downtown Montréal, and was spending most of his time there rather than in Dubai. I called him and arranged a meeting the next morning. I had already printed a copy of the draft offer, with the important points highlighted and my own personal notes in the margins. Rasheed was not computer literate, so I made sure everything was clear on a hard copy. By this point, I hadn't spent a great deal of time on that file, but I knew that if the vendor accepted the offer, I would likely have to devote a good portion of my time advising Rasheed on running the business.

The next morning, Rasheed and I met at my office. I reviewed the details of the offer with him, point by point, to ensure that the document reflected his wishes. Strangely, he started to negotiate with me on the price.

"You don't have to negotiate with me, Rasheed. Just tell me how much you would like to offer and I will write it in," I said. He was adamant about submitting an extremely low offer.

"The next point is the deposit, Rasheed. Usually the purchaser posts a deposit of about ten percent of the purchase price in a lawyer's trust account. If the offer is accepted and everything goes well, the deposit will be applied against the purchase price upon closing. If not, it will be returned to you."

"No, no ," Rasheed said. "I will not make a deposit."

I sighed and rolled my eyes. "We are going to ask them to consider the offer with no deposit? Rasheed, they won't take us seriously."

Even though he was insistent, I explained the accepted North American business practice of deposits. He was highly resistant to the idea, but grudgingly agreed to include a deposit.

"The next important aspect of your offer to purchase is due diligence. Your offer stipulates a ninety-day period in which you can verify facts about the business and its operations. It also outlines a list of documents we will need, which you and I discussed the other day with Marc."

Rasheed nodded in approval as I went through the offer.

"I have their financial statements from last year," I said. They provide a surface-level view of the business, but we will have to go deeper. Look at the first page. You can see last year's revenue, expenses, assets, liabilities, and the net profit. The details of each line are listed throughout the following pages. But there is an important notice on the cover page. These numbers have not been audited.

"What is the difference?" Rasheed asked.

"This financial statement has been prepared using information provided by the client, although with respect to Generally Accepted Accounting Principles. An audited financial statement is certified by an accountant, who actually visits the client's business and verifies the financial records in person. It is important for us to request audited financial statements. With what we have now, we are not able to verify the receivables, payables, and many other items that can easily be deferred. The other important thing is to verify that the value of the equipment leasehold improvements and any goodwill is realistic. Finally, it is important to recognize something that can never be measured by a financial statement: the relationships the company has with its suppliers, customers and employees. Those areas are intangible keys to business success," I said.

I was rather surprised by Rasheed's lack of leadership. For a person submitting a multi-million dollar offer to purchase a business, I expected him to engage more in the details of this offer. But he seemed interested in only the price. I was convinced that, without my guidance, he would have simply submitted an unconditional binding offer. But I couldn't, in good conscience, let him do so.

"Break-even is enough," Rasheed said. "I am interested in its real estate value."

Jonathan happened to walk into the room at that point, and asked if he could bring us some coffee.

"Jonathan," I said, "Have a look at these documents and photos." I showed him the listing for the entertainment centre Rasheed was planning to purchase.

"Oh, I know that place. It's been there forever. I used to go there when I was a teenager. It is getting pretty old," Jonathan said. Rasheed gave him a look that clearly suggested his opinions were not welcome.

"Thanks, Jonathan. I would appreciate the coffee," I said. He brushed off the situation and went to the other room.

"You see, Rasheed, the business might break even today, but as soon as you take over, you may not get the same type of leverage from suppliers. Because they don't know you, they might ask for deposits or change their payment terms."

He nodded, and seemed to be listening.

"We have to make sure that the equipment is not at the end of its lifecycle. Ongoing regular maintenance is another important consideration. For example, we should find out if the equipment requires costly regular maintenance," I said. "Also, you need to consider that inflation is very stable in North America. Prices don't increase as quickly here as what you are accustomed to in Dubai. Real estate always tends to increase in value, but we don't experience price increases brought on by high inflation."

"How we know that business is making good money?" Rasheed asked.

Jonathan returned with a couple of cups of coffee. His timing was perfect. I was dying for a cup.

"It would be the ratio of income to the capital investment. With that figure you can compare the return of your investment in this business with any other investment that interests you. For example, by looking at the financial statements, you can see that your investment in this family entertainment business would produce a return of around fourteen percent. It is an important consideration if you are evaluating other opportunities. However, like I said before, there are other contributing factors you should be aware of that influence the profit of this business."

Rasheed sat in complete silence. I couldn't tell whether he was listening to me or if he simply tuned me out because he thought I was incompetent. We had covered a lot of ground that morning and I wanted to end the conversation for the day. With the details finalized, I would be taking his signed offer to my lawyer for review, and presentation to the vendor and his lawyer. I asked Rasheed if he wanted to go back to his place. I knew he had some other affairs to take care of. I wanted to prepare a list and a schedule to start the due diligence investigations.

I spent considerable time that afternoon making a list of all the factors we needed to research during the due diligence period. High on my list was identifying the entertainment centre's direct and indirect competitors. But given the size and nature of this business, it was challenging. I identified a small variety of entertainment businesses that I thought would attract young families. I also looked at large theme parks in the region, which were publicly held companies whose financial and other information was available over the Internet, or from local land registry offices.

I called Rasheed at the end of the day. "Rasheed, I was busy this afternoon preparing a list of competitors, and a list of factors to include in a competitive analysis. I would like to pick you up tomorrow and visit some of them," I said.

"Excellent, Reza."

"Also, since most entertainment centres are more active on the weekend, we can visit some of them on Saturday," I suggested.

"Okay, see you tomorrow."

On the way to Rasheed's apartment the next morning I was thinking about how difficult it was to connect with him on a personal level. At this point, I had known Rasheed for eight months. But he could still only talk about nothing but business with me. I reflected on the character of people typically involved in the family entertainment industry. Rasheed definitely did not fit the mould. I had difficulty imagining him having fun! The few times I had tried to introduce him to others, he seemed to recoil. The only thing that seemed to occupy his thought was making a deal. Alarms were going off in my mind. I still firmly believed that this business was not compatible with his personality.

Rasheed was waiting outside as I drove up to his building. He grabbed my car door before I had even stopped, jumped in and slammed the door closed.

"What's up? Are you all right?" I asked.

He started to curse in Arabic.

"What happened, Rasheed?" I asked again.

"Door man! I had to repeat myself three times! I don't understand how they give him job!" Rasheed said, furiously.

I didn't know what to say. I was learning quickly that Rasheed could be rather acerbic. Perhaps that is why he was successful at business, but I could also see the steep price that he paid for that success.

We first drove to the entertainment centre for which he had submitted an offer to purchase. We wanted to have a fresh picture of it in our minds before visiting competitors. It was an old place, in need of a serious facelift. Most of our conversation focused on the property, rather than the business operations. I made some notes about the entrance, the activities that I saw, and the customer service. Ironically, Rasheed was completely satisfied.

He found the property very appealing. It was actually the first time I saw him express a bit of positive emotion.

We stayed there for about an hour. We spent the remainder of the day visiting direct and indirect competitors, to get a general feel for the industry. At the end of the day, on our way back to Rasheed's condominium, he asked me if I had gleaned the information that I was looking for. "Yes," I said, "but I am going to spend some time with it and write a report for you." I said.

"I just want to hear what you think," he replied.

"I have to do some Internet research and try to get some more comparable market information."

"Reza, I just want to know what you think."

I paused to collect my thoughts. "I think it is a nice place, and although it is unique it would be very hard to do anything fast," I said. I knew Rasheed wanted me to tell him what a great deal the business was, and that we shouldn't wait too long to remove the conditions.

"You give your report by Monday?"

"No," I said. "Tomorrow is Sunday. Sunday is my day to spend with my family.

He tried to negotiate with me. Playing the family card did not deter him one bit. Since I didn't want to argue with him, I said I would try to give him something early in the week.

The best part of my day is when I arrive home and my kids run up to the door and give me a huge hug. The stress and fatigue just melt away at that moment. That day was no different. I parked my car and walked up the stairs to open the door. While I was looking for my key, one of my kids opened the door and jumped into my arms.

"Hi, I'm home," I called out to my wife.

"Did everything go well with Rasheed?" she asked.

"Alright, I guess. But he does not listen well. Much of the advice I give him goes in one ear and out the other."

"Well, your responsibility is to tell him your honest opinion. He has to then take responsibility for his actions."

I told her that I agreed with her. But I didn't want to talk about work at home. I always had great weekends with my family.

Rasheed was waiting for me outside my office on Monday morning when I arrived.

"Rasheed, what are you doing here so early?" I asked.

"How about your report?" he replied.

"Rasheed, it is nine o'clock Monday morning!" I wasn't making any effort to be diplomatic. "You are welcome here anytime. But, I will call you as soon as I have some information."

"Alright, I have something to do." He wasn't offended. For the first time, I had set a boundary with Rasheed. It worked. He respected it.

I went upstairs and got settled in for work. Jonathan had already arrived. I made a list of people I needed to contact about the business and the building. The first was a list of business services people: a public notary, a real estate appraiser, a building inspector, and city officials. The second list concerned aspects of the business I needed to evaluate, such as competition, further capital investment required, cash flow, market trends, customer base, relations with suppliers, and all existing contracts binding the company.

"Here you go, Jonathan," I said, handing him a sheet of paper. This is the list of the reports we need."

In sharp contrast to Rasheed's haste, it took me two weeks to gather the information I needed to evaluate his offer on the business. Even at that, the environmental assessment wasn't complete. The Phase One environmental assessment of the building was not satisfactory, so we had to request a Phase Two evaluation, which would take at least another week. You can imagine Rasheed's reaction when he found this out.

Rasheed came over to review my report on a Tuesday morning. Upon entering my office, he expressed surprise at seeing all of the supporting documentation. He sat down and I began going through the various reports I had gathered over the past two weeks.

"This is the appraisal report. It offers an unbiased opinion of the value of the building." I said. "It uses three different methods to determine the value of the real estate."

"Which way this building was evaluated?" Rasheed asked.

"By market comparison, replacement cost, and the revenue it is generating," I said.

"And what is the value?" Rasheed asked.

"The lowest of the three values is based on its revenue. But it is good. Look here," I said, pointing to the figure. "The appraiser is valuing just the building significantly higher than what you are offering," I said.

"Then why we wait?" Rasheed asked. "Why it took you two weeks to tell me that? I know this from beginning. You really are a business consultant. You tell me something I already know," Rasheed said.

I had come to know Rasheed, and his gruff interpersonal skills. But with that comment, he came close to crossing a line with me. Business was business, however. I bit my tongue and retained professional composure.

"Looking at this report, Rasheed, the appraiser has kept some capital for reserve. He doesn't give much value to the equipment. Some of the existing equipment is leased and is nearing the end of its contract. So, by renewing any contract, the cost of the operation might increase. By how much it could increase, I'm really not sure. Certain aspects of this business have come to the end of their lifecycles and need attention immediately."

I could tell that it wasn't sinking in. Rasheed was fixated on the fact that the building itself, without the family entertainment business, was appraised at a much higher value than what he was offering. But I continued to walk him through the information Jonathan and I had collected over the past two weeks.

"Jonathan can explain the competition report."

I motioned to Jonathan, although I could tell from Rasheed's body language that he was not going to absorb Jonathan's presentation.

"We looked at different categories of the family entertainment industry," he began. "We included direct competitors and indirect substitutes. Most of the businesses we looked at were much smaller operations being run directly by the owner, although we did include a couple of large theme parks in the region. All of the businesses we reviewed, large and small, were in much better condition than this business. Both Reza and I feel that to compete effectively with them, this business would need a fairly large capital investment to bring it up to industry standards."

Actually, Rasheed was listening closely for a change.

I jumped back into the conversation. "Rasheed, I also believe that as soon as you take over this operation, its revenue will decrease."

"Why?" he asked.

"There are a couple of factors. First, based on our research of revenue streams of publicly held entertainment companies in this region, the industry is experiencing a slight downturn. But perhaps more importantly, whenever a business assumes a new owner, all of the established relationships change. Some employees will inevitably leave, which will affect your customer service. You will likely lose some regular customers until you establish new relationships. Similarly, it appears that the owner has been using many of the current suppliers for a long time, which suggests that he is getting favourable terms from them. Upon taking over this business, your costs could very well increase."

"There are other points that I want to bring to your attention Rasheed. For instance, let's take a look at the financial statements. One of the most important aspects of any business is cash flow. Businesses breathe with cash. Without sufficient cash, a business suffocates. Usually, when you take over a business, in addition to having enough money on hand for advertising, payroll, and other immediate expenses, you need to make deposits with suppliers. If you decide to go ahead with the purchase, we have to make a financial projection for you, which would include a cash flow projection, too. I have sent all the documents to a lawyer for comments. He should be able to provide his feedback by early tomorrow," I said.

"What can be wrong with the contracts?" Rasheed asked.

Again, I was surprised that such a successful business person did not appreciate the importance of a solid contract.

"The contracts can be binding for any purchaser, so we should study them well. For example, as I mentioned before, some can renew automatically with predetermined payments and services, which would not be to your benefit," I said. "The last time I structured a purchase for one of my clients, there was an old photocopier that came with the business. It had a five-year lease with rather steep monthly payments. I knew I could have gotten a brand new colour copier for a fraction of the price, but it would have cost a lot of money to break the contract—"

"I don't understand what you say. What is the bottom line? Do you think it is good deal or not?"

I shrugged. "It all depends on what you want to do with that building," I said. I was trying to make sure that Rasheed fully understood every dimension of this transaction, and what he was offering to purchase. On the other hand, all Rasheed could see was the apparent bargain. My father always said that the price you pay for something is not nearly as important as the price you could get if you had to turn around and sell it.

"Rasheed, if you wanted to buy the building and rent it out, I would recommend it as a great deal. Of course, with having no tenant lined up, you are not likely to get a bank to finance the purchase. Until you found a solid tenant, you would have to have enough cash to carry the entire cost of operating the building. Renting the building would give you around a twenty-five percent return on offer, based on the appraiser's report. Now, in the event that you wanted to maintain the existing family entertainment business there, you might need to invest additional capital to modernize it. However, I don't think you have either the industry experience or the proper team to run this business for you," I said. I paused to let Rasheed ponder my thoughts.

"I think you should take some time to consider it. I don't know how much capital you have behind you. Nobody but you can tell you if you should purchase this building. Only you know can judge your previous experiences, if you are committed to this idea and have the passion to make it a success. Take some time and think about it," I said, and closed the file.

Rasheed sat stone- faced.

"Would you like to get some lunch, Rasheed? I am hungry."

"I am not hungry," he replied, "but I come with you."

I spent the rest of the day with Rasheed, talking about the building and the business.

The next morning, Marc, Jonathan, and I sat down with Rasheed in my office.

Rasheed was deep in thought. He said very little, and his body language showed that he was unhappy. He wanted some help to make the decision about the purchase, but I had had enough experience to know that such advice would also give him somebody to blame if things went badly.

"You know, Rasheed, by Friday we have to either waive all the conditions or cancel your offer," I said.

"Do we *have* to answer by Friday?" Rasheed asked.

"Yes," Marc replied, "the due diligence period will end on Friday. If you don't answer, you can lose your deposit."

"What do you think, Reza?" Rasheed asked me, yet again.

"Rasheed, I'll be honest with you. From the very beginning I have said that I do not think you should do this deal. If you had a blue chip tenant lined up, it would be the deal of century. But since you have to maintain the family entertainment operation, I do not think this deal would provide a decent return, if any, on your investment," I said.

Marc quickly jumped in. "At least not in the short term," he said. Marc had an interest in Rasheed making the purchase. He stood to lose a hefty commission if the deal didn't go through.

"Okay," Rasheed said. "We go ahead, but we lower the offer price."

"And how would you do that?" Marc asked.

"Marc, the building inspector's report, appraisal, and the environmental report give us plenty of justification to go back with a lower offer," I said.

Rasheed loved the idea. Marc wasn't too keen because his commission was based on the selling price. I wasn't being driven by emotion, so I was able to be much more objective and blunt. I told Marc to arrange a meeting the following morning with the vendor. Rasheed backed me up. Marc walked over to the next room and called the vendor's broker on his cell phone. He came back a few minutes later with an unsettled look on his face.

"What?" I asked.

"Mr. Marc, is it all right?" Rasheed asked.

"Yes," he replied, "but they know why you want to meet."

We submitted a number of offers and counter offers over a period of four days. Finally, Rasheed and the vendor were able to strike a deal in which Rasheed would purchase this two-hundred-thousand- square- foot building and the family entertainment business for cash. There was no conversation about financing. We waived all the outstanding conditions and sent the final documents to the vender's lawyer for review.

Rasheed called me that evening. "Reza," he said, "how much of a loan we can get on this deal?"

"Loan?!" I cried. "Rasheed, don't you remember? You signed an all-cash offer! That is one of the primary reasons they accepted your low-ball offer! It makes no financial difference to me if this offer closes or not. But if it doesn't close because you can't come up with the money, I will lose my reputation! Montréal is not a very big market. Everyone knows everyone in the real estate business around here. This is a big transaction. Many people have their eyes on it." I was furious, and wasn't shy about making sure that Rasheed knew it. We had spent days negotiating back and forth with the vendor.

"You need to think of a solution, Rasheed. There is no way I can get you a mortgage."

He shrugged me off as if the problem was mine, not his. "I don't have all the cash needed to close that deal. You have to talk to Marc and either delay closing or try to get loan," he said.

I was stunned. But there was little I could do. I knew Rasheed well enough to know that his word was final.

I let out a big sigh and shook my head. "Let me talk to Marc," I responded, exasperated.

Before calling Marc, I took a step back to analyse the situation. I tried to think of a financial institution that would fit the circumstances. Usually the banks have preferences when giving out loans. Some are interested in residential lending, while some prefer commercial lending, but only under specific conditions. To get a loan on a dilapidated family entertainment centre would be practically impossible.

Regardless, there was no choice but to go ahead. I called three friends in three different financial institutions. Even if I could prepare all the necessary documentation in a week, it would take weeks for any bank to approve a multi-million dollar loan. We had only a few days before the notary was to close the deal.

I got to my office and, with Jonathan, started to prepare the documents necessary for a loan application. The banks would need the same documents that we had compiled for due diligence, and information about Rasheed's background and financial position. I gave the list of required documents to Jonathan and asked him to make three copies, one for each bank.

The phone rang and Jonathan answered. It was Marc. He passed the phone over to me.

"Marc, we have to meet the vendor again," I said.

"Why is that? What else do you need to see him for? Not another haircut! Reza, you know we can't go back for any more!" He was agitated.

"I know, Marc. Calm down. We're not going to ask for another haircut. Rasheed needs some time to come up with the money, so we want to see if the vendor would accept a balance of sale in the event that he can't get financing," I said.

"And if not? What if the vendor is not willing to accept the idea?" Marc asked.

"Then, the deal might be off," I said.

Marc was understandably upset. He had spent a tremendous amount of time on this file. He would only be compensated if the deal went through. But Rasheed left us no other option but to approach the vendor about the new developments. Marc had no choice. It was awkward, but he was able to convince the vendor to sit down with us once again the next day.

I picked up Rasheed and met Marc outside the vendor's office. The vendor greeted us inside. He was surprisingly cordial with us, considering that we were, in effect, re-opening negotiations. I was careful to maintain professionalism with him because he was a high-profile real estate developer with an extensive network in Montréal.

I took the lead in the meeting, laying out the scenario that Rasheed had created for all of us. I was expecting to be treated harshly by the vendor, as we had all spent almost two full weeks negotiating and renegotiating the details of the transaction, only to now have Rasheed renege. I proposed having a sixty percent balance of sale that would last only for five months. After that period, Rasheed would face a very high interest rate until the balance was paid in full.

With surprisingly little resistance from the vendor, we struck a new agreement based on those terms. I have to say that I was shocked that the vendor would even reopen the negotiations. He agreed to hold a loan for sixty percent of the transaction price for five months at the going market interest rate. Obviously he didn't hold much hope of finding another buyer for this property.

Marc, Rasheed, and I left the vendor's office and walked toward the lot where we had parked our cars. Marc and I were quite happy, realizing full well that the deal could easily have fallen apart. Rasheed, however, was visibly agitated. After seeing in person how flexible the vendor was, Rasheed was convinced that we could have gotten an even better purchase price.

I came very close to boiling over. "Look, Rasheed. Marc and I have invested a tremendous amount of time on this project. We found the opportunity for you, negotiated your first offer on your behalf, conducted a thorough market study and building inspection, and then re-negotiated the terms you initially agreed to. You signed off on a set of conditions, only later to ask us to approach the vendor again to change them. You have now waived those conditions. At this stage, I will not approach the vendor again. We have gone far beyond what is reasonably expected to accommodate you. I will go no further!"

Rasheed knew that I was angry, and that he was pushing a very sensitive button. He backed off, although I knew full well that he truly wanted to go back to the vendor a third time to lower the offer price. Marc and I were prepared to walk away, and Rasheed clearly sensed it. Without us, our knowledge of the Canadian real estate market and our network of professional services providers, Rasheed would be helpless.

The vendor's legal firm drafted the agreement to reflect the new terms. In essence, the agreement had to be completely rewritten, as the new terms added a great deal of complexity to the transaction. It took two weeks for the lawyers on both sides to finalize the wording of the new agreement. The vendor stipulated that the added legal costs, which totalled tens of thousands of dollars, had to be borne by Rasheed.

I picked up Rasheed to go to the notary's office for final signatures. Well, guess what? Rasheed began questioning why he had to pay more than his initial calculation—due to a number of adjustments along the way—even though we had drafted the final deed of sale. But Marc and I stopped him in his tracks. We simply would not accept the overtures he was making to again reduce his offer price.

The deal was finalized. Rasheed became the owner of the family entertainment business and the two-hundred-thousand-square-foot building in which it was housed. It was one of the most frustrating deals I had ever negotiated on behalf of a client.

If the negotiation process was riddled with headaches, then managing the family entertainment business itself proved to be downright chaotic for Rasheed. He had to put up tens of thousands of dollars just for a cash float. He was required to post a deposit with the utility supplier, and the first payment for payroll, among other costs. To top things off, within the first two weeks of taking possession of the business, the general manager handed Rasheed his resignation and took three employees with him to start their own family entertainment business. That is when I got a phone call from him. He wanted to see me, as soon as possible, in his new office. I held my hand to my forehead and winced. I knew it was just the beginning. The nightmares I had envisioned when Marc introduced this opportunity to Rasheed, the ones that prompted me to steer Rasheed away from this business, were materializing.

In the months that I had known Rasheed, I had seen him in some pretty foul moods, but nothing compared to his mood when I walked into his office at the entertainment centre.

"How are you, Rasheed?" I asked.

"Angry, Reza, very angry!" he screamed. "Everything is wrong. Too many things happening that you did not prepare me for. My general manager left. When we talk with him in due diligence process, he seemed okay and he would stay here."

Rasheed needed a scapegoat and I was the natural choice.

"Rasheed, I have good news for you," I replied, trying to deflect his anger towards something more positive. "The mortgage broker called me this morning to say that the bank is interested in financing this building," I said.

It seemed to work. He calmed down.

"Rasheed, your goal in purchasing this property was to close the business and rent it out," I reminded him. "Have you decided what you want to do?"

"Yes, I will keep the business. It has lot of potential."

It was yet another flip-flop in his thinking. He seemed to change his mind day by day. On one level, I was at wit's end dealing with this man. But he was a client.

"But Rasheed, you could spend money on anything and it would have great potential. This is a tired business. It needs a big capital injection to bring it up to date. I tried to make this clear to you in the negotiation process."

"What can I do now?" he asked. "Reza, I invest in this company in Canada because I know you and I trust you. If I didn't know you, I would never do that."

Rasheed was casting blame on me. He crossed a line again, and I had to let him know it.

"Well, if you trusted me, you should have listened to me! I told you in clear terms, from the very beginning, the risks associated with this business! But you did not listen to me. You were too focused on the price versus the market value." I walked over to the window and looked outside. "Rasheed, you know that I didn't think this was a good business for you."

I paused to let it sink in. "Anyhow," I said, in a calmer voice, "let's see what we can do."

After two months, I miraculously got a mortgage approved for him. Perhaps I should not have been so amazed because there were a number of strict conditions that came with it, one of them being that I would be involved in the management of the family entertainment centre, and in the event that I was removed from the business, the bank would call the loan. Rasheed and I agreed that I would spend two days a week, from that point forward, working at the centre to manage operations. It meant one less thing for Rasheed to worry about, in terms of closing the deal and running the business, but it also meant a huge new commitment for me. The problem was that I had no personal interest whatsoever in the family entertainment business — indoor games, bowling, hamburgers, and children's birthday parties. To do well in business, you must live your passion every day. But I took it on as a personal challenge. Admittedly, there was a good deal of potential to grow this business,

I had to get to know the business from the inside out. There were so many details about it that I didn't understand. Half of the existing equipment needed to be replaced, which was not a big surprise. What we failed to uncover during the due diligence process was that most of the suppliers had gone out of business. The closest ones to deal with were located on the west coast of the United States. In some cases, it was easier to source used parts from other entertainment centres that had been mothballed by their owners. I didn't have connections with anybody in this line of business, so talking to knowledgeable people about the challenges we faced was impossible. By not thoroughly understanding the issues, I had difficulty finding proper solutions.

In the end, it took three years of work and an enormous capital injection from Rasheed to bring the operation up to par. I became an expert on an industry in which I had no true passion. The business did not live up to Rasheed's profit expectations, but the real estate portion of the deal proved to be a lucrative investment.

Meanwhile, I met someone who had developed a very successful self-storage business. I asked him about his preparations and how long it took for the business to become a success. He told me that he spent three entire years studying the self-storage industry and planning his business before he launched the venture. Three years. And it was profitable within the first year.

Lessons Learned

The events I have described in this chapter are precisely the kinds of business experiences that motivated me to write this book. I have endured a tremendous amount of grief as a result of diving into business acquisitions without thoroughly checking beneath

the surface for rocks. Not doing extensive homework before making an acquisition can debilitate you as a small business manager, sometimes fatally. I want readers to learn from my mistakes.

It goes without saying that it is important to be careful about details when considering an acquisition. A professional can help you identify scenarios that an unseasoned business owner would never imagine. A well-designed contract will help protect you against the unknown. But don't think that professionals hold the only key to a transaction's hidden insights. If you're thinking about buying a business or a franchise, question everyone you possibly can about the business and the industry in which it operates. Talk to the customers who support the business. Talk to the employees, even ones who may appear to have the most menial responsibilities, to get their insights into how the business is being managed, . Talk to competitors and suppliers about market trends. Stop at nothing to talk to as many people as possible about the business. Eventually you will form a clear picture that will help you determine if your acquisition is going to be a sound investment.

My experience with Rasheed taught me the supreme importance of having a clear goal, as well as a personal interest, in the business you are buying. Rasheed was a capital investor, interested solely in making money. He had no emotional connection to the entertainment business. For that matter, neither did I, yet I was pushed into the position of running the business on his behalf. While he made a very good real estate investment, the entertainment business itself was only a footnote in Rasheed's mind to the overall package. The most successful business owners face their line of business every day with enthusiasm for what they do. It isn't just about the financial rewards at the end of the line. Do not think that because you have been successful once, a new venture will be successful, too. Stick to what you know best and have a clear goal. Changing your strategy is fine, but don't lose sight of your goal.

Finally, any acquisition will involve negotiations. Do your homework before negotiating, so you know the fair value of the business you want to purchase, as well as how much room you have to negotiate on either side of that mark. Negotiate hard. But never, ever, give your counter party more than what they ask for. Business is business, after all.

Chapter 10: Plan Your Exit Route

During the Qajar dynasty in nineteenth century Persia, Amir Kabir, a famous chief minister known for his reformist policies, walked around a mosque. A man sitting on the ground at the centre of the inner square caught his attention. The square was encircled by a chain, which had great mystical power. Anybody who sat within its perimeter would be sheltered from persecution, regardless of their previous actions. Amir Kabir knew the man, and was aware that he was evading punishment for having stolen a great deal of money. He became angry, and immediately ordered the chain to be removed and destroyed, as it was being used for the wrong purpose.

Standing at the side, the keeper of the mosque questioned the minister on the wisdom of his decision. "You never know, Your Excellency, you may need it yourself someday,." he said.

The minister snickered and spitefully pulled down the last length of chain. The criminal within its perimeter was seized immediately.

Amir Kabir went on to enact reforms that led to some of the greatest changes in Persia's history. Like any drastic change, the reforms were not without cost. He was soon targeted by a group of corrupt bureaucrats, whom he had removed from high-ranking positions in his government. But they did not go quietly. Dozens of them banded together and tried to capture the Amir at his official home. It was a coup attempt.

It was a terrifying show of force the Amir had never before experienced. He fled to the square in that same mosque, hoping to find another chain encircling an area that would protect him. The very same keeper he had met months before saw him and asked why he had come.

"I need protection! A group of evil rebels is hunting me down," *he said.*

The mosque keeper replied, "Your Excellency, you should have left a length of that special chain in place to protect yourself."

I have always passionately believed that you can achieve anything you set your mind to, so long as you have the will. Perhaps that belief is what enabled me to create an impressive business group within just a few years of immigrating to Canada. However, I have experienced many situations in which I did absolutely everything in my power to achieve my goal, only to have my efforts result in failure. Remember,; you may have all the determination in the world, but you will not teach a pig to fly.

In my many experiences as a small business owner and manager, I believe that exiting successfully from a business is the exception, not the norm. I have seen many small business operators fall into bankruptcy, or close to it, while chasing their dream. I try to instil in other small business owners the importance of not allowing yourself to get painted into a corner. You should always have an exit strategy that will allow you to safely walk away from trouble.

A couple of chapters back, I briefly mentioned my experience opening - and closing - a large home furnishings outlet in Quebec City, called Titish. I want to provide a closer look at that saga here, because I learned some hard lessons from it that could help other people. I didn't design a proper exit plan from Titish, which left me in a vulnerable position. I ended up incurring huge costs in terms of time, money and energy. The experience prompted me to start thinking in a more holistic way about business. There is a natural starting and finishing point to everything, and the finishing point is not necessarily the multi--million dollar buyout that many entrepreneurs naively envision in the planning stages.

Marc, my real estate broker, had long been encouraging me to expand my business. He was always on the watch for retail space that would be suitable for my needs. He eventually came across an excellent space that appeared on the market in Quebec City. It was located in a shopping mall that was managed, by coincidence, by a business acquaintance of his, Michel Collinette.

Marc and I drove to Quebec City to view the space. The mall in which the store was located was one of the largest shopping centres in all of Canada. With about three hundred stores, it was practically a self-contained city. It was a destination that attracted hundreds of thousands of visitors each year. I was immediately impressed by the number of people in the mall, even for a Tuesday afternoon. We learned that the mall had been expanding in size on a regular basis since the 1960s, and that the interior had been regularly updated to appeal to contemporary consumer tastes.

We made our way inside and up to the property management office on the second floor. Michel, the mall manager, greeted us, took our coats, and offered us something to drink after the three-hour drive from Montréal. I quickly developed a favourable impression of him.

Michel walked us over to the vacant space, which was hidden behind window coverings and a sign that read, "Exciting retail opportunity coming soon." There is not much one can say about an empty store in the middle of a shopping mall. At twenty thousand square feet, it was one of the larger outlets in the mall. It was flanked by an electronics chain store on one side, and a sporting equipment store on the other. It had an additional entrance at the rear that led directly to the parking lot, a large storage area in the back section, and its own loading dock. The space had previously been occupied by a national discount department store.

The three of us returned to Michel's office to discuss the specifics of a lease. The rent seemed reasonable to me. Michel was quite motivated to get the space filled. Of course, a lot of renovations— new lighting, partitions, bulkheads, risers and paint—were required in order to bring the space in line with my vision. Michel suggested that the mall owners might be willing to pay for those renovations, if my offer to lease was appealing.

Marc and I drove back to Montréal that evening. The drive gave us three hours to discuss the details of what we had seen and the possibilities the space would offer me. Marc was quite enthusiastic about the space and strongly encouraged me to submit an offer to lease it. Of course, he stood to gain personally from brokering the deal, but aside from that, he made some good points about the suitability of this space for my furniture outlet.

I made up my mind that evening. I would submit an offer to lease the space for ten years at the rate they were asking, which included a small annual increase to cover inflation. My only conditions were rent-free access to the space for three months to complete the necessary renovations, and a lump sum of money paid back from the mall owners within thirty days of opening, to cover the cost of my renovations. This practice is not uncommon in the industry. Otherwise, it was a very strong offer.

Four days later, after Marc and Michel discussed the details back and forth over the phone, the signed offer was ready to send to

Michel. Marc and I anticipated smooth sailing, based on the groundwork he had done with Michel. However, one of the partners who owned the mall expressed deep concern over the lump sum payment clause for the leasehold improvements. Marc went to bat for me, pointing out that the owners stood to gain handsomely from a ten-year lease, and that the reimbursement of leasehold improvement costs was entirely normal. The fact of the matter was the owners knew this, and were simply driving a hard bargain. Marc negotiated back and forth on my behalf for two weeks. The owners eventually conceded, and accepted the lump sum payment clause on the condition that I would guarantee the entire ten-year lease with my other stores in Montréal.

I had been advised in the past never to guarantee a lease. But this space was very appealing to me. My Tapis en Gros stores were doing well. Together, they could easily cover the monthly lease payments for this space if necessary. I believed wholeheartedly that the business model I crafted for this furniture and home décor store was solid. I had successfully built up Tapis en Gros to five stores and was confident that I would be no less successful executing my vision with Titish. In my eyes, there was nothing to fear. I really wanted this excellent location. So, I accepted the owner's condition and guaranteed the ten-year lease with my corporation that held the five Montréal-based Tapis en Gros outlets. The landlord accepted the offer and the space was mine.

Rather than jumping through the hoops of borrowing start-up capital from a bank, I borrowed the funds from the corporation that held Tapis en Gros. This move put a little bit of strain on Tapis en Gros' cash flow, but it would only be for a short time. I felt secure knowing that the landlord would pay back the cost of the leasehold improvements thirty days after I opened, which would allow me to immediately recover a portion of that cash outlay.

Dream Beyond Borders

It was June 2001, and my goal was to open the store for business in early September. As there was quite a lot to do in a short time, I hired a design firm that specializes in retail interior design to bring my vision to life. Marc then helped me find a local construction crew to do the renovations. It took five weeks from signing the lease to reach the point where hammers started to swing, which left about eight weeks to finish the renovations, hire a manager and staff, purchase computer and phone systems, run an advertising campaign to promote the grand opening and stock the store with inventory. Eight weeks may sound like plenty of time, but considering the businesses I needed to manage back in Montréal, not to mention a new-born at home, I was under a lot of pressure.

For the most part, my other businesses kept me tied to Montréal. I monitored progress of the Quebec City renovations daily over the phone with the construction manager, but I also made the five-hundred -kilometre round trip to Quebec City a couple of times a week to monitor the renovations in person.

My plan was to launch Titish with inventory already on hand in my Montréal warehouse. With only three rent-free months, there was not enough time to select merchandise directly from Chinese manufacturers, and have it shipped across the Pacific to Vancouver and then over land to Quebec City. I didn't want to risk being out of the country while the renovations were under way, so I planned to open the store in early September, and then immediately fly to Guangzhou, China, to attend a large semi-annual trade show to order the inventory.

Those three months leading up to the grand opening are now a blur in my mind. I worked sixteen-hour days, seven days a week, to keep all the balls in the air in Montréal and Quebec City. I was absolutely exhausted for the entire summer. When I was finally able to hire a store manager in August, the workload subsided a bit. Construction finished slightly ahead of schedule, and it was smooth sailing from there. I hired staff, purchased advertising in two local newspapers, and had five truckloads of merchandise shipped from Montréal just after the Labour Day weekend in preparation of the grand opening on Wednesday September 12. I even arranged for a local public figure to attend the opening, and a radio station to broadcast live from inside the store.

The grand opening day arrived under tense circumstances. Just the day before, the entire world watched in shock as the World Trade Centre and the Pentagon came under attacks by terrorists. Immediately, the global economy entered a state of paralysis. On the day of the attacks, literally in the final hours after weeks of preparations, and with two dozen staff on hand looking to me for direction, I had to decide whether I would proceed with the grand opening of Titish. Around the world, people had no idea what the next few days or weeks would bring. Further attacks on other countries seemed like a very real possibility. But in Quebec City and across Canada, people continued to go about their daily business, albeit with their eyes and ears glued to their radios and televisions. My read on what was happening on the streets of Quebec was that people were shocked, but not panicked. I decided to forge ahead.

I would have preferred to have had more merchandise on display in this cavernous store, which was almost half the size of a football field, but I had enough to get by until I could place orders in China. On opening day, the newly hired staff did a very good job of welcoming people and tending to their needs. The radio station, although a bit costly, successfully attracted people's attention to the store. Overall, I was pleased with the outcomes of the day, especially considering the events of September 11. The punishing amount of work I had endured that summer paid off.

The manager I had hired for Titish had many years of retail experience and excellent leadership skills, which gave me confidence to leave the store in his hands for a week while I went to China to order merchandise. I was taking a gamble, because I was heading to China with basically no money in my pocket to pay for my purchases. My contract with the landlord called for him to pay me a large sum of money thirty days after opening Titish, to cover the cost of the leasehold improvements I made to the space. I intended to use that money to pay for the twenty or so containers of merchandise I intended to order. I would be in China when the funds were scheduled to be transferred from the mall owners. The money would be available when it was time to pay the Chinese suppliers. I got on the plane for China feeling that I could rely on that contract.

The retail trade fair in Guangzhou attracted tens of thousands of buyers from around the world. It's hard to describe the sense of awe I felt when I entered the convention centre. There were literally hundreds upon hundreds of merchants displaying their goods in an area about the size of five football fields. Electric mini-buses were being used to shuttle people from one zone of the exhibition floor to another! To give a sense of just how many people attended, the McDonald's restaurant had a row of sixty cash registers to serve customers.

Anything you could possibly imagine for your home—from paper clips to refrigerators—was on display. The prices were hard to believe. A dining room table that would typically cost me three hundred dollars from a North American wholesaler cost only about seventy dollars direct from the manufacturer at the fair. In fact, the cost of transporting a container of goods back to North America could easily be more than the value of its contents. On the other hand, buyers could only order in very high volumes.

I spent four days at the show negotiating with about two dozen manufactures of furniture, glassware, ornaments, wall hangings, table coverings, kitchen and bath accessories, linens and light fixtures. I placed orders that would fill twenty shipping containers. I paid each manufacturer a small deposit to hold my order. The balance would be paid before I would return to Montréal. By that time, the mall owner would have transferred transfer money to my account, as per our agreement. I would have my wife wire me the money.

Meanwhile, I called Marc, my real estate broker, every day to get updates regarding my payment from the mall owner. He assured me that there would be no problem. Then, on my last day at the show, Marc called me on my cell phone.

"Reza, it's Marc."

He caught me off guard.

"Hi Marc. So, the money has been transferred?"

"The mall owner has been told there is not enough merchandise in the store, and that you haven't spent much on leasehold improvements. They are refusing to release the funds."

"What? Those are subjective judgments and are not a condition in the contract! You've seen what I have done with that store! Marc, I'm in China at a trade show! I was counting on that money to seal these purchase orders!"

"I know, Reza. He is flatly refusing to pay. There is nothing I can do."

Marc was just the messenger. There was no use in attacking him. If anything, he was on my side and would be an important ally.

"What does Michel have to say about all of this? He's been watching all the renovations," I said.

"Michel left. He's not working at the mall any longer. I don't know what happened."

I paused for a moment and let out an audible sigh.

"Okay. I'll be home in two days. I'll deal with it as soon as I get back."

What to do? I was forced to place a hold on all of the orders I had made at the trade show that week. I was angered beyond description. That evening (morning in Canada), I called the manager at Titish and told him to close the store immediately until further notice, even though it contravened mall policy. I was determined to send a message to the mall owner that I would not be pushed around.

I was back in Montréal three days later, and visited my lawyer right way. Days of correspondence between him and the mall owner's lawyer resulted in the mall owner himself flying to Quebec City to meet us at the store, and judge for himself the legitimacy of my renovations to the space. Ironically, he had not visited that mall in person for a few years. He simply entrusted everything to Michel, his recently departed mall manager.

Michel's replacement felt I had not spent enough money on leasehold improvements to justify the financial payout stipulated in the contract. In effect, he felt that I was not living up to my end of the bargain. My meeting with him and the owner of the mall was tense. The three of us walked through my store so that I could show the owner in person the improvements and modifications I had made. Granted, merchandise was a bit sparse in the store because I was relying on stock that I could spare from my operations in Montréal. Otherwise, I had spent well into six figures making the necessary renovations to accommodate my business in the space. The new property manager only saw the higher than average number of blank spaces on the floor of the store, and sounded the alarm. I saw all of the cosmetic and layout changes that I had made since signing the lease.

Although not thrilled, the landlord acknowledged the renovations I had made. Legally, we were both in a very ambiguous position, but I think he realized that an agreement was an agreement, and that I would have the upper hand if it came down to a legal challenge. Besides, he had a ten-year lease, and stood to lose more in legal costs than if he just stuck to his original financial plans for the store over the long term. He reluctantly agreed to transfer the money that week, and I agreed to re-open the store the next day.

The most challenging part of starting a new business is attaining financial sustainability in the first year. Compounding those natural challenges, I launched the Quebec City store in the eye of an economic storm. The 9/11 attacks had a lingering effect on the world economy. North American consumer confidence had been dramatically destabilized. It took the stock markets months to regain their twenty percent drop in value in the wake of the attacks. The chilly economic climate may have been a major factor behind the store not living up to my financial predictions. I had expected phenomenal growth in the first year, based on my experience with Tapis en Gros in Montréal. In any case, by the end of that first year, I came to the harsh realization that Titish was not going to be financially sustainable. It was costing me a lot of money, not to mention being a tremendous drain on my time. The store had simply not taken off in the way I had expected.

I would be forced to close the store. The business was losing money and I didn't see a quick way out of the problem. I wanted to cut my losses, lick my wounds and rack it up to a good lesson learned, except that I was contractually bound to leasing this twenty-thousand-square-foot space for another nine years.

I approached the mall manager and informed him that I wanted out of my lease. He relayed this request to the landlord, who was categorically unwilling to renegotiate the terms of our contract. The only thing that he and I could agree on was that my other corporation had guaranteed the lease.

I had no options. The contract was clear. The only thing I could do was renege and simply stop paying rent. My theory was that the landlord would conclude that I was a problematic tenant who was not worth the effort to keep on board, and would cut me loose.

Unfortunately my strategy just aggravated him. He and I had been on speaking terms, albeit barely, but my actions sacrificed what little sense of civility was left between us. His reaction, which naively I had not anticipated, was to take me to court. And he knew he held the winning hand: a clearly written contract that identified my Montréal-based corporation as the guarantor of the ten-year lease of his space, all being defended by a powerful law firm. The only card I had left to play was to try and delay the court proceedings.

In Quebec, if a tenant stops making rental payments, a landlord can obtain a safeguard order, which forces the tenant to continue paying the lease until a final judgment is issued by the court. This landlord went ahead and secured such an order against me.

Personally, I was feeling drained of all the energy I knew I would need to face this challenge. I had a young baby at home. The demands of running my business group had prevented me from spending more than a few minutes each day with him, a personal dilemma that was tearing me apart. The cash flow issues with this new store compounded my stress.

In defiance of the court order, I defaulted on my next payment. The landlord then exercised his judgment and took legal action to begin seizing Tapis en Gros. He went to Montréal and sized up the assets of my five Tapis en Gros outlets in person, which galvanized his conviction to uphold the terms of our contract. One by one, his legal team began to register the contents of my stores for eventual seizure. Fuelled by my brazen actions, he was determined to take my other business down in order to recover what our agreement spelled out as rightfully his.

It was at this point that Michel, the original manager of the Quebec City mall, appeared on the scene. He was an acquaintance of my broker, who tracked him down on my behalf. It turns out that Michel had left the mall of his own free will, and was still in contact with the owner. In fact, Marc was able to reason with the owner on my behalf through Michel.

With Michel's intervention, and a series of prickly negotiations between our respective lawyers, the mall owner and I came to an agreement. Instead of seizing Tapis en Gros, the owner registered a lien on one of my commercial buildings for the amount equivalent to one year's lease payments. The condition was that I would keep Titish operating in his mall for one more year. After that, I would be free to exit our contract. I succeeded in getting the mall owner to back off from his attempt to seize Tapis en Gros.

For twelve more months I continued to operate Titish, losing money every step of the way. But it was less money than I would have lost had the mall owner seized control of Tapis en Gros. It was a huge relief to close that store and free myself from yet another costly and stressful legal battle. After closing the store, I was left with a fair bit of merchandise I was not able to sell by the time I vacated the space. But I was absolutely confident there was a profitable market for my home décor business concept.

Successful people learn from their failures, and consider them stepping stones to future success. I refused to simply crawl into a hole and give up. Rather than liquidating the merchandise for pennies on the dollar, I decided to open a store in Montréal, but on a much smaller scale.

Within about three months, I converted one of my existing commercial properties in Montréal to accommodate a furniture and home décor business, which I named Kolbé. Armed with a great deal of experience, the preparations were much easier for me this time around. I also had my younger brother to help with the launch. He had come to Canada from Iran a few months earlier, and had expressed an interest in working with me in a family partnership.

One of the advantages I had this time was that I located the store in one of my own commercial buildings, which alleviated pressure on my cash flow. This move would help compensate a major strategic shift I would make with Kolbé, which was to source products from Canadian, rather than Chinese, wholesalers. I just couldn't continue to run back and forth to China anymore to select products.

Kolbé was turning a positive cash flow within six months, albeit with the benefit of free rent. It was following the path that I had originally envisioned, one that more closely resembled the successful rise of Tapis en Gros. Feeling the same sense of invincibility that I did when growing Tapis en Gros, my brother encouraged me to open a second Kolbé store in Montréal just months after launching the first one. He convinced me that if we opened a similar store in an area with higher incomes, sales would be stronger and we would make better margins. He argued that he could easily take on managing a second store. It made sense to me.

Looking back, I wasn't being guided by clear objectives. I was purely focused on getting bigger and bigger, but I lacked a set of principles to guide that growth. Opening a second Kolbé store seemed like a logical progression. But I would have to rent commercial space. This time around I decided to work with a different real estate broker, Bertrand Gervais, with whom I had done business in the past. I asked him to search for a location.

Of four available retail spaces that Bertrand found in suburban Montréal, one in particular appealed to me. It was a six-thousand-square-foot space in an upscale suburban Montréal shopping centre. My brother felt there was no need to look any further. The mall drew exactly the type of clientele we were seeking for our products.

The mall manager's enthusiasm for our business was infectious.

"Mr. Sarshoghi," she said, "there's no question that this shopping centre would be a fantastic fit for your furniture and home décor business!" She then rhymed off a number of impressive statistics that sounded too good to be true.

"Did you see the big furniture store on the opposite side of the corridor?" She pointed to a familiar national chain. "It's generating about fifty million dollars a year in sales. You just need a small fraction of that pie!"

It was déjà vu; Quebec City all over again. This time, however, I was much, much wiser when I submitted an offer through Bertrand to lease the space.

The mall owner and I then spent the next couple of weeks negotiating the terms of the lease. The very last point to settle was the matter of providing a guarantee for the lease on behalf of the corporation that held Kolbé. But I flatly refused to provide a guarantee. My harsh experience in Quebec City with Titish had taught me the risks of doing so.

"Look," the mall manager said to me, "if you truly believe in your business concept, why won't you provide a guarantee?"

My brother saw it exactly the same way. His body language told me that he was siding with the landlord.

"No," I replied, shaking my head. "I will not include such a clause."

She kept a poker face. My brother was silent.

"Madam," I said, "I'm not here to try to take advantage of you. I would be happy to do business with you under the terms we have negotiated, but I just cannot provide the guarantee you are looking for."

The mall manager, my brother and Bertrand looked to each other for cues.

I continued. "You are a business person. So am I. All business people have to assume a degree of risk. Nobody is guaranteeing my business, so how can I guarantee yours?"

I then calmly stood up, picked up my bag, and extended my hand to shake hers. "You know where to reach me if you want to talk further about this agreement." My brother, Bertrand, and I then left her office.

Three days passed without hearing from the mall manager. I assumed that she wasn't willing to accept the terms I proposed for the lease, and that I would have to continue my search for a retail space. I have to admit that refusing to provide a guarantee is rather unorthodox in the real estate business. Triple A tenants, such as banks or any large national chain, are more apt to be excluded from such requirements, as they represent a lot less risk. But I was practically unknown.

My cell phone rang just before six o'clock on the third day. It was my broker.

"Reza," he said, "the mall manager says that you drive a hard bargain, but she is willing to do business with you."

"Very good. I am pleased."

"She said that if you fax her a signed offer that incorporates all of the negotiated terms we discussed, she will accept a year-to-year lease agreement," he said.

"I'll come by first thing tomorrow morning."

This time around, given my brutal experience with the Quebec City mall's owner, I took a strategic approach to signing my lease. I established two separate corporations to operate the new store. The first corporation, a numbered company in which I held all the shares, was the one I used to sign the lease. This company would carry liabilities, but never any assets on its books. Money for the monthly lease payments was lent to this company by a second corporation, Kolbé Inc., which was used to handle all of the store's other transactions. Inventory or money flowing in or out of the store was recorded on Kolbé's financial records. It was a perfectly legal mechanism that provided protection in the event the landlord tried to seize my assets. With no relationship between the two corporations, the landlord could not threaten to seize any of my other business operations.

I came to learn that the statistics the mall manager had provided about the shopping centre were grossly inflated. I never saw the traffic levels inside the mall that she had touted during her sales pitch. For example, her claim that the big furniture store opposite mine was generating sales of about fifty million dollars annually was complete rubbish. According to other mall retailers I got to know, it was likely only generating a fraction of that figure in annual sales.

Early into the second year of operations, the second Kolbé outlet was still losing a lot of money. The store wasn't generating enough revenue to even cover its monthly lease payment. I was subsidizing it with cash from my other businesses. The hole had to be plugged. With nine more months left on the annual lease, I saw no invisible hand that would magically increase mall traffic and sales. The writing was on the wall. I needed out. My brother wanted to hang on for a while longer, but when I pressed him for ideas on how to increase sales to the point where this store would no longer drain cash from my business group, he accepted my reasoning. I was not in this business to lose money. I had already racked up debt with my suppliers. This store was putting me further into the red with every month that passed.

I had to stop making lease payments in order to pay suppliers and operating expenses. After the second missed payment, the mall's corporate owner, unsurprisingly, launched legal proceedings. Based on my experience in Quebec City, I knew exactly what was coming at me. The landlord secured a judgment against me, which would force me to resume lease payments until the case was heard in court. However, this time, I was able to follow the exit path that I had engineered from the beginning. Before getting to that point, I simply cleared the inventory out of the store and handed the keys back to the mall manager.

The judgment was against the corporation that held the lease, one of the two corporate structures I had created to operate the store. However, that corporation was basically worthless because it held no assets. When the landlord's lawyer realized that it had no value, he let the case go. He knew that the mall owner would be grasping at straws.

What could have been another costly and exhausting legal case for me ended before it even got off the ground. I walked away personally unscathed, despite having a mountain of inventory on my hands, some supplier agreements to discontinue and some debts to pay. I didn't feel good about reneging on my annual lease agreement, but the space was leased again less than three months later. The landlord surfaced relatively unscathed, too.

Lessons Learned

Dream Beyond Borders

My venture into the furniture and home décor market was motivated by my success in growing a small carpet shop into a five-store chain of large retail floor covering outlets. What I learned from starting and running those businesses, and from my failures along the way, made me extremely confident. Tapis en Gros, in my mind, was proof that I would not and could not, fail with Titish in Quebec City. Despite all of my careful planning, the Titish venture ended with a hard landing because I didn't engineer an appropriate exit strategy.

The point I want to emphasize— a life lesson that I will always heed— is that regardless of your personal strengths and determination as a small business manager, you must always recognize that something completely beyond your control can destabilize your business. The risk for a young, single entrepreneur with no dependents is much different than it is for a middle-aged person with a mortgage and children who will soon head off to university. Business is a game of survival.

In the case of Titish, I legally, perhaps foolishly, committed myself to a ten-year lease on a very expensive property. Granted, nobody predicted the financial fallout from the 9/11 attacks. But if Titish had simply failed on its own, I would still have been legally bound to a costly ten-year lease.

I am not suggesting that one should shirk his or her moral responsibility as a small business person. Far from it. But be smart. Protect yourself by always planning an exit route, within the boundaries of the law, in the event that the walls start to cave in.

With the second Kolbé store in Montréal, the landlord pressed me to guarantee the lease, as I had done in Quebec City. But all a guarantee does, in effect, is download more risk onto the lessee. By not agreeing to guarantee the lease, I was simply requiring the landlord to share some of the risk with me, which is not unethical.

Despite my best efforts, Kolbé flatlined. I handed the landlord the keys to her property. She tried to sue me, which was her right, but she didn't have a legal leg to stand on. This time, I had prevented legal headaches by planning an exit route at the outset. Because it took the landlord less than three months to lease that store again, my actions did not inflict irreparable harm on the owners.

My years of experience launching and managing small businesses have taught me that time is the only way to determine if a business decision is good. Certainly market studies, financial projections, and business forecasts helped inform my decisions, but all of those tools are based on the assumption that the future will be stable. Nobody predicted the 9/11 attacks or the sudden meltdown of the global financial system in 2008.

I have come to realize that over exuberance, combined with the rapidly growing economy in the late 1990s and again in the early 2000s, gave me a sense of invincibility. It took a very challenging legal case against me to recognize the powerful forces, outside of my control, that could bring on my demise. Those experiences taught me to always have a plan in place that would allow me to land on my feet in the event of an emergency.

Epilogue

It was not long before I ended up closing both Kolbé stores in Montréal, which marked the final chapter of my effort to diversify my floor covering business into the furniture and home décor market. At that time, I was still operating the five Tapis en Gros outlets and a few commercial buildings. But the three-year ordeal that began with expanding my business group into Quebec City made me realize that I needed to focus on my strengths. Too many times since buying Collage Tapis, my first business, I unknowingly bit off more than I could chew. Perhaps it was over-exuberance, but I think my unprincipled focus on growth at any cost distracted me from looking carefully before I leapt.

I sat in my office one day and reflected on what I needed to do to strengthen my business group, and avoid becoming vulnerable again to such costly mistakes. Making money was easy for me. But it seemed even easier to find myself embroiled in situations that took severe financial and personal tolls. My family paid a price for these ordeals, too.

I recognized that I needed to learn more about identifying and managing risk. Out of curiosity one day, I Googled a few terms related to risk management. A number of university MBA programs appeared in the search results, which got me thinking about the prospect of continuing my education. The more I explored these programs, the more intrigued I became about the idea of going back to school. I spent a few hours that day searching the websites of a number of Canadian and distance MBA programs.

That evening at home I sat down with my wife, and raised the idea of going back to school to pursue an MBA. She lived through all of the hardships I endured over the previous three years, and saw what a toll they had taken on me. But she also recognized that I had dreams. She had stood by me through many difficult times, providing moral support when my world was caving in around me.

"Honey," she said, looking me in the eye, "if this is something that you truly want to do, I will stand behind you. Education is important, as is the example you will set for our children."

She paused for a moment and smiled at me. I was surprised at just how supportive she was. I had basically been a stranger in my own home for the last three years. A full-time MBA program would not exactly allow me to devote more time to my family. But she understood how important it was for me to continue my education.

I did some serious soul searching for a few days and ultimately concluded that going back to school was an option that I could not afford to pass up. I had experienced phenomenal success since landing in Canada, growing from humble beginnings as a carpet flipper to presiding over a multi million dollar business group. But I had run out of fingers on which to count the number of times I had to hire legal help to either pursue somebody or to defend myself. I had experienced phenomenal growth with Tapis en Gros, but The Home Depot suddenly emerged on the scene and squeezed me out of the market. They beat me at my own game. Perhaps I was so determined to prevent anything from slowing me down that I was not wary enough about what might be hiding around that next corner. I needed to learn more. The smart thing to do was to admit to myself that there was much more I could learn from an MBA program.

Montréal is home to two well- respected business schools. There was also Queen's University's School of Business, located about three hundred kilometres away in Kingston, Ontario, which offered an Executive MBA program on weekends in a downtown Montréal boardroom. A host of overseas universities offered online MBA programs, but I wasn't convinced that online learning was the experience I was seeking.

There was something about the Queen's Executive MBA program that appealed to me. The admissions staff responded immediately whenever I had a question or sent them an email, the timing of the program worked for me, and Queen's University has a strong reputation. I talked it over with my wife, weighed the pros and cons of each program, and decided to apply to Queen's.

I didn't anticipate the application process to be such a challenge. I learned quickly that they don't admit just anybody with a cheque book. I had to gather written recommendations, write the GMAT examination, and have an interview with an admissions officer. Each of these steps was a challenge, but the greatest challenge, frankly, was obtaining a certified copy of my engineering degree from Iran. I actually had to ask my parents to order it in person.

I have been in war zones as a soldier, lived through the Revolution in Iran, and experienced the hardships of many legal battles in court. Ironically, the personal anxiety I experienced during the application process to the Queen's MBA program seemed to be on the same level as those situations. It was a tough process. The entire admissions process took about four months.

I received a written offer of admission to the Queen's Executive MBA program, delivered to my office by courier, in May 2007. It was one of the happiest days of my life. I immediately packed my briefcase and raced home to share the news with Azita and my boys. She gave me a big hug when I showed her the letter, and said that she wanted to go out for dinner with the kids that night to celebrate my accomplishment.

In July 2007, I drove to Kingston to take part in the first of three on-campus residential sessions. I would spend the next two weeks immersed in challenging business cases and intensive group study, followed by months of bi-weekly classes in downtown

Montréal linked to other Queen's classrooms across the country by live video feed. Two more residential sessions at Queen's would follow over the next twelve months, as well as team-based assignments and challenging individual projects.

The intensity of the experience is hard to describe. Every waking hour of the program's sixteen months was filled with working on the program's approximately ninety-five deliverables on top of managing the demands of my business and family. The intensity was compounded by the fact that English is my second language. I typically had to read materials multiple times to develop a clear understanding of their main points. Writing assignments in English that met the university's standards was just as challenging.

The MBA experience was many things wrapped into one experience: enlightening, gruelling, and yet one of the most satisfying accomplishments of my life. It uncovered questions about managing a business, leadership, and about myself as a business leader that I had never before thought to ask. I finished the program feeling as though my perspectives on business, and life in general, had been greatly broadened.

Walking in the convocation procession into Grant Hall at Queen's University that beautiful May morning in 2009 was one of the proudest moments of my life. My wife, children, and parents were in the audience to share the glory of my accomplishment. They stood up and cheered for me as the MBA program director placed the graduation hood over my head and handed me my degree. It was the completion of another step of a journey that has led me from my hometown in Iran to my accomplishments in Canada.

Canada has been incredibly good to me. I am living proof that Canada offers riches to anybody with the right business vision and the willingness to work hard. I have learned a lot of lessons in my twenty years of starting and running small businesses here. As I have recounted throughout this book, there has been a lot of hardship along the way, which I could have avoided if I had known then what I know now. This book is my attempt to give something back by sharing the lessons I have learned with other small business managers who haven't gained extensive experience. I hope that it will help you avoid some of the challenging experiences that I endured along the way.

Everybody has weaknesses. The MBA program taught me that the key to success is to capitalize on your strengths and simply avoid your weaknesses. If you are a hundred-metre sprinter, don't fool yourself into believing that you can win marathons. Winning in this highly competitive world requires you to perform at your best. In the words of my marketing professor, Ken Wong, "If you're going to play, play to win."

I am now taking a completely different approach to running my businesses, thanks, in part, to some of the things I learned in the MBA program. I haven't lost money, nor have I had to defend myself in court, since the program finished. More importantly, I am spending more time with my family, and only rarely work more than five days per week. I am working to live, not living to work.

These days I have completely moved away from the retail sector, having sold Collage Tapis, and the coffee and gift shops. I now concentrate on real estate development and helping other people manage their real estate assets. Real estate is the area in which I enjoyed the greatest success over the years.

I am still working with Rasheed, the Dubai-based investor who purchased the indoor family entertainment centre. Rasheed and I have come a long way over the years. I still manage the entertainment complex for him, as well as a couple of other major real estate holdings around Montréal. Rasheed now gives me autonomy to manage the entertainment business and his real estate holdings. We currently have plans to close the entertainment business, demolish the building, and convert the surrounding property into a high-rise residential housing complex.

As for Tapis en Gros, I sold the remaining stores to a group of buyers, who felt they could create a new competitive advantage in the market. After all was said and done, Tapis en Gros was not a profitable venture for me. Court challenges, competition from big-box stores such as The Home Depot, and the unforeseen cost of expansion eroded the gains I could realize from this venture. On the other hand, I didn't lose money from Tapis en Gros, either. Yes, Tapis en Gros represented three years of hard work for no overall financial gain, but I certainly don't regret the experience of building that business. I now know what I am capable of achieving, if I put my mind to it.

What happened to the people with whom I have shared this journey? Fred, my first salesman at Collage Tapis, who was instrumental in supporting my expansion to Tapis en Gros, got back together with his wife after being separated for ten years. Today they are closer than ever as a couple and their teenage children are happy to have both their parents back living under the same roof. It was a beautiful ending to a turbulent decade for his family. Perhaps Fred's story is another example of being able to achieve anything, if you are determined.

The saga with the National Bank of Greece represented some of the greatest drama of my early business days. The truth eventually came out when I approached Nick, the CEO, after I had found alternative financing from another bank. I came to learn that NBG was marketing itself as an acquisition target to other banks, and they needed to strengthen their numbers in certain areas. My loan was simply an easy target. Soon after I concluded my dealings with NBG, one of the big chartered Canadian banks acquired NBG's Canadian branches.

My business dealings involved family members over the years, as you will recall my experiences with Kevin Bronson, the carpet retailer from the United States who got me tangled up with Credit Suisse First Boston. Kevin was introduced to me by my cousin. I certainly don't have a connection to Kevin any longer, but I have heard that today he runs his own import-export business in New York City. My cousin is now much more careful about involving family members in business deals. The ordeal with CSFB was just as taxing on him as it was on me because he felt responsible for the situation.

You will recall my experience of rushing back to Iran to tend to my ill father during the middle of a full audit by the Canada Revenue Agency. Having to leave his side at the hospital bed in Iran to return to Canada was one of the most stressful things I have ever had to do. It was a defining point in my life that taught me what is truly important. It turned out that my father had had an allergic reaction to a new medication his doctor had prescribed. He fully recovered in the coming months, but the experience prompted me and my siblings to bring my parents to Canada. Today my parents live close to me in Montréal, where I can easily be there for them when necessary. They spend three months of each year in Iran.

Years after wrapping up my retail businesses, I found myself reminiscing on the chapter of my life that began with arriving in Canada and eventually purchasing Marta's designer rug business. I came a long way since those days as a new Canadian who flipped carpets to make ends meet in his adopted country. I decided one day to connect again with the past, and some of the people who were a part of my business journey. I was curious to know where life had taken them, so I went for a drive.

My first stop was at the store across from the cemetery, the first new space I had leased for Collage Tapis. The entire area had been transformed into offices and factory outlet stores.

My next stop was Sherbrook Street, the first piece of property I purchased in Canada, for the "new" home of Collage Tapis. The store is now being used as an art gallery. The new owner did a magnificent job of restoring the historical façade, which honestly was the only thing that now makes me feel good about selling that property and closing the business. I walked into the gallery and introduced myself to the salesperson.

"I owned this building before you moved in," I said.

She smiled at me and said, "Then you must be Reza."

I smiled and nodded in response.

"We still get your customers coming in and asking for you." She welcomed me to take my time and look around. The walls brought back so many memories. I had to craft so many solutions to business problems every single day in that store. I don't believe that any other high-end carpet store in Montréal has been able to achieve the distinction and prestige of Collage Tapis.

From Sherbrook, I crossed the river to check out one of the coffee shops, Café Saison. It was completely different than when I sold the business. However, the tin plated ceiling and the chandelier I had imported from Iran had not changed. It was still being operated as Café Saison, but the old-world style had been replaced by a new age theme of soft colours, ambient music, and water trickling from a fountain in the back corner. I didn't feel compelled to introduce myself to the owners.

I drove to the bistro where I met Sara. I walked in and, there she was, standing behind the cash counter. As soon as she saw me, she got up and ran toward me with her arms outstretched and a huge smile on her face. It had been at least four years since I had last seen her. She had tears in her eyes, and I have to say that I welled up a bit, too. We sat down and talked for a while. She explained that I was like a knight in shining armour, who magically appeared out of nowhere and helped her through a very difficult period of her business. She said she would be forever grateful for my mentorship. Today, Sara is married and owns three successful coffee shops with her husband.

I couldn't complete the journey down memory lane without passing by the second building I had leased to Tony, the owner of the Japanese restaurant. This was the building that sat empty for months and months without Tony beginning his promised renovations. I had long since sold that building (although today I still own the one in downtown Montréal whose roof collapsed), and it was converted into a steakhouse. I will never forget the headaches Tony created for me. Apparently, he left Canada long ago with a huge trail of debt, and has never been seen since, or at least not around Montréal.

I could not think of Tony without also thinking of Charles, the real estate broker who lined up so many deals and partnerships for me. Charles and I had worked quite closely together. But I eventually realized that he structured deals for me, such as the deal with Tony, the National Bank of Greece, and the Quebec City store, to serve his interests first, not mine. Ultimately I was the one who paid the price, but in each case, I have nobody to blame but myself. Charles and I naturally drifted apart.

What a ride the last twenty years have been! I have to say, though, that the rewards of achieving my business dreams have only been equalled by the personal satisfaction of helping other entrepreneurs succeed in this game we call business. The ultimate aim of any business is to solve somebody else's problem. Reflecting that afternoon on the journey that led me to a life of opportunity in Canada, I committed myself to not only continuing to grow my business goals, but to earnestly pursuing a new type of wealth that money cannot buy: helping others. I have learned, especially from my interactions with Sara and Rasheed, that helping others gives me a sense of pleasure and accomplishment that I could never get from a diamond, sports car or a Mediterranean cruise. And what better way to begin sharing my experience than to write a book with lessons that I think are the keys to successfully managing a small business.

It all begins with a dream, a tenacious belief that your dream can be achieved, and an unwavering personal commitment to make it happen. But that is just the starting point. Along the way, you will need to make smart decisions, which I hope will be informed by the lessons I have learned along the way and shared in this book. Success in business is the exception, not the rule. But look around. Thousands of businesses have been built on uncertainty. If I could do it from my humble beginnings as a newcomer to Canada, you can too.

Dream Beyond Borders